JEWISH CIVILIZATION
IN THE
HELLENISTIC–ROMAN PERIOD

Edited by

Shemaryahu Talmon

Published in cooperation with
The International Center for University
Teaching of Jewish Civilization, Jerusalem

Trinity Press International
Philadelphia

Published by
Trinity Press International
3725 Chestnut Street
Philadelphia, PA 19104

Library of Congress Cataloging-in-Publication Data

Jewish civilization in the Hellenistic-Roman period / Shemaryahu
    Talmon, editor. — 1st Trinity Press International ed.
        p.   cm.
    Includes bibliographical references.
    ISBN 1-56338-034-X
        1. Judaism—History—Post-exilic period, 586 B.C.-210 A.D.—
Congresses. 2. Jews—History—586 B.C.-70 A.D.—Congresses.
3. Dead Sea scrolls—Criticism, interpretation, etc.—Congresses.
I. Talmon, Shemaryahu, 1920-
BM176.J42   1991
296'.09'014—dc20   91-25560
                                                       CIP

Typeset by Sheffield Academic Press
Printed in the United States of America

Dedicated by
Ceil Feinberg
in loving memory of her husband
PETER I. FEINBERG
an ardent supporter of learning

CONTENTS

PART I
History, Society, Literature

PART II
Qumran Between Judaism and Christianity

PREFACE

In the summer of 1986, the Continuing Workshop on Teaching Jewish Civilization in Universities and Institutions of Higher Learning with Emphasis on Comparative Religion held its first international work-shop on the teaching of Jewish civilization in the Hellenistic–Roman period. Another workshop was convened the following summer, to deal with a related topic, the academic teaching of Qumran scrolls, forty years after the first discovery of these ancient Jewish documents in the Judaean Desert close to the shores of the Dead Sea. The Qumran scrolls can be securely dated in the time-span between the third century BCE and the first century CE. They throw welcome light on a 'dark age' in the history of Judaism which is not documented by any other contemporaneous sources—'the turn of the era' which is of paramount importance in the development of both Judaism and Christianity.

Because of the intrinsic affinity of the issues which were brought under review it was decided to publish jointly the papers presented for discussion in both workshops. The first part of this volume contains essays which arose out of the first workshop. They focus on themes relating to Jewish civilization in the late Second Temple period, with the first essay sketching the background against which the then unfold-ing developments should be assessed. The second part of the book includes papers which bear directly on the role that should be assigned to the Qumran scrolls in the academic teaching of the period.

The topics discussed herein span a wide spectrum of scholarly pur-suits drawn from a variety of disciplines, and thus reflect the inter-disciplinary character of the workshops. The approach taken by the authors differs from case to case. Some papers present a broad picture of basic phenomena in the civilization of the period. Students should be exposed to such a perspective regardless of where their specific major interest lies. Other papers focus in depth on specialized subject matter, but point out ways and means for integrating such information into a more general curriculum. It hardly needs stressing that the views expressed are the sole responsibility of the respective authors.

While this volume, like the workshops of the International Center for University Teaching of Jewish Civilization from which it emerged, brings under scrutiny pivotal aspects of Jewish civilization in the Hellenistic–Roman period, restrictions of time and space required that a selection of issues be made. It is hoped that the project will continue, and that participants in future workshops will consider curricular implications, the preparation of bibliographical guidelines suited to various types of students and institutions of higher learning as well as the publication of pertinent literature translated from the Hebrew.

Shemaryahu Talmon
Jerusalem

Acknowledgments

Emanuel Tov's article, 'Hebrew Biblical Manuscripts from the Judean Desert: Their Contribution to Textual Criticism', is a revised and updated version of one published in *JSS* 34 (1958), pp. 5-37. It is included here with the kind permission of the editor of that journal.

Shemaryahu Talmon's 'The Internal Diversification of Judaism in the Early Second Temple Period' is an adaptation of 'Jüdische Sektenbildung in der Frühzeit des Zweiten Tempels. Ein Nachtrag zu Max Webers Studie über das antike Judentum', in Max Weber's *Sicht des antiken Christentums. Interpretation und Kritik* (ed. W. Schluchter; Frankfurt: Suhrkamp), pp. 233-80. In English it appeared under the title 'The Emergence of Jewish Sectarianism in the Early Second Temple Period', in S. Talmon, *King, Cult and Calendar in Ancient Israel* (Jerusalem: Magnes Press, 1986), pp. 165-201.

Professor Talmon's 'Between the Bible and the Mishnah: Qumran from Within' was published in S. Talmon, *The World of Qumran from Within* (Jerusalem: Magnes Press, 1989), pp. 11-52. Permission to reprint both articles is gratefully acknowledged.

The International Center for University Teaching of Jewish Civilization gratefully acknowledges the assistance of the Joint Program for Jewish Education (State of Israel Ministry of Education–The Jewish Agency for Israel–World Zionist Organization) and of the Memorial Foundation for Jewish Culture in support of its overall program.

ABBREVIATIONS

AB	Anchor Bible
AES	*Archives of European Sociology*
AJS	*American Journal of Sociology*
AJ	Max Weber, *Ancient Judaism*
Ant.	Josephus Flavius, *Antiquities of the Jews*
BA	*Biblical Archaeologist*
BAC	Biblioteca de autores cristianos
BASOR	*Bulletin of the American Schools of Oriental Research*
BETL	Bibliotheca ephemeridum theologicarum lovaniensium
Bib	*Biblica*
BIES	*Bulletin of the Israel Exploration Society* (= *Yediot*)
BTB	*Biblical Theology Bulletin*
BZAW	Beihefte zur ZAW
CBQ	*Catholic Biblical Quarterly*
CRINT	Compendia rerum iudicarum ad Novum Testamentum
CSSH	*Comparative Studies in Society and History*
DBSup	*Dictionnaire de la Bible, Supplément*
DJD	Discoveries in the Judaean Desert
EI	*Eretz Israel*
EncBrit	*Encyclopaedia Britannica*
EncJud	*Encyclopaedia Judaica* (1971)
GARS	Max Weber, *Gesammelte Aufsätze zur Religions-Soziologie*
HSM	Harvard Semitic Monographs
HSS	Harvard Semitic Studies
HTR	*Harvard Theological Review*
HUCA	*Hebrew Union College Annual*
IDB	G.A. Buttrick (ed.), *Interpreter's Dictionary of the Bible*
IEJ	*Israel Exploration Journal*
IOSCS	International Organization for Septuagint and Cognate Studies
JAOS	*Journal of the American Oriental Society*
JBL	*Journal of Biblical Literature*
JJS	*Journal of Jewish Studies*
JQR	*Jewish Quarterly Review*
JQRMS	Jewish Quarterly Review Monograph Series
JSHRZ	Jüdische Schriften aus hellenistisch-römischer Zeit

JSJ	*Journal for the Study of Judaism in the Persian, Hellenistic and Roman Period*
JSOT	*Journal for the Study of the Old Testament*
JSS	*Journal of Semitic Studies*
JTS	*Journal of Theological Studies*
KCC	S. Talmon, *King, Cult and Calendar in Ancient Israel*
PAAJR	*Proceedings of the American Academy of Jewish Research*
PAPS	*Proceedings of the American Philosophical Society*
PSBA	*Proceedings of the Society of Biblical Archaeology*
QHBT	F.M. Cross and S. Talmon, *Qumran and the History of the Biblical Text*
RB	*Revue biblique*
RBén	*Revue bénédictine*
REJ	*Revue des études juives*
RevQ	*Revue de Qumran*
SAJ	Max Weber, *Studie über das Antike Judentum*
SBL	Society of Biblical Literature
SBLSBS	SBL Sources for Biblical Study
ScrHier	*Scripta Hierosolymitana*
SJLA	Studies in Judaism in Late Antiquity
SOR	*Social Research*
STDJ	Studies on the Texts of the Desert of Judah
ThWAT	G.J. Botterweck and H. Ringgren (eds.), *Theologisches Wörterbuch zum Alten Testament*
VT	*Vetus Testamentum*
VTSup	Vetus Testamentum, Supplements
WQW	S. Talmon, *The World of Qumran From Within*
ZAW	*Zeitschrift für die alttestamentliche Wissenschaft*
ZKT	*Zeitschrift für katholische Theologie*

LIST OF CONTRIBUTORS

Joseph M. Baumgarten
Baltimore Hebrew College, Baltimore

Gerald J. Blidstein
Ben-Gurion University of the Negev, Beer-Sheva

James H. Charlesworth
Princeton Theological Seminary, Princeton

Devorah Dimant
Department of Bible Studies, University of Haifa

Maurice Gilbert
Pontifical Biblical Institute, Jerusalem

Thomas A. Idinopulos
Miami University, Oxford, Ohio

Jacob Milgrom
University of California, Berkeley

George W.E. Nickelsburg
University of Iowa, Iowa City

Uriel Rappaport
Department of Jewish History, University of Haifa

Lawrence H. Schiffman
New York University, New York

Hartmut Stegemann
Georg August Universität, Göttingen

John Strugnell
Harvard University

Shemaryahu Talmon
The Hebrew University of Jerusalem

Emanuel Tov
The Hebrew University of Jerusalem

PART I

HISTORY, SOCIETY, LITERATURE

THE INTERNAL DIVERSIFICATION OF JUDAISM IN THE EARLY SECOND TEMPLE PERIOD

Shemaryahu Talmon

I

This paper focuses on the beginnings of internal socioreligious diversification in Judaism between the fourth and the second century BCE. The discussion will not encompass the groups of dissidents that made their appearance in the Judaism of the late Second Temple period and have long been a subject of intensive scholarly investigation. Concomitantly it attempts to re-evaluate some central aspects of Max Weber's work concerning post-exilic Israel, bringing under scrutiny new materials discovered since his day and the results of post-Weberian scholarly research. Thus, the paper may be seen as an addendum to Weber's *Ancient Judaism*.[1]

I shall attempt to integrate into the presentation of the issue new evidence which was not available when Weber wrote his book.[2] A host

---

1.   This study was published originally as a series of essays entitled *Das Antike Judentum* in *Archiv für Sozialwissenschaft und Sozialforschung* (1917–1919), and was republished posthumously by Marianne Weber as volume three of Weber's *Gesammelte Aufsätze zur Religions-Soziologie* (hereinafter: *GARS*) (Tübingen: Mohr, 1921). The English translation, *Ancient Judaism (AJ)*, was prepared and edited by H.H. Gerth and D. Martindale (Glencoe, IL: The Free Press, 1952).

2.   Research carried out since Weber's days has decisively changed scholarly appreciation of the history and sociology of Judaism in the pre-Pharisaic, Pharisaic and Rabbinic periods. In the framework of this study, even a most restricted selective listing of pertinent publications in this area of inquiry cannot be attempted. It must suffice to draw attention to only a few titles which reflect the impressive results achieved by scholars in Israel, the United States and Europe: J. Klausner, *Jesus of Nazareth: His Life, Time and Teaching* (trans. from Hebrew; London: Allen & Unwin, 1925); A.C. Schalit, *König Herodes. Der Mann und sein Werk* (trans. from Hebrew and enlarged; Berlin: de Gruyter, 1969); A. Ben-David, *Talmudische*

of recent discoveries, such as the Gnostic materials from Nag Hammadi[1] and, foremost, the Scrolls from Qumran,[2] throw welcome light on dissenting religious groups and trends in the Second Temple period. They help in illuminating, even though only partially, the otherwise undocumented age in the *Geistesgeschichte* of the late biblical and the early post-biblical era, which from a Christian point of view has been termed the 'intertestamental' period. The decisively richer information on the socioreligious profile of Judaism in the Second Temple period that the new documents provide, calls for a reassessment of Weber's typology and his presentation of some phenomena pertaining to post-exilic Israel and its socioreligious structure.

Ökonomie (Hildesheim: Olms, 1974); D. Sperber, *Roman Palestine, Money and Prices* (Ramat Gan: Bar Ilan, 1974) and *Roman Palestine 200–400, The Land* (Ramat Gan: Bar Ilan, 1974); M. Stern and S. Safrai, *The Jewish People in the First Century* (Assen: van Gorcum, 1974–76); E.E. Urbach, *The Sages, their Concepts and Beliefs* (trans. from Hebrew; Jerusalem: Magnes Press, 1975); G. Alon, *Jews, Judaism and the Classical World* (trans. from Hebrew; Jerusalem: Magnes Press, 1977), and *The Jews in their Land in the Talmudic Age (70–640 CE)* (trans. from Hebrew; Jerusalem: Magnes Press, 1980); S. Safrai, *Das Jüdische Volk im Zeitalter des Zweiten Tempels*; (trans. from Hebrew; Neukirchen–Vluyn: Neukirchener Verlag, 1978), and *Die Wallfahrt im Zeitalter des zweiten Tempels* (trans. from Hebrew; Neukirchen–Vluyn: Neukirchener Verlag, 1982); S. Lieberman, *Greek in Jewish Palestine* (New York: Jewish Theological Seminary, 1942), and *Hellenism in Jewish Palestine* (New York: Jewish Theological Seminary, 1950); J. Neusner, *Early Rabbinic Judaism: Historical Studies in Religion, Literature and Art* (Leiden: Brill, 1975), and *First Century Judaism in Crisis* (Nashville: Abingdon Press, 1975); G. Stemberger, *Das klassische Judentum: Kultur und Geschichte der rabbinischen Zeit* (Munich: Beck, 1979), and 'Das rabbinische Judentum in der Darstellung Max Webers', in *Studie über das antike Judentum* (hereinafter: *SAJ*) (ed. W. Sohluchter; Frankfurt am Main: Suhrkamp, 1978), pp. 185-200.

1. The new insights have been fully assimilated by K. Rudolph, *Die Gnosis. Wesen und Geschichte einer spätantiken Religion* (Göttingen: Vandenhoeck & Ruprecht, 1980), which goes beyond the classic study of H. Jonas, *The Gnostic Religion: The Message of the Alien God and the Beginnings of Christianity* (Boston: Beacon Press, 1963). See further, H.G. Kippenberg, 'Intellektualismus und antike Gnosis', *SAJ*, pp. 201-18. Rudolph and Kippenberg provide up-to-date bibliographies.

2. A concise description and evaluation of these discoveries may be found, *inter alia*, in F.M. Cross, *The Ancient Library of Qumran and Biblical Studies* (New York: Doubleday, 1961); and G. Vermes, *The Dead Sea Scrolls: Qumran in Perspective* (London: SCM Press, 1977; London: Collins, 1982).

A case in point is his treatment of the Samaritans to whom he refers only *en passant*.[1] The diametrical opposition of Jews versus Samaritans (as a prefiguration of the dichotomy Pharisaism versus heterodoxies) now must be viewed in the light of the Qumran finds which add a new dimension to the phenomenon of incipient Jewish sectarianism.[2]

An investigation of the new materials, and especially of the Qumran writings, may throw light on processes which Weber traced in *Ancient Judaism* and on concepts which constitute the warp and the woof of his typology. Let me mention just a few to which reference will be made in the ensuing discussion:

1. Weber's crucial assumption that post-exilic Israel experienced a decisive transition from peoplehood and nationhood to a (mere) 'confessional community' (*Glaubensgemeinschaft*) must be put to the test by its application to the self-understanding of the Samaritans and the Qumranites.

2. In this connection also, his contention that Israel then developed traits of a pariah community in an increasing measure will come up for review. An analysis of the Qumran (and Samaritan) world of ideas provides tools for a reconsideration of the 'in-group–out-group morality', which in Weber's view is rooted in the early biblical ethos, grew stronger in the setting of the Babylonian exile, and since Pharasaic times has shaped the attitude of Jews towards the non-Jewish world. Concurrently some attention must be given to the question whether, and if so in what degree, the presumed dual morality indeed was conducive to or precipitated the crystallization of a stringent behaviour pattern which consolidated Judaism from within, and at the same time cut it off from the surrounding society.

3. The constitution of the Qumran community may serve as a test for Weber's proposition that in the last centuries before the rise of Christianity, a rigid cultic code, the rabbinic halakhah, prevented Jews from engaging in agricultural

---

1. *AJ*, pp. 360ff., 415f.
2. See S. Talmon, 'Types of Messianic Expectation at the Turn of the Era', in *King, Cult and Calendar* (hereinafter, *KCC*; Jerusalem: Magnes Press, 1986), pp. 204-24.

occupations which by their very nature engender infringements of ritual prescriptions, and that, as a result, Judaism developed an intrinsically urban ethos.[1]

4. The study of the dissenters' commune of Qumran may bear on the more general question of how the socioreligious phenomenon 'sect' should be defined in distinction from other socioreligious structures.[2] The results of this inquiry may prompt a re-evaluation of Weber's description of the Pharisees' religious stance as 'sectarian religiosity' (*Sektenreligiosität*).

5. The presentation of the Righteous Teacher, the dominant figure of leadership in the Qumran writings, invites a reconsideration of Weber's typology of religious leaders.

6. The Qumran writings also reflect the progressive dénouement of the *Rationalisierungsprozess* which plays such an important role in Weber's thinking, as well as the increasing democratization of one-time esoteric religious learning. However, because of their many ramifications, these developments require a rather involved exposition which cannot be attempted here.

II

At this stage of our inquiry, a characteristic of the sources on which all observations concerning biblical Judaism are based must be brought under consideration. Any attempt to retrace the social and religious development of Israel in the pre-exilic period is perforce based almost entirely on inferences drawn from the interpretation of literary materials which already in the biblical age had been handed down over centuries, and now are before us in the forms and formulations which the latest tradents or redactors gave to them. While the

---

1. *AJ*, pp. 363f.

2. See, *inter alia*, T.F. O'Dea, 'Mormonism and the Avoidance of Sectarian Stagnation: A Study of Church, Sect and Incipient Nationality', in *AJS* 60 (1954–55), pp. 285-93; P.L. Berger, 'The Sociological Study of Sectarianism', in *SOR* 21 (1954), pp. 467-85; B.R. Wilson, *Sects and Society* (London: W. Heinemann, 1961), and 'Patterns of Sectarianism', *CSSH* III (1963); *idem, Messianische Kirchen, Sekten und Bewegungen im heutigen Afrika* (ed. E. Benz; Leiden: Brill, 1965).

extent of the time-lag between the occurrence of a particular event and its recording remains a matter of scholarly debate, that fundamental characteristic of the biblical traditions is generally recognized in modern biblical scholarship.

No such chronological gap between the historical circumstances and their reporting manifests itself in the biblical account of the early post-exilic times. The books which relate the details of the Return from the Exile—especially Ezra, Nehemiah, Haggai and Zechariah—are contemporaneous with or were composed shortly after the actual events which they record. While the contemporaneity does not allay the scholar's concern over the 'objectivity' of these presumed eyewitness reports, for once the biblical records are practically synchronous with the historical situation and reflect, *grosso modo,* the ideational stance of that age. In that sense, the Qumran scrolls have a special significance. They are the only extensive contemporary documentation relating to a Jewish group that flourished in the last centuries before the turn of the era. These documents are first-hand records, penned by scribes of the New Covenant commune for the benefit of its members, and have reached us in their pristine form. Therefore they are of unsurpassed value for a sociological case study of a religious group in antiquity.

III

Let me stress once again that I am concerned here with the beginnings of the internal differentiation which affected Jewry between the late fourth and the early second century BCE. My thesis is that the emergence at that time of varying interpretations of the shared heritage must be viewed in conjunction with Judaism of the sixth and fifth century BCE, as revealed to the scholar in the post-exilic biblical literature. The diversification which then arose and ultimately found its salient structural expression in the formation of sects, can be fully appreciated only against the backdrop of the experience of the Babylonian Exile and the Return from the Exile. Viewed from this angle, the very phenomenon of Jewish sectarianism in the following period links directly with the history and the *Geistesgeschichte* of early post-exilic Israel in the sixth and fifth centuries BCE.

I shall direct my comments to two pivotal aspects of the socio-religious transformation to which the biblical body politic was exposed in the wake of the cataclysmic events of 586 BCE, viz. the destruction of the Temple, the capture of Jerusalem, and the concomitant loss of political sovereignty: (1) changes in the social structure of the Israelite society and in the interaction of the main societal agents of leadership: king–priest–prophet; (2) the transformation from the pre-exilic monocentric nation, defined by the geopolitical borders of the Land of Israel, to the post-exilic people characterized by a multicentricity which resulted from deportations and voluntary or semi-voluntary migration.

1. The social structure of Israel in the monarchical period hinged upon the interaction of three pivotal socioreligious institutions—kingship, priesthood, and prophecy—which safeguarded a basic cohesiveness and unity, notwithstanding social and economic differentiation and the political division into two realms.

The societal integrity of Israel in the monarchical period rested upon the equilibrium maintained between the forces of constancy—kings and priests, and the generators of creative movement—the prophets. An undue gravitation toward institutional realism could impair Israel's uniqueness shaped by the precepts of biblical monotheism. An overemphasis on utopian idealism could intensify eschatological speculations and messianic dreams to a degree that would undermine the will to live in actual history. Neither of these extremes appears to have materialized in the First Temple period.

2. In the days of the monarchy, and essentially also in the preceding stages of the Hebrew tribes' implantation in the Land of Canaan, the life of the people was marked by a fundamental geographical circumscription which furthered social, religious, and political cohesion. Traditions of a common ethnic extraction and of a shared historical past caused the division into two rival kingdoms (since approximately 900 BCE) to be considered a temporary breach that would be healed at some future time in history. It did not sap the Ephraimites' and the Judaeans' inherent consciousness of being one nation. The external pressure of the surrounding 'foreign nations', and ongoing contacts between Judah and Ephraim—war, intermittent alliances, commerce, and the two-way migration of groups and individuals—helped preserve the pathos of an intrinsic oneness, symbolized in the tradition of the 'Twelve Tribes'.

Even when no single place was recognized by all Israel as the nation's religious and political pivot, the very boundaries of the Land sufficed to circumscribe Israel's monocentricity. Not even the recurrent deportation of Ephraimites in the wake of the conquest of Samaria by the Assyrians in 722 BCE materially affected this geographical focus. No constituted group of Israelites established itself beyond the space of the divinely promised and sanctified Land. There is no tangible evidence suggesting that the relocations effected an emergence of 'Ephraimite centres' in Mesopotamia or elsewhere. Even if this should have been the case, as is sometimes surmised, those presumed exilic communities disappeared within a comparatively short span of time. In any event, there is nothing to show that a new, lasting understanding of Judaism, which differed significantly from that of pre-destruction Samaria, ever was conceived by Ephraimites in exile.

To sum up, throughout the First Temple period, homogeneity prevailed in Israel over heterogeneity, and uniformity over diversity, thanks to internal cohesion and geographical compactness.

IV

All this changed abruptly after the debacle of 586 BCE, when Judah and her capital city fell prey to the Babylonians. With the political framework in shambles, the monarchy lost its practical *raison d'être*. However, the idea and the ideal of 'royalty', in the configuration of the 'anointed shoot of the house of David' (cf. Isa. 42.1-3 with 11.1-5),[1] gained strength and became the embodiment of a restoration hope and ideology. With the Temple sacked, the cultic paraphernalia looted and carried away by the conqueror, the priests were in effect deprived of their sphere of function and influence. This did not result in a religious reorientation leading to a search for new means and forms of worship, but rather in the emergence of an intensified dream

---

1. The anointed King-Messiah concept has been abundantly discussed in scholarly publications which are too numerous to be listed here. For an overview and selected bibliography, see Talmon, 'Kingship and the Ideology of the State in Ancient Israel', in *KCC*, pp. 9-38; and 'Types of Messianic Expectation', *ibid.*, p. 215. See also Talmon, 'Der gesalbte Jahwes. Biblische und früh-nachbiblische Messias- und Heilserwartungen', in *Jesus Messias?* (Regensburg: Pustet, 1982), pp. 27-68; K. Baltzer, 'Das Ende des Staates Judah und die Messias-Frage', in *Studien zur Theologie der alttestamentlichen Überlieferung* (ed. R. Rendtorff and K. Koch; Neukirchen–Vluyn: Neukirchener Verlag, 1961), pp. 33-44.

of a future restitution of the time-honoured holy place and the sacrificial cult.[1] In short, the 'institutionalized' political and religious agencies, and their representatives who had been imbued with the charisma of office, survived the historical setback by a temporary transfer from the place of factuality to that of conceptuality. Their reactivation in historical reality was considered a certainty, depending on the conduct of the people, which would lead to a reconciliation with God and the restitution of its fortunes.

Most severely affected was the prophetic leadership and the very phenomenon of prophecy. The prophet's personal charisma lacked the staying power which institution conferred upon monarchy and priest-hood, and the fall of Judah and Jerusalem signalled the wane of prophecy. There was indeed a short-lived re-emergence of prophecy in the period of the Return (Haggai, Zechariah and Malachi); but there was an acute need for a replacement of personal inspiration as a prin-ciple of public guidance by more rational and controllable forms of instruction, which triggered the emergence of new classes of spiritual leaders—the Scribes, and then the Sages. Their authority rested on the expert extrapolation of the hallowed traditions by techniques whose reliability can be objectively ascertained, rather than on personal inspiration which cannot be subjected to any generally acknowledged controls.

Concomitant with the developments which affected the leadership, the original geographical compactness of Israel was shattered. An era of multicentricity set in: multiformity replaced uniformity; hetero-geneity supplanted the former homogeneity. It is to these features that we must now turn our attention.

After the fall of Jerusalem, the Babylonians, emulating a strategy introduced by the Assyrians, deported segments of the Judaean population and settled them in various localities in Mesopotamia. Some of these are mentioned by name in the biblical sources, e.g. Tel-Abib (Ezek. 1.3; 3.15) and Casiphia (Ezra 8.15-20). The concen-tration enabled the exiles to maintain their identity and, in effect, to further their tradition in ways that were not shared by the 'remnant'

---

1.   See S. Talmon, 'The Emergence of Institutionalized Prayer in Israel in the Light of Qumran Literature', in *Qumrân, sa piété, sa théologie et son milieu* (Bibliotheca Ephemeridum Theologicarum Lovaniensium, 44; ed. M. Delcor; Paris: Duculot, 1978), p. 265 = *WQW*, pp. 204ff.

left by the conquerors in the Babylonian province of Judah (Jehud). Thus, there emerged in Babylonia a new 'centre' of Judaism in which a particular understanding of biblical monotheism was cultivated. The Babylonian community entertained a fervent messianic hope for an imminent return to the homeland, which restrained them from sinking roots in the foreign soil (Jer. 29.4-7); thus it could provide echelons of returnees when the liberating edict of Cyrus the Great (538 BCE) made this possible. However, not all exiles returned. Those who remained were to become the matrix of a flourishing community which in later days would compete with and, at times, surpass Palestinian Judaism in literary achievements and social weight.

Another centre crystallized in Egypt. Information on Jews in Egypt comes from two disparate sources which are some 150 years apart. One set of evidence derives from Jeremiah 43–44. It is reported that an unspecified number of Judaeans fled to lower Egypt a short while after the fall of Jerusalem, fearing Babylonian reprisals for the murder of Gedaliah, the governor whom the conqueror had appointed over the province (Jer. 41).

More detailed evidence can be gleaned from the archives of a Jewish garrison stationed in Elephantine in Upper Egypt.[1] The documents pertain to a period of approximately forty years, between 420 and 380 BCE. However, references therein to earlier historical events indicate that the settlement preceded the conquest of Egypt by the Persian king Cambyses in 525 BCE. Of special importance for our purpose is the knowledge gained from the Elephantine papyri on the internal structure of this community and its religious outlook,[2] as well as on its relations to the homeland. We learn that these Jewish soldiers had built a temple in Elephantine before 525, that is, merely decades after the destruction of the Jerusalem Temple. The construction of a permanent sanctuary outside Jerusalem, in a foreign land, constitutes a significant departure from biblical concepts. The very existence of the

1.   See A.H. Sayce and E.A. Cowley, *Aramaic Papyri of the Fifth Century BC* (Oxford: Clarendon Press, 1923); E.G. Kraeling, *The Brooklyn Museum Aramaic Papyri: New Colony in Elephantine* (New Haven: Yale University Press, 1953); G.R. Driver, *Aramaic Documents of the Fifth Century BC* (Oxford: Clarendon Press, 1954).

2.   For a comprehensive analysis of the material, see B. Porten, *Archives from Elephantine* (Berkeley, CA: University of California Press, 1968); A. Vincent, *La religion des judéo-aramaéens d'Elephantine* (Paris: Geuthner, 1937).

sanctuary in Elephantine flouted the uniqueness of the Jerusalem Temple and its exclusive legitimacy, and implies that Egyptian Jewry had adjusted to their 'Diaspora' conditions. They had accepted life 'outside of the Land' as final, and did not entertain any hope for a restoration in historical times.

It may be presumed that this attitude ultimately led to their severance from their former compatriots and coreligionists in the Land of Israel and in the Babylonian Diaspora. In consequence, Egyptian Jewry had no share in the founding of the new community in the Land by the returnees from the exile in the wake of Cyrus's declaration.

The estrangement of Egyptian from Babylonian and Palestinian Jewry was deepened by one other historical-political factor. Egypt was conquered by the Persians only in 525 BCE, in the reign of Cambyses. Thus, the Jews in Egypt were not included in the decree of 538 which had been addressed mainly to the exiles in Babylonia–Persia (Ezra 1.2-4; 4.3), and probably also to other Jews living in territories of the Persian Empire (cf. Ezra 7.11-25).

A synoptic view of the composition of the Jewish people after the fall of the Kingdom of Judah in 586 reveals a situation which is fundamentally different from the one that obtained in the First Temple period. Not only has multicentricity replaced the former monocentricity but, what is more, the different Jewish communities present diverse sociological and spiritual, in short existential, profiles. The 'remnant' who had been permitted by the Babylonians to remain in the 'Land', in essence did not change their life style, economic structure, and religious-cultic customs, notwithstanding the loss of political sovereignty and cultic institutions, and the incurrence of economic hardship. They clung to their established system of values, despite the changed circumstances.

In Egypt there emerged a community of emigrants who had elected to leave their homeland, even though under pressure. The severance of ties with the 'Land' and with basic precepts of biblical monotheism severely undermined their staying power and their will to resist the inroads of the surrounding society and its conceptual universe. They embraced an accommodating syncretistic stance which ultimately caused their community to wither.

In contrast, the community of exiles in Babylonia–Persia persisted in its particularity.[1] They indeed 'reformed' and reinterpreted traditional values in order to cope, as a stubborn minority, with the situation into which they had been hurled. Their unmitigated sense of being in exile reinforced their insistence on the strict adherence to their spiritual heritage, and furthered the formation of societal structures adjusted to exilic conditions. More than that, their consciousness of being expatriates intensified the hope for repatriation in an appreciable historical future, and for a reconstitution of a political sovereignty under an anointed king of the Davidic line. It stimulated an intrinsically activist stance.

Before proceeding to the next stage of my inquiry, I must highlight some salient characteristics of Israel in the exilic times which seem to have a special bearing on the appreciation of Weber's conceptual framework.

1. Post-destruction Palestinian Jewry was not divorced from agriculture nor did it become urbanized. Quite the opposite appears to have been the case.[2] The cities became the pivots and mainstays of the imperial civic and military administration, with the concomitant influx of foreign bureaucrats, army personnel, and foreign population groups which the Assyrian suzerain transplanted into the conquered territories of Samaria (see 2 Kgs 17.24-41), and the Babylonians most probably introduced into Judah (see Ezra 4.7–6.5; Neh. 3.33–4.2; 6.1-7; 13.16). It may be postulated, in fact, that the Jewish population of the 'Land' became increasingly de-urbanized, being forced out of the cities and pushed into the rural periphery.

The continued attachment of considerable parts of the Jewish populace to agricultural pursuits persisted into the period of the return from exile, and beyond it into rabbinic times.[3] This fact clearly

---

1.   The Book of Esther appears to reflect an 'adjusted' exile community in the Persian period. See S. Talmon, 'Wisdom in the Book of Esther', *VT* 13 (1963), pp. 119-55; W.L. Humphreys, 'A Life-style for Diaspora: A Study of the Tales of Esther and Daniel', *JBL* 92 (1973), pp. 211-13; S.A. Meinhold, *Die Diaspora-novelle–eine alttestamentliche Gattung* (PhD dissertation, University of Greifswald, 1969), and 'Die Gattung der Josephsgeschichte und des Estherbuches: Diasporanovelle, I, II', *ZAW* 87 (1975), pp. 306-24.

2.   Some of the legal documents found at Elephantine demonstrate that in Egypt as well Jews owned land, and presumably engaged in agriculture.

3.   This fact has been abundantly documented in post-Weberian research. See the literature cited on p. 16 n. 2 above.

emerges from the accounts preserved in the post-exilic biblical writings which indicate that the *Landbevölkerung* played an important role in the returnees' reconstituted body politic. Recurrent references to cattle, vineyards, fields and crops, and the failure of crops (Hag. 1.6, 10, 11; 2.15-19; Zech. 8.10-12; Ezra 3.7; Neh. 5.1-15, 18; etc.), point to the existence of a substantial rural class with agricultural interests, and not to a landless urbanized *Bürgertum*. Biblical reports have it that Nehemiah was forced to have recourse to the conscription of every tenth member of the returnees' families for settlement in Jerusalem, so as to ensure that former exiles would predominate in the citizenry of the capital (Neh. 7.4-5; 11.1-2). Equally revealing is the 'roster of returning exiles', preserved in two slightly diverging versions (Ezra 2.1-70 and Neh. 7.6-72), which served Nehemiah as the basis for the repopulation of Jerusalem with trustworthy men. In part this list is arranged according to localities in the Land of Israel (Ezra 2.21-35), mostly villages and rural townships. The arrangement reflects the returnees' intention to re-establish themselves in locations where their forebears had been settled: 'The (returning) priests...Levites...and all Israel (settled) in their villages' (Ezra 2.70 = Neh. 7.72; cf. 11.11).

2. The enforced status of *konfessionelle Glaubensgemeinschaft* was regarded by the Babylonian exiles as a mere temporary adjustment to prevailing adverse circumstances. However, as will be explicated, once this new form of communal life had come into existence, it would not be discarded, even when the conditions which had brought it about were seemingly reversed or attenuated by the return to the Land. The structure of the credal community would be absorbed into the future societal framework of Jewry, in transformations which are concordant with its changing religio-societal configuration. A symbiosis of credal community and nation evolved and coalesced.

3. The continuing adherence to pre-exilic socioreligious structures also finds expression in the circumstance that immediately upon their return to the land, the former exiles began to rebuild the Temple (Ezra 3.2-3; 4.1-3; cf. Hag. *passim*; Zech. 3.1-7; 6.9-15 etc.) and reinstituted the sacrificial service (Ezra 3.3-6; 6.1-22; 7.11-24; Neh. 10.35-40; 12.43-47; 13.30-31; cf. Mal. 1.6-14; 2.12-13; etc.). As in the past, the Temple was not considered an institution exclusively dedicated to 'religious' concerns, but was also a symbol of nationhood and political sovereignty. This was well understood by the

local Persian officials (see Ezra 4.12-22; 5.6-8, 24).

4. Weber's contention[1] that, since access to the *religiöse Glaubens-gemeinschaft* was regulated primarily by 'ritual law', proselytism became a constitutive phenomenon of post-exilic Judaism, certainly does not apply to the returnees' community. The above-mentioned roster of returning paternal houses obviously is intended to help preserve the ethnic-national circumscription of its membership, and to block altogether or at least brake the infiltration of outsiders. The restrictive effect of the thus achieved self-identification becomes exceedingly visible in the ensuing campaign of Ezra, Nehemiah and their followers against the intrusion of foreign women into the Judaean society. The traditional endogamy principle which precludes intermarriage with ethnic foreigners, now is expanded to apply also to non-Judaean Israelites whose version of the biblical faith was at variance with the returnees' understanding of biblical monotheism. One again encounters the concentric structure of credal community within nation: because of the religious-credal factor, *connubium* becomes operative solely within the society of the former exiles. Only returnees can be counted among the 'holy seed' whose preordained restoration the pre-exilic prophet Isaiah had announced, so that it might become the stock out of which the people (nation) of Israel will rise again (cf. Ezra 9.2 and Neh. 9.2, with Isa. 6.13). A triad relationship which would prevail in later Second Temple Judaism emerged:

credal-nation	in-group
national	in-group
religious–ethnic–foreign	out-group

This pattern would determine, to a large degree, the interrelation of the diverse factions in Judaism that are but structured societal manifestations of diverging interpretations of the common tradition shared by all.

V

The multicentricity and heterogeneity of Judaism effected by the dispersion constitute the backdrop against which one must view the

---

1.   *AJ*, pp. 362-63, 417-21.

overall population in the land after the return of the contingents from the Babylonian–Persian exile, and appreciate their internal diversification and the conflicts and clashes which resulted from it.

The 'in-group–out-group' ethos which had characterized Israel's relations with its pagan neighbours in the land during the monarchic period, and in the Diaspora during the exile, now manifested itself in new configurations. The need for a close circumscription of Jewish identity, which had been especially pressing in the setting of a surrounding pagan foreign majority in Babylonia–Persia, was turned inward. Insistence on the observance of religious ritual norms—especially Sabbath, festivals, and circumcision—in the Diaspora had acted as a defence mechanism in the quest for self-preservation *vis-à-vis* ethnic 'others'. After the return, the question at issue progressively became internalized. Compliance with the specific-particular execution of these rites now became a criterion which set apart constituents of one Jewish 'inner group' from others.

The biblical sources indicate that the Israelites in the Land at first expressed a readiness to join with the returnees in the effort to rebuild the Temple. The Book of Ezra reports that as against 'the people(s) of the Land' who sought to prevent the restoration of the Temple (3.3), some inhabitants proposed to participate actively in the building operations. These petitioners are designated 'adversaries of Judah and Benjamin' (4.1). This implies that they were considered opponents of the returnees whose community was predominantly, if not exclusively, constituted of exiled Judeans and Benjaminites (see Ezra 1.5; 2.11 = Neh. 7.6; Ezra 10.9; 2 Chron. 34.9; etc.), citizens of the former Kingdom of Judah. The precise specification of the petitioners' identity suggests that the report concerns an internal Israelite group and raises the question whether the returnees should completely separate themselves from the 'Palestinian' Ephraimites (and possibly also from Judeans) who had not undergone the exile experience, or whether they should agree to integrate them in their midst. Zerubbabel and his followers rejected them (Ezra 4.1-3), obviously acting under prophetic pressure. The refusal caused bad blood between the two factions. But this apparently did not prevent the 'locals' from trying again in the days of Ezra and Nehemiah to win acceptance into the Judaean *res publica,* once more to no avail.

The finality of the rift between the two strata of Israelites in the Land comes to the fore in the pronouncements of the last biblical prophet Malachi, who was presumably active at that time. At the end of his book, which signals the closure of the collection of prophetic writings and the termination of biblical prophecy, the author records a controversy between two (certainly 'Jewish') factions: 'those who fear God and serve him' and 'those who do not fear God nor serve him' (Mal. 3.11-21). The first are promised fortune and salvation, the other misery and damnation at the (appointed) day when God will sit in judgment over his people.[1] It goes without saying that the author sides with those whom he considers to be obedient to God. They may be regarded as akin to those 'who revere (or abide by) the word of God' (Isa. 66.5; cf. 65.11), to the *anawim*, 'humble', or *ṣaddikim*, 'righteous' of the Psalms, and as forerunners of the later *ḥasidim*, the 'pious' of early Maccabaean times.

Having been repeatedly spurned by the returned Judaeans, the Ephraimites or Samarians[2] (subsequently also known as Shechemites) abstained from further overtures. Approximately a century later, they struck out on their own. Renouncing any adherence to the Jerusalem Temple, they reportedly built a rival sanctuary on Mount Gerizim near the city of Shechem. Josephus relates that Menahem, a member of the high priestly family whom Nehemiah had ousted from Jerusalem (Neh. 13.28), then married the daughter of Sanballat, whom the Samaritans consider to have been the leader of their community at that time. The priest had taken from the Temple in Jerusalem a Torah scroll which he placed in the sanctuary on Mount Gerizim.[3] Josephus's story is not without difficulties. He appears to have telescoped historical events, linking the priest whom Nehemiah drove out of Jerusalem (approximately 430–425) and who may have been the son-in-law of the Sanballat of Nehemiah's days, with another Sanballat, probably the third,[4] who flourished a hundred years later,

---

1.   The 'day' does not necessarily have an eschatological connotation, viz. 'the end of days', but rather connotes a future-historical, preordained point in time. See S. Talmon, *Eschatology and History in Biblical Judaism* (Occasional Papers, 2; Jerusalem: Tantur, 1986).

2.   Note: not 'Samaritans'. This latter designation applies to the Shechemites only after their final separation from the Jews in or after Alexander's days.

3.   *Ant.* 11 (Loeb), pp. 306-47.

4.   See F.M. Cross, 'The Discovery of the Samaria Papyri', *BA* 26 (1963), pp. 110-21; *idem*, 'Papyri of the Fourth Century BC from Daliyeh: A Preliminary Report on their Discovery and Significance', in *New Directions in Biblical*

in the time of Alexander. But these inaccuracies and inconsistencies do not invalidate Josephus's statement on two points.

First, by the end of the fourth century, the erstwhile Samarians, who now would become known as the Samaritans, had entirely severed their links with the Jerusalem community. The establishment of a 'holy place' on Mount Gerizim, whatever form it took, gave finality to the break.

Second, the secessionists adopted the Torah as the fundament on which they built their communal life.[1] Thus, both major derivates of pre-exilic Israel—the returnees from Babylon and the Palestinian Israelites—proclaimed the Torah the mainstay of their beliefs and practices.[2] Each conceived of itself as 'the Torah community', and strove to outdo the other in professing and exhibiting faithfulness to Torah laws. Paganism had been totally overcome.[3] On this common platform of basic consent, each faction emphasized particular aspects in the execution of the shared tradition. 'Dissent' expressed itself in differences of interpretation resulting in deviating norms. Technicalities in the execution of circumcision, precision in the observance of the Sabbath and the festivals,[4] matters concerning the Temple and the cult, now achieved exceeding prominence. The opposition to *derekh hattorah*, 'the (proper) way of the Torah', would be *derekh aheret* 'another (heterodox) way'.[5] The internal boundary lines between one faction and the other proved to be no less rigid than those which had separated and continued to separate all Israelites from the 'other nations'.

Archaeology (ed. D.N. Freedman and J.C. Greenfield; New York: Doubleday, 1969), pp. 41-62; *idem*, 'Aspects of Samaritan and Jewish History in Late Persian and Hellenistic Times', *HTR* 59 (1966), pp. 202-11; *idem*, 'A Reconstruction of the Judean Restoration', *JBL* 94 (1975), pp. 4-18.

1.   This was correctly pointed out by Weber, who specifies that they accepted the Torah 'in the revision of the Exilic priests' (*AJ*, p. 360).

2.   One is inclined to find an expression of this intense Torah consciousness in Psalm 119.

3.   See Urbach, *The Sages*, pp. 286-314; Safrai, *Das Jüdische Volk*, pp. 39-40.

4.   See *b. Sanh.* 91a; *b. Zeb.* 13a. Weber saw these issues entirely within the framework of the relations of Jews and foreigners, i.e. in the compass of his 'in-group–out-group' model (*AJ*, p. 354).

5.   See S. Lieberman, 'Light on the Cave Scrolls from Rabbinic Sources', *PAAJR* 20 (1951), pp. 395-404.

Attention should be drawn to some less conspicuous but no less weighty discords which are apparent in the Jewish–Samaritan controversy. In discussing the formative impulse which the destruction of Jerusalem and the ensuing deportation lent to the emergence of the post-exilic community, I singled out the transformation of the former monocentricity into multicentricity, and the dislocation of the previously balanced social structure of pre-exilic Judah. It is in these two spheres that the divergent developments of mainstream Judaism and the Samaritan community became eminently manifest.

By tracing their descent to the tribe of Joseph, the Samaritans claim a share in the history of the Northern Kingdom in which the Joseph clans predominated. They know and tell of the destruction of Samaria, and of the deportation of contingents of Samarians to Mesopotamia. However, in contrast to Judah, the geographical compactness of the Ephraimite population in the monarchical period was not transformed into a plurality of centres after the fall of the Northern Kingdom. As already stated, we have no information on any Ephraimite collectivity that was constituted outside Palestine and developed a life stance which differed from that of the Palestinian centre. The original monocentricity of the ten tribes whom the Samaritans claim to represent became utterly fragmented. Only the population that had been allowed to remain in the territory of the former Northern Kingdom preserved vestiges of an Israelite identity. The Ephraimite Diaspora appears to have fallen prey to a process of internal dissolution, leading to its eclipse within a comparatively short time after the fall of Samaria. Thus the Samarians, and later the Samaritans, were never exposed to the fructifying impact of the 'Diaspora and Restoration experience' which etched the contours of the post-exilic Judaean community. First the Samarians, and then the Samaritans, persisted in their severely curtailed monocentric uniformity into Hellenistic times. Then, under the impact of various internal and external factors, dissent became rife in the Samaritan community and generated sectarian secession in its ranks.

Non-acceptance of the prophetic and historiographical literature into the Samaritan biblical canon, and the concomitant accordance of authoritative sanctity to the Pentateuch alone, accounts for additional conceptual divergences from Judaism. The rigorous exclusive Torah, i.e. Pentateuch steadfastness, precipitated in Samaritanism the emergence of an utterly ritualistic religiosity that lacks the inner tension which prophecy bestowed upon Judaism. In the Samaritan religious stance, exact adherence to behavioural norms assumes paramount importance. Samaritanism experienced only restricted spiritual movement, as if religious development had come to a halt in the early stages of its genesis. Since then, Samaritan men of learning and letters have produced few new insights or literary innovations, certainly nothing comparable to the intellectual fecundity of Second Temple and post-Second Temple Judaism.

It may well be that this spiritual immobility was bolstered by the non-existence in the Samaritan world of the utopian ferment which the messianic hope imparted to mainstream Judaism, to the Qumran community (see below), and then to Christianity. Their opposition to the Davidic dynasty, concomitant with the rejection of the biblical prophetic books and the historiographies, impeded the articulation of a messianic vision in the Samaritans' conceptual universe. Although they do foresee a future time of divine mercy, in which they expect to be transported from their adverse historical situation into a shining perfect one, the depiction of that era remains rather vague, with no 'royal anointed' showing on the horizon. The indistinct references to a central figure which will arise in that ideal future age seem to pertain to a new Moses (Moses *redivivus)*, designated *taheb*. This latter term may be translated 'restorer'. The future aeon is conceived as a replica of the Mosaic era in which the restorative thrust is fully dominant, and which lacks altogether the utopian cosmic superstructure which prophetic inspiration had envisaged.[1]

Samaritanism embraced only one of the two principles which became the mainstays of mainstream Judaism. Concentrating on the regulation of life in actual history by the normative Torah code, they lost the spiritual tension with which messianism and the idealistic vision of the future had imbued Judaism. While adherence to normative practice may well have been a major factor in the preservation of a structured Samaritan community over two millennia, it also generated a rigidity which prevented this community from dealing creatively with history by absorbing changes through an ongoing process of interpreting and, to a degree, re-formulating traditions.

The 'inner-group' relationship (in the framework of the above proposed three-tier model) which determined the attitude of the Judaean

---

1. See Talmon, 'Types of Messianic Expectation', in *KCC*, pp. 207-209.

returnees towards the non-exiled Israelites, obtains also in respect to the Samaritans. In this case, too, their self-identification as people and creed defined their posture *vis-à-vis* the contemporary Jewish nation and state. By establishing a separate central sanctuary on Mount Gerizim as the religious pivot of their 'national entity', the Samaritans in fact reactivated a political-religious pattern which arose out of the secession of the northern from the southern tribes after the death of King Solomon (c. 900 BCE), and culminated in the establishment of the Kingdom of Samaria and its schismatic *Reichsheiligtum* Beth-El which was meant to serve as a counterpoint to the (*Reichs*) Temple in Jerusalem (1 Kgs 12.25-33).

VI

At this juncture, it is appropriate to make reference to an aspect of the issue under consideration which is of special importance in the Second Temple period, namely, the diversity of impacts which the civilizations of successive empires that subjugated Israel had on the cultural, religious and societal outlook of Judaism. The issue is much too multi-faceted and involved to be discussed here in detail. We must content ourselves with a mere delineation of its contours and its relevance for the diversity of configurations in which Jewish schismatic tendencies expressed themselves at the time.

It cannot go unnoticed that the concept of socioreligious diversification, as it figures in our discussion, does not apply to cases of internal cultic-political dissent in periods when Israel was in the sphere of the political and cultural influence of Semitic (Assyrian and Babylonian) or Oriental (Persian) overlords, i.e. before c. 300 BCE. After Alexander's conquest of the ancient Near East, Judaism in the Land, and to a large degree also in the Diaspora, became enfolded in a political framework whose cultural profile was shaped by influences which flowed from the Occident, from Greece-Hellas. At that juncture in history, the Samaritan schism crystallized. The situation changed radically when, in 163 BCE, the Hasmonaeans re-established Jewish political sovereignty for one hundred years, after which time Rome subjugated the Jewish state. It is precisely in that 'Hasmonaean Century' that the commune of the Qumran Covenanters flourished. Its inception, though, may have preceded the Hasmonaeans' success by a decade or two. No definite correlation between the status of political independence and the specific mode of Qumran secession can be readily established. But it must be noted that at this stage in Jewish history, dissent assumes a form which differs considerably from that of the Samaritan schism, and will reflect in the features of Jewish heterodoxies which emerged in the late Second Temple period.

VII

I can now turn to an analysis of the Qumran Covenanters' community. The above outlined chronological coalescence of events in the post-exilic period is even more pronounced in reference to the commune of the Covenanters of the Judaean desert. No other ancient group or community has left such a rich literary legacy, authored by some and intended for all of its members, which enlightens the reader on its history, societal structure, and conceptual universe. The details gleaned from these literary remains together form a mosaic which is a true to life model of a secessionist faction in Second Temple Judaism, like no other ever encountered by students of that period or, for that matter, of the entire biblical era. Being contemporaneous with the events described in them, the Qumran writings constitute the best conceivable basis for the study of any ancient social entity, in this instance of an early Jewish dissident movement (or inter-local sect).

In addition, these materials afford the viewer a rear-window view, so to speak, of the mainstream Jewish society from which the Covenanters had separated and with which they were engaged in an ideational struggle over the exclusive right to legitimately represent 'true Israel'. Thus, the Qumran Covenanters may be considered in Weber's terminology a 'historical object' of interest in itself, but even more so a 'heuristic instrument'[1] for testing theoretical concepts appropriate to the study of Judaism in the Second Temple period (and possibly also of 'sect' as a socioreligious phenomenon).

Scholars have attempted to identify the Qumran Covenanters' commune with practically every Jewish sect or religious stream of the Second Temple period that had been known from ancient sources before the discovery of the new material. The most widely accepted theory identifies them with the Essenes. In comparing those two

1.   See M. Weber, *The Methodology of the Social Sciences* (trans. E. Shils and H. Finch; Glencoe, IL: Free Press, 1959), p. 156.

groups, one tends to highlight affinities which by no means can be disregarded,[1] but may not pay sufficient attention to telling differences.[2] For reasons of method, and not only because of historical considerations,[3] I prefer to view the Covenanters for the present as a *sui generis* phenomenon, the examination of which is bound to add a new dimension to the study of early Jewish dissent.

The founding members of that community can be best defined as a group of millenarian-messianic Jews who had reckoned the advent of the 'Kingdom to Come' by attaching a real-historical interpretation to a biblical prophecy. The utopian messianists seem to have read a message of hope into the prophet Ezekiel's symbolic act performed in the face of the Babylonian siege of Jerusalem, which originally was meant to announce a period of punishment which for Israel (Ephraim) would last 390 years, and for Judah forty years (Ezek. 4.4-6). The Qumranites interpreted this to mean that, 390 years after the destruction of the First Temple in 586 BCE, Israel's fortunes would be restored. In anticipation of this great event, they separated from their fellow Jews and repaired to the desert, there to prepare themselves body and soul for the imminent salvation. The date at which they arrived by taking the prophet's visionary figures at face value astonishingly dovetails with the prevalent dating of the emergence of the Qumran community to the beginning of the second century BCE. In the resulting high-tension situation, the traditional forms of normal social life lost their meaning. Standing on the threshold of a new age which they expected to be governed by an ideal code of religious, social and political values, those millenarians saw no reason for

1. See S. Lieberman, 'The Discipline in the So-Called Dead Sea Manual of Discipline', *JBL* 71 (1952), p. 206 n. 77.

2. See S. Talmon, 'The Calendar Reckoning of the Sect from the Judean Desert', *ScrHier* 4 (Jerusalem: Magnes Press, 1958), pp. 162-99.

3. As does Lieberman, in 'The Discipline': 'Jewish Palestine of the first century [the historical horizon must be widened to include the last two centuries BCE—ST] swarmed with different sects. Every sect probably had its divisions and subdivisions. Even the Pharisees themselves were reported to have been divided into seven (a round number of course; see *ARN* 37, ed. S. Schechter, (New York: Feldheim, 1945) 37, 109 and parallels) categories. It is therefore precarious to ascribe our documents definitely to any known of the three major [I would include also 'minor'—ST] sects.'

abiding by accepted notions and maintaining established societal institutions.[1]

The millenarian spirit generated in the first Covenanters an anarchistic anti-establishment stance, such as can also be observed in other millenarian movements.[2] Qumran anarchism, though, was not a deep-seated principle, but rather an *ad hoc* reaction to existing circumstances, a necessary step to be taken for paving the way that would lead to the messianic age. In the Qumranites' vision of the 'Age to Come', the sociopolitical and cultic institutions will be reinstated in accordance with their concepts, customs and codified law. This vision is patterned upon the basically this-worldly conceptions of the Hebrew Bible, or at least of some major strata of that literature, which put a premium on a good life, on family and kinship, and on an orderly social structure.[3]

Qumran theology and the structure of the Qumran commune illustrate the issue of 'change and continuity'. They oscillate between a highly idealized concept of the historical biblical Israel and a utopian vision of a future historical world which is conceived as a glorified restoration of the biblical past.[4] The Qumranites viewed their own community as the only legitimate remnant and representative of the biblical people of Israel. They had been chosen to experience in an appreciably near future a restitution of Israel's fortunes, culminating

---

1.   A concise presentation of these aspects may be found in S. Talmon, 'The New Covenanters of Qumran', *Scientific American* 225. 5 (November 1971), pp. 73-81.

2.   See, *inter alia*, N. Cohn, *The Pursuit of the Millennium* (New York: Essential Books, 1957); P. Worsley, *The Trumpet Shall Sound* (London: Macgibbon & Kee, 1957); A.J.F. Kobben, 'Prophetic Movements as an Expression of Social Protest', *International Archives of Ethnography* 49 (1960), pp. 17-64; Y. Talmon, 'Pursuits of the Millennium. The Relation Between Religious and Social Change', *AES* 3 (1962), pp. 125-48; S. Thrupp (ed.), *Millennial Dreams in Action, CSSH* 2 (The Hague, 1962; New York: Schocken, 1970); B.A. Wilson, *Millennialism in Comparative Perspective, CSSH* 6 (The Hague, 1963), pp. 93-114; Y. Talmon, 'Millenarian Movements', *European Journal of Sociology* 7 (1966), pp. 159-200.

3.   See L. Dürr, *Die Wertung des Lebens im Alten Testament und im antiken Orient* (Münster: Aschendorff, 1926); S. Talmon, 'Die Wertung von "Leben" in der hebräischen Bibel', in *Der Herr des Lebens. Jüdische und christliche Interpretation in der Ökumene* (ed. H.G. Link and M. Stoehr; Frankfurt am Main: Haags Herchen, 1985).

4.   See Talmon, 'The New Covenanters'.

in the re-establishment of the Temple in Jerusalem.

One finds at Qumran some mystical inclinations. But these play only a minor role in that spiritual framework. The type of millennialism which flourished in that community does not dovetail with the mystical chiliasm on which Weber based his typology.[1] Qumran exhibits a quite different development: the initial temporary anarchistic posture, which never seems to have been antinomistic, will be supplanted by a hypernomistic stance which exceeded the nomism of most if not of all other religious trends in Judaism of the time.

The conviction that the exact details of the unfolding latter-day drama had been revealed to them appears to have induced in the Qumran members an elitist consciousness which their Jewish contemporaries undoubtedly interpreted as a sign of unwarranted arrogance. They viewed themselves as the divinely appointed elect. They were the 'Sons of Light' who had been authoritatively commanded to part company with the 'Sons of Darkness', their fellow Jews, so that in their community the divine promise, as it is spelled out in some biblical prophecies, could finally be realized. Their communal life was an expression of the revitalization of biblical Israel before the conquest of Jerusalem by the Babylonians. They believed that the New Covenant which they established was the realization of Jeremiah's vision of the covenant which the God of Israel would renew with his liberated people (Jer. 31.30).

The elite-consciousness which appears to have put its stamp on the self-understanding of the Qumran Covenanters is utterly discordant with their apparent 'pariah status'. The Qumran commune displays all or most of the qualities by which Weber sought to define the pariah character of the post-exilic Jewish *'religöse Glaubensgemeinschaft'*, that is, ritualistic segregation, enmity towards non-members, in-group morality (*ökonomische Sondergebarung*), and lack of political autonomy.[2] This obvious contradiction between subjective self-understanding and objective classification altogether escaped Weber's attention and was not taken into account in his treatment of ancient Judaism. It would seem that the omission should be remedied and that this phenomenon should find an expression in an adjusted typology. Like the returnees from Babylon and the Samaritans, the Qumranites

1. *GARS*, I, p. 533.
2. *AJ*, p. 336.

also viewed themselves as both a nation and a credal community and thus present one more case of a mediating or mixed type which resists being subsumed under Weber's dichotomized typology.

Similarly, the Qumran commune defies Weber's counter-positioning of 'church' into which one is born and which has a 'compulsory-associational' and 'ascriptive' character, and of 'sect' which is a 'voluntary association' and therefore of an 'elective' nature.[1] In the 'New Covenant', these (according to Weber) 'polarized' principles become inseparably fused; only Israelites by 'ascription' can achieve membership in this 'elective' association.

The description of their lifestyle which the Qumranites provide in their writings, and the preservation and augmentation of legislation pertaining to agriculture in Qumran law literature, prove that agricultural pursuits persisted in practically all divisions and subdivisions of Second Temple Judaism. Arguing *a fortiori* from the intensely nomistic Samaritans and Qumranites, whose rigid ritualistic law code did not prevent them from engaging in agriculture, we certainly cannot present the comparatively speaking more 'liberal' Pharisees as having been estranged from such occupations. The same holds true for rabbinic Judaism: 'The Mishnah knows all sorts of economic activities. But for the Mishnah the centre and focus of interest lie in the village... The Mishnah class perspective described merely from its topics is that of the undercapitalized and overextended upper class farmer... The Mishnah therefore is the voice of the Israelite landholding proprietary class. All Israel had was villages.'[2]

According to Weber, the waning of agriculture and village orientation was contiguous with the waxing of a preponderant *städtische Ethik*. Nothing in the Qumran conceptual universe gives evidence of this transformation. Since the presumed precondition was, in fact, missing—the abandonment of agriculture—the posited development towards 'urban ethics' did not materialize, neither at Qumran nor in

1.   See 'The Protestant Sects and the Spirit of Capitalism', in *Essays in Sociology* (trans. and ed. H.H. Gerth and C. Wright Mills; London: Kegan Paul, 1947), pp. 305ff.; M. Weber, *The Protestant Ethic and the Spirit of Capitalism* (trans. T. Parsons; New York: Scribner's, 1958), p. 145 and n. 173; pp. 152-53.

2.   J. Neusner, 'Max Weber Revisited', in *Religion and Society in Ancient Judaism with Special Reference to the Late First and Second Centuries* (Oxford: Clarendon Press, 1981); Safrai, *Das jüdische Volk*, pp. 2, 4, 21, 25-26, and authorities quoted there.

other groupings of Second Temple Judaism. One suspects that Weber at times retrojected his own experience of a denationalized and non-agrarian urbanized Jewish bourgeoisie and its ethos into earlier stages of Jewish social history.

When the foreseen date of the onset of the 'Kingdom to Come' passed uneventfully, the Covenanters were in danger of losing their bearings. There and then, a Moses-like figure arose out of their midst, the Teacher of Righteousness. His origins and biographical data are not explicated. However, he was obviously born out of the existential stress generated by the non-realization of the community's millenarian expectations.[1]

In Weber's conceptual framework, the Teacher would rate as a leader whose charisma resulted from *soziale Zuschreibung*.[2] Unlike Jesus, whom Weber considers to be representative of the religious 'founder-type', the teacher did not create but rather solidified a pre-existing *neue soziale Gemeinschaft*[3] which, however, was also in conflict with family and clan. But, like the biblical prophets (see, e.g., Isa. 3–4), his main aim was not to undo, but rather to reform the established society and its institutions, so that ultimately it would embrace and act out the traditional values which he and his followers were determined to preserve in their purity.

At the same time, embedded within this figure are characteristics which, *pace* Weber, could be ascribed separately to two different types of religious virtuosi. While the Teacher is never reported to have executed cultic functions (either as a priest or a prophet), he is presented as a priestly preceptor invested with the spirit of prophecy. Thus, *Amtcharisma* coalesces with *persönliche Berufung* in his personality. It follows that he cannot be placed securely and adequately in any one category of Weber's neat schema of four types of religious leaders: *Kultpriester* and *Kultprophet, Lehrpriester* and *Lehrprophet*.[4]

---

1.   Since the nucleus-community existed before that leader came onto the scene, he is correctly designated 'Teacher' in the Qumran scrolls. He cannot be classified as an 'archegetes' (*AJ*, p. 331), i.e. as a 'founding prophet' (*GARS*, I, pp. 540-41). See F.A. Isambert, 'Fondateurs, papes et messies (XIX siècle)', *Archives de Sociologie et Religion* 3.5 (1958), pp. 96-98.

2.   See W. Schluchter, 'Altisraelitische Ethik und okzidentaler Rationalismus', *SAJ* p. 65.

3.   *GARS*, I, p. 542.

4.   See Schluchter, 'Altisraelitische Ethik', p. 23; D. Emmet, 'Prophets and their

While the essential typology may be upheld in theory, more attention should be given to *Mischtypen* which in reality constitute the majority of cases.[1]

The Teacher apparently did not innovate any religious concepts and maxims, but rather was an inspired interpreter of the traditional lore. He was instrumental in forging the group's anarchistic utopian messianism into the basis of a new social and religious structure. During his term of office and through him, the amorphous cluster of men who had reckoned the dawn of the 'World to Come' by millenarian speculations developed their own religious and societal structures. The erstwhile anarchistic dissenters' community hardened into an institutionalized socioreligious establishment which soon was to surpass in social rigidity and legalistic exactitude the old order from which they had seceded.

This transformation generated at Qumran a gradual increase in specific covenant precepts which culminated in their codification. Before long, the particular tenets of the Covenanters solidified into what may be termed a written appendix to the traditional law. Some parts of the Qumran legislation are preserved in the legal portions of the Zadokite Documents, others in the Manual of Discipline, and still others in the Temple Scroll, etc. With all due caution and reservations, this particular body of laws may be viewed as a sectarian parallel to the rabbinic law codified in the Mishnah. But, unlike the latter, the Qumran Code is not formulated in the 'question and answer' pattern without a specific 'address',[2] but rather is expressly aimed at a specific audience, the 'members of the Commune'.

The rapid transmutation of the Qumran Covenanters, within the time-span of one generation, from the status of a secessionist, anarchistic, inspired, millenarian fellowship into a structured religious establishment again makes this phenomenon an incompatible object for inclusion in Weber's clear-cut typology of socioreligious bodies. The dichotomy of Cult versus Word, Law versus Spirit, Church versus

---

Societies', *JAOS* 86 (1956), p. 18.

1. In other instances, e.g. in 'Magic and Religion', Weber displayed interest not only in pure manifestations of the suggested types, but also in '*Mischverhältnisse*'. See Schluchter, 'Altisraelitische Ethik', p. 23.

2. See Neusner, 'Max Weber Revisited', p. 3.

Sect,[1] simply does not apply to the Qumran community.

The exclusive regulations had, at one and the same time, a centripetal and a centrifugal impact on the Covenanters. On the one hand, they effected a marked cohesion between the individual members, and bestowed a distinctive uniformity upon their community; on the other hand, they clearly set it apart from the surrounding Jewish society.

In this context, the issue of in-group versus out-group morality does not apply to the separation of Jews from non-Jews, but rather pertains to the internal diversification which had already manifested itself distinctly in Judaism of the days of the Return, intensified at the height of the Second Temple period, and reached its apex in the first century of the Christian era. Thus the nature of the Qumran 'ethical dualism' is intrinsically different from Weber's understanding of this feature in relation to Pharisaic Judaism. The difference is apparent in his treatment of 'inner worldly asceticism' which he believed to be incompatible with in-group–out-group morality: 'this all-pervasive ethical dualism meant that the specific puritan idea of proving oneself relgiously through "inner-worldly asceticism" was unavailable [for Second Temple Judaism—ST]'.[2] This assertion has become untenable in the face of the Covenanters' theology and practice. As a matter of fact, the discoveries at Qumran have irrefutably shown that 'inner-worldly asceticism' was not first practised by Protestantism, nor was it innovated by nascent Christianity, but rather is a religious stance which has its roots in a (or possibly some) trend(s) which can be traced in the Judaism of the second century BCE. It went together with (possibly only temporary) celibacy and monasticism,[3] and with 'vocational' life, like that of ascetic Protestantism which, according to Weber, 'was absent [from Judaism—ST] from the outset'.[4] While the circumstances pertaining to the genesis at Qumran of these religious facets, which go counter to the familistic orientation predominating in the biblical world, still escape our knowledge, the facts in themselves are indisputable.

---

1.   *GARS*, III, pp. 220ff., quoted approvingly by Schluchter ('Altisraelitische Ethik', p. 65); further, E. Troeltsch, *Die Soziallehren der christlichen Kirchen und Gruppen* (Tübingen: Mohr, 1919; repr. Aalen, 1977), p. 189.

2.   *AJ*, p. 343.

3.   See Talmon, 'The New Covenanters'.

4.   *AJ*, p. 343.

The socioreligious phenomena brought under scrutiny in the foregoing discussion highlight the internal diversification which affected Jewry in the Hellenistic–Roman period. They must be taken into account in any attempt to recapture the historical conditions in which nascent Christianity arose within Second Temple Judaism, a belief structure from which it ultimately became divorced.

THE MATERIAL CULTURE OF THE JEWS
IN THE HELLENISTIC–ROMAN PERIOD

Uriel Rappaport

The history of the Jewish people in the Hellenistic–Roman period cannot be fully comprehended without an acquaintance with the material culture of the land of Israel. Such knowledge enables the lecturer to present a vivid historical picture that will spark the students' interest by revealing to them a land small but varied in landscape, poor in natural resources yet rich in culture, insignificant in area yet important in world history. At the same time, information about the realia of the land provides the means for a better understanding of the general background of many relevant historical, philosophical or literary issues of the period.

I realize that it is generally not feasible to follow the methodology of the *Ecole des Annales* and provide a 'total' history of any given subject. Nevertheless, it seems highly desirable to strive for an encompassing view of the society that produced the culture with which we are concerned. The importance of a proper assessment of the situation in the country and in the society at large can be seen even when we deal with subgroups, sects, and trends within the wider community. In the writings from Qumran, for instance, the term *harabbim* recurs; scholars interpret it as referring to 'the many', the people in general. If this interpretation is correct and the sectarians were aware of *harabbim*, the contemporary historian should also be concerned with them.

Focus on sociopolitical issues does not imply in any way that the religious history of the period is of lesser importance. I am fully aware of the significance of the ideas which emerged at that time and were so influential. Yet I propose that whatever we consider to be the 'upper' tiers of the historical construction, we must turn our attention to the foundation, which is the physical land.[1] This inclusive approach will contribute to the search for historical truth. I can easily imagine that at this very moment, somewhere in the land of Israel, someone is chancing upon an object which may cause us to turn some of our well-established conceptions upside down.

The consideration of realia in the teaching of Israelite history presents no difficulties. The instructor now has access to a wide spectrum of teaching aids related to the geography of the country, its ancient cities, archaeological excavations and objects, artefacts of daily life, epigraphy and numismatics. Dealing with these objects in themselves is, obviously, not the aim of the historian. They can, however, be used to illustrate an academic lecture on the history of the period, particularly in introductory courses; and, more important, they can be integrated into classroom discussions of historical issues.

I would like to mention, briefly, some discoveries which are of vital importance for updating our knowledge of the period and are also relevant to our understanding of some of the historical problems which it poses.

1. Of great interest are new sources of information that have come to our attention in the last two decades, discoveries which can be dated to the Persian and the early Hellenistic period.[2] Examples of such new data are the tiny silver coins bearing the inscription YHDH, the Ptolemaic eagle, and a royal portrait.[3] The discovery of these coins raises problems which require consideration: does the change of the inscriptions in this group from the Aramaic YHD to the Hebrew YHDH testify to a renaissance of the Hebrew language? What do we learn from these coins about the Jewish attitude, during that period, towards human and zoomorphic representations? Which authority minted these coins? What was the status of the High Priest at that

1.   See W.D. Davies, *The Gospel and the Land* (Berkeley: University of California Press, 1974), *passim*.

2.   See especially the recent English edition of the monograph by E. Stern, *The Material Culture of the Land of the Bible in the Persian Period, 538–332 BC* (Warminster: Aris and Phillips, 1982).

3.   L. Mildenberg, 'YEHUD: A Preliminary Study of the Provincial Coinage of Judea', in *Greek Numismatics and Archaeology* (ed. O. Moerkholm and N.U. Waggoner; Wetteren: Editions NR, 1979), pp. 183-96. Subsequent to the writing of this paper, two articles appeared on this subject by A. Spaer and by D. Barag, in *Israel Numismatic Journal* 9 (1986–87), pp. 1-3 and 4-21 respectively.

time? What was the position of the province of Judaea under the early Ptolemies?

This material can be used to engage the students in a discussion of such sub-topics as the economy of the period, art, palaeography, the impact of hellenization on Jewish society, etc.

2. Another revolutionary discovery from the same period and the same field are the small Samaritan silver coins which bear the inscription SMRN (= Samaria), and a coin inscribed YRB'M (= Jeroboam). This discovery[1] requires that we review some of our ideas about the province of Samaria, its position *vis-à-vis* Judaea, the self-image entertained by its population or its ruling class, etc. Such pieces of information can serve as a starting point for an extremely interesting discussion of an important chapter in the history of this period.

The above two examples, of the YHD–YHDH and the SMRN coins, suffice to demonstrate the importance of numismatic finds for any scholarly discussion, and their potential contribution to the academic teaching of the period. In this context, mention must be made of N. Avigad's recent publication of bullae from post-exilic Judaea. These finds shed new light on the governors who ruled that province in the period after the Return to Zion, and on other related issues.[2] Fortunately, almost all this material is now available in an original publication in English (Mildenberg, 1979; Spaer, 1979), in a bilingual Hebrew–English edition (Avigad, 1976), or in translation (E. Stern, 1982).

I will now turn my attention, somewhat arbitrarily, to several additional discoveries relating to the later Roman period.

3. The excavation of Hirbeth El Hamam, a tell on the western slopes of the Mountains of Ephraim, revealed a settlement and clear traces of siege: camps, circumvallation and a mole were found there. It appears that the besiegers were Romans. The excavator, A. Zertal, suggests

1.   The SMRN coins have not yet been published. The YRB'M coin was published by A. Spaer, 'A Coin of Jeroboam?', *IEJ* 29 (1979), p. 218.

2.   N. Avigad, 'Bullae and Seals from a Post-Exilic Judean Archive', *Qedem* (1976). Avigad also deals with problems concerning the general background and period of the texts which appear on these seals. It is worth mentioning here two other publications on newly discovered bullae from an earlier period but bordering on ours: N. Avigad, *Hebrew Bullae from the Time of Jeremiah* (Jerusalem: Israel Exploration Society, 1986 [Hebrew]), and Y. Shiloh, 'A Hoard of Hebrew Bullae from the City of David', *EI* 18 (Jerusalem: Israel Exploration Society, 1985), pp. 73-87.

that the remains give evidence of the Roman siege of Narbetha.[1] Josephus mentions this locality in relation to the expedition of Cestius Gallus (*War* 2.509). Although there are differences between the account of Josephus and the finds of the excavation, the identification of Hirbeth El Hamam with Narbetha should be considered favourably.

Examination of this interesting site raises important questions. Can it indeed be identified with biblical Aruboth, or with later Narbetha or Narbathein? Is the account in Josephus dependable, in the light of the excavation? What are we able to learn about Roman siegecraft from this site?

4. Gamla, on the Golan Heights, has been excavated by a team under the direction of Shemaryah Gutman. This site provides impressive visual testimony for the Jewish rebellion, comparable in certain aspects to Masada. It also presents a historical-geographical problem of identification: a building found there has been identified tentatively as a synagogue. If the identification is correct, this is the most ancient synagogue building ever discovered. In short, Gamla is one of the most impressive and important sites currently being excavated in Israel.[2]

5. The recently discovered and explored underground hideout complexes found in large numbers in the south and southwest of the Judaean mountains have been related by archaeological scholars to the Bar Kokhba revolt. Alternative explanations and interpretations of the significance, use and chronology of these underground tunnels have been proposed. The current discussion raises questions of economic, sociological, and historical importance which enrich our knowledge and understanding of the country and its history. The discovery of the tunnels has led to further consideration of the Bar Kokhba revolt, as well as to a new appreciation of the account of the revolt by Dio Cassius, and the reference to the Jewish underground hideouts contained therein.[3]

1. On the site and excavations, see A. Zertal, 'The Roman Siege System at Khirbet el Hammam (Narbetha) in Samaria', *Qadmoniot* 14 (1981), pp. 112-18 (Hebrew); and *Arrubboth, Hepher and the Third Solomonic District* (Tel Aviv: HaKibbutz HaMeuhad, 2nd edn, 1984 [Hebrew]), esp. pp. 133-36.

2. S. Gutman, *Gamla* (Tel Aviv: HaKibbutz HaMeuhad, 1985 [Hebrew]).

3. See, most recently, A. Kloner and Y. Tepper, *The Hiding Complexes in the Judean Shephela* (Tel Aviv: HaKibbutz HaMeuhad, 1987). See further, Discussion: 'Subterranean Hideaways in the Judaean Foothills and the Bar Kokhba Revolt',

The examples mentioned here cover but a small part of the relevant material data available to historians of the Graeco-Roman period.

In conclusion, I would like to comment briefly on some current literature and source material. It is important to bear in mind that a familiarity with modern Hebrew has become almost indispensable for anyone who wishes to become acquainted with the period under discussion. At the same time, a great amount of literature, whether originally written in a Western language or translated from the Hebrew, is available.[1] The following brief list of basic source books is not intended to be exhaustive.

E. Stern, *The Material Culture of the Land of the Bible in the Persian Period, 538–332 BC* (ET; Warminster: Aris and Phillips, 1982 [Hebr. 1973]).

The first volume of the *Cambridge History of Judaism* (ed. W.D. Davies and L. Finkelstein; Cambridge: Cambridge University Press, 1984) includes contributions by American, European (including some from the USSR), and Israeli scholars.

M. Hengel, *Judentum und Hellenismus* (Tübingen: Mohr, 1969) was published in English in two volumes, *Judaism and Hellenism* (Philadelphia: Fortress Press, 1974).

M. Stern, *Greek and Latin Authors on Jews and Judaism* (3 vols.; Jerusalem: Academy of Sciences and Humanities, 1974–84), contains important introductions, notes, and translations of non-Jewish sources.

A rich selection of literature on the Hellenistic period is available for academic teaching in English, German, French, Italian and Spanish. Indeed, increasing interest in these subjects is being shown in Italy and Spain. Useful material for student use can also be found in course books of The Open University of Israel (Tel Aviv), several of which have been translated into English.[2]

Cathedra 26 (1982), pp. 4-46 (Hebrew); A. Kloner, 'Hideout-Complexes from the Period of Bar Kokhba in the Judean Plain', in *The Bar Kokhba Revolt. A New Approach* (ed. A. Oppenheimer and U. Rappaport; Jerusalem: Yad Yitzhak Ben Zvi, 1984 [Hebrew]), pp. 153-71, and, in English, A. Kloner, 'The Subterranean Hideaways of the Judean Foothills and the Bar Kokhba Revolt', *The Jerusalem Cathedra* 3 (1983), pp. 114-35.

1. See M. Mor and U. Rappaport, 'A Survey of 25 Years (1960–1985) of Israeli Scholarship on Jewish History in the Second Temple Period', *BTB* 16 (1986), pp. 56-72.

2. E.g.: *Jerusalem to Jabneh* (Tel Aviv: The Open University, 1980); *The World*

The availability in English of scholarly works, as opposed to teaching materials, constitutes a more difficult problem. Unfortunately, translations from Hebrew (or other languages) of some academic publications only appear on the library shelf or in the bookshops long after the date of their original publication; others are not translated at all. A wide variety of Hebrew source books, anthologies, and monographs could serve teaching needs abroad, were it not for the language barrier.

Information about current literature is nowadays easily accessible in various forms and on a variety of levels. Some bibliographies and lists are more complete, others less so; some are more up-to-date than others; some are annotated, others not. But all serve a wide range of interests and needs.[1]

Special note should be made of L.H. Feldman, *Josephus and Modern Scholarship (1937–1980)* (Berlin: de Gruyter, 1984), and of HEROD, the HEllenistic ROman Data on-line bibliographical text system for the Hellenistic–Roman period at the library of the University of Haifa.[2] The data are supplied on line and will be connected to data banks of various kinds in scholarly institutions throughout the world. Progress in the use of computers in libraries is providing better and easier access to bibliographical data than at any time in the past.

of the Sages (Tel Aviv: The Open University, 1983).

1. I have in mind such publications as the *Elenchus* of *Biblica*; *Internationale Zeitschriftenschau für Bibelwissenschaft und Grenzgebiete*; *RAMBI—Index of Articles on Jewish Studies*, 1–28 (Jerusalem, 1966–88). Several other periodicals, e.g. *JSJ*, have good bibliographical sections.

2. This is a special application of the general system called HOBITS in use at the library.

RELIGIOUS AND NATIONAL FACTORS
IN ISRAEL'S WAR WITH ROME

Thomas A. Idinopulos

Anyone teaching Jewish civilization of the Hellenistic–Roman period must inevitably deal with the war of 66–74 CE, the Great Revolt as it is called. How to teach this traumatic event in the context of Jewish historical and religious development poses its own questions and difficulties.

The Great Revolt was a tragic turning point in the long struggle for Israel's national independence. The struggle began in 167 BCE with the successful revolt of the Maccabees against the Seleucid state, and ended in 135 CE with the catastrophic defeat of the Bar Kokhba rebels. During the war of 66–74 CE the Jerusalem temple, the symbol of religious and political autonomy, was destroyed, ending the tradition of priest-led ritual worship and elevating the Torah-minded Pharisees as the guardians of Israel's faith and future. The wars of 66–74 and 132–135 together sealed the fate of the Jewish nation for the next 1,800 years: Israel would lose her sovereign civil life and become one of a multitude of minor nations, subject to the will and whim of Christian and Muslim rulers. Finally, the Jews as a nation would become a conglomerate of isolated communities, each religiously insulated from the surrounding world by rabbinical leaders who protected their communities by suppressing political impulses.

Few today have pondered these facts more than Professor Yehoshafat Harkabi, who urges us to learn the bitter lessons contained in them.[1] If we accept his arguments, we should teach the Great Revolt as the heroic but essentially foolish effort of Jewish leaders to win a freedom that could not be, a move that sacrificed thousands of

---

1. Yehoshafat Harkabi, *The Bar Kochba Syndrome: Risk and Realism in International Politics* (New York: Rossel Books, 1983), pp. 6-23.

lives for unrealistic political goals, and relinquished the security of a people in its own land in response to obsessive religious ideals. The arguments are not without point. There was ample foolishness and obsessiveness in Israel's violent opposition to Rome. One need only remember that in 70 CE, when Roman soldiers were approaching the gates of Jerusalem, rival Jewish factions, instead of pulling together, tried to destroy each other and burned the city's food supply.

If judged solely by criteria that are military and political, then indeed the Great Revolt was a horrendous mistake. But can the revolt be so judged? I ask the question because what impresses me in the historical accounts is not the outbreak of violence, which seemed inevitable, but rather the long period of Jewish restraint which preceded the violence. For several decades before violent revolt, Jews sought political or administrative solutions to problems created by Roman violations of Jewish religious law.

What also emerges from historical accounts is a picture of Jewish-populated Judaea, where life, as throughout the Mediterranean world, could not be neatly divided into 'political' and 'religious' categories, certainly not according to the meanings those words have today. In the first century, Israel was in the last period of a thousand-year-old theocracy in which no distinction was recognized between the cultic and the administrative, between ritual and politics. I believe this fact has great bearing on how we should understand, and therefore teach, the Great Revolt. For if, as I contend, politics and religion were intimately and organically related in the minds of first-century Jews, no less than of Romans and Greeks, the events of that period cannot be evaluated, as Professor Harkabi would evaluate them, according to modern, secular, pragmatic values.

Harkabi faults the Jewish revolutionaries for launching a war without realistic regard for military and political consequences. These revolutionaries who 'built a bridge only to the middle of the river' were followed by the Bar Kokhba rebels who imitated their example. Harkabi's criticism does not arise from dry, dispassionate investigation of the past. He addresses his arguments to the present and future leaders of the State of Israel, urging these leaders to learn the lessons of ancient Israel's failed rebellions and avoid unrealistic, religiously inspired war-making.

But a word of caution must be interjected at this point. The theocracy of ancient Israel is not the modern State of Israel where Jewish religion plays a 'role' and occupies an 'office'. Modern history is an unreliable perspective from which to understand and evaluate morally events of the past.

What further impresses me in the historical accounts of the Great Revolt is the positive pattern of those events, by which I mean that Jews were not only protesting against Roman abuses of their religion, but were also fighting for something. That 'something' was the uniqueness of the Jewish nation, a uniqueness rooted in religious law. The late historian Michael Avi-Yonah fixed our attention on the ultimate threat facing Jewish communal leaders through 650 years of pagan Graeco-Roman cultural dominance.[1] Physical survival of the community was threatened in this period, but the ultimate threat was more spiritual and cultural than physical. The threat was represented by the allure of Greek language, religion, art, sport, dress, social and sexual customs. To preserve the religious integrity and political autonomy of the Jewish nation, Jews found themselves fighting first Greeks, and then Romans.

The two Roman–Jewish wars of 66–74 and 132–135 CE should not be viewed, as Harkabi seems to view them, as disruptions or deviations in the long course of Jewish history. For if we examine Jewish history from David's time to Alexander's conquest of Palestine, we find that the single most dominant energy sustaining the Jewish people is what we today would call 'national consciousness'. The national consciousness of ancient Israel was complex, inextricably religious, political, social, and territorial, an energy source which gave shape to the nation throughout its stages of development. I cannot claim credit for this insight. I borrowed it from Avi-Yonah, whose words are worth quoting:

> . . . the Jewish nation as such, and not any metaphysical force, has been the main factor in shaping Jewish history in all periods, from the time of Moses to the present day. National consciousness is like a pulse—sometimes it beats strong and clear, and sometimes it is difficult to catch—but there is no life without it. The national strivings of Israel, the manifestations of which have varied from time to time, existed at all times throughout Jewish history.[2]

1. Michael Avi-Yonah, *The Jews under Roman and Byzantine Rule: A Political History of Palestine from the Bar Kochba War to the Arab Conquest* (Jerusalem: Magnes Press, 1984), p. xviii.

2. Avi-Yonah, *The Jews under Roman and Byzantine Rule*, pp. 13-14.

Avi-Yonah's rejection of the influence of divine providence and metaphysical force in shaping Jewish history requires methodological clarification. For what truly matters in appreciating the depth and complexity of ancient Israelite national consciousness is not what individual Jews believed about God, but the influence of religious beliefs in shaping the society. Here theology must defer to sociology. The implications of this for the study of the Great Revolt are clear and convincing. However foolish or obsessive Jewish religious feelings were in the first century, the outbreak of violent revolt against Rome sprang from those feelings and cannot be separated from them, as we shall now see.

Our primary source of knowledge about the Great Revolt is Flavius Josephus's *The Jewish War*, which unfortunately is not wholly trustworthy on the subject. Josephus wrote his account partly to justify his own switch from the Jewish to the Roman side of the war, partly to convince his readers that further revolt against Rome was futile and impious, and partly to blame the war on a hard-core Jewish revolutionary element which had supposedly sown seeds of dissension in Palestine for some fifty years before the outbreak of the violent conflict. As we cannot study the Great Revolt without Josephus's text to hand, the text itself must be critically scrutinized at every point. Fortunately, the American scholar David Rhodes has made it possible to separate the bias in the account from the likely pattern of events described in it, by a superb sifting of Josephus's narrative.[1] In addition, in tracing the roots of the Great Revolt back to the Maccabaean war, William Reuben Farmer demonstrates a religious and political logic in the 66–74 conflict that Josephus would never have admitted.[2] Relying on these works and others, what do we learn of the Great Revolt that should guide our teaching of the event?

The proper context for understanding the Great Revolt is the so-called Davidic covenant, the idea of the God-blessed Davidic dynasty which shaped and sustained Israelite national consciousness for 1,000

---

1. David Rhodes, *Israel in Revolution: 6–74 CE. Political History Based on the Writings of Josephus* (Philadelphia: Fortress Press, 1976).

2. William Reuben Farmer, *Maccabees, Zealots, and Josephus: An Inquiry into Jewish Nationalism in the Greco-Roman Period* (Westport, CT: Greenwood Press, 1973 [repr. of original 1956 edition]).

years, from the break up of the monarchy to the crushing of the Bar Kokhba rebellion. The divine blessing was extended to nation, land, capital, government, law, temple—that is, to all the institutions of Israel's freedom and faith. The belief in the Davidic covenant and its blessing can be credited with providing Judah with more than 300 years of stability denied to Samaria, her sister kingdom to the north.

After the fall of Judah, the belief in the Davidic covenant did not die, but rather gave added significance to the messianic idea that a Davidic prince chosen by God would inaugurate the era of redemption. In time, messianism and nationalism fused in Jewish minds, reinforcing the sense of Jewish national unity and purpose.

The period of restoration under Nehemiah and Ezra did not replace Jewish national hopes with a narrow cultic religiosity, as Christian scholars often write;[1] rather, Israel's reformers found fertile resources for expressing the nation's particularity or self-identity in law and ritual. Their strategy was very different from David's promotion of the dynastic covenant, but the goal was the same: national cohesion.

It is that same feeling of national cohesion which explains the Jewish rebellion against Greek Seleucid rule in the second century BCE. The Jews of Seleucid-ruled Palestine faced two problems: physical survival, and peaceful assimilation into the Greek environment which included the acceptance of the Greek language, religion, thought, dress, and customs. In 198 BCE it seemed that these threats could be averted. In that year the Greek ruler Antiochus III issued a charter in which Jews were given the right to live according to the law of their ancestors. But twenty years later the king's successor, Antiochus IV Epiphanes, introduced a policy of enforced hellenization of Jews, including the compulsory worship of the Greek gods. The crowning insult to Jewish national pride was Antiochus's decision to rededicate the Jerusalem temple to the god Dionysius Sabazius. The Jewish reaction to this religious persecution—the first in history, according

---

1. As examples see: Bernard Anderson, *Understanding the Old Testament* (Englewood Cliffs, NJ: Prentice-Hall, 1957); Martin Noth, *The History of Israel* (New York: Harper, 1958); John Bright, *A History of Israel.* For a counterview within Christian Old Testament scholarship, see: Walter Harrelson, *Interpreting the Old Testament* (New York: Holf, Rinehart and Winston, 1964); T.C. Vriezen, *The Religion of Ancient Israel* (Philadelphia: Westminster Press, 1973).

to Avi-Yonah—was a rebellion which eventually produced an independent Jewish state under the Hasmonaean rulers.

The persecution of the Jewish nation under Antiochus IV was the first major crisis faced by Jews after the Babylonian Exile; the second was the fall of the Hasmonaean state in 63 BCE at the hands of Roman soldiers. The Jewish response to this crisis is important for understanding the roles of faith and nationalism, religion and politics, in the Great Revolt. Or, rather, we should know what the response was not. It was not the response of the biblical prophets to the Assyrian destruction of the Northern Kingdom and to Babylonia's destruction of Jerusalem—namely, that God is punishing Israel for its sinful idolatry. In the period following the destruction of the Hasmonaean state, there probably were any number of urban Hasidim-Pharisees who adopted the theodicy of the prophets and who, like them, were prepared to come to terms with Israel's foreign rulers. But the old prophetic theodicy was not convincing to the overwhelming majority of Jews, most of whom led a simple, pious life in the countryside. These villagers grieved the loss of Jewish independence under the Hasmonaeans, and detested the Romans as alien intruders. They could not interpret the loss of their freedom as God's punishment of their idolatry, because they did not practise idolatry. Their sense of nationhood and attachment to land, capital, city, government, law and temple was reinforced by the memory of the Hasmonaean state and its betrayal under the Roman puppet-king Herod and his descendants.

The subjugation by Rome intensified Jewish messianic expectation, making it seem not only a metaphysical hope, but a practical possibility. Under Roman rule, the Jews of Palestine numbered more than half a million. They were mostly peasants, deeply nationalistic, and resentful of Jewish aristocratic 'assimilationists' in Jerusalem and other large towns. The *am-ha-aretz*, the peasant 'people of the land', became the willing recruits of the armies led by revolutionary zealots against Rome.

The Great Revolt began in 66 CE when Florus, the Roman procurator of Judaea, attempted to rob the temple treasury. In reaction, temple priests were persuaded by Jewish rebels to suspend the daily sacrifice of a bull and two lambs on behalf of the Gentile emperor and the Roman people. That sacrifice symbolized Jewish loyalty to the government, and its sudden termination was interpreted as an act of sedition. Thereupon, Roman soldiers fought the Jewish rebels who were soon joined by thousands of peasants, merchants, minor-level priests, some Pharisees, and even members of the aristocratic high priest caste. By the end of 67 CE, when the provisional Jewish government was in control of Jerusalem, Jews of every class and every religious group were engaged in the revolt.

The Great Revolt was a truly popular uprising, and not the product of some die-hard revolutionary group conspiring in defiance of Roman law and Jewish national will, as Josephus would have us believe. Josephus wished to trace the revolt back sixty years to the year 6 CE when the obscure Judah the Galilaean mounted a revolt against the Roman tax census, which in his eyes was blasphemous because it forced Jews to acknowledge Caesar, not God, as their lord. Doubtless Judah was a religious extremist who caused trouble for the local Roman government; but there is little evidence to support Josephus's contention that he was the spiritual ancestor of the Zealot party that would make its appearance in 67–68 CE, when the more militant rebels were seeking to wrest control of the provisional government from the high priests and other moderates.

David Rhodes argues that serious strife between Jews and the Roman authorities developed only twenty years prior to the Great Revolt. Before that, in the decades that followed Judah's anti-tax rebellion there were sporadic instances of Roman religious intolerance or bad judgment, to which Palestinian Jews responded in non-violent political ways, by appealing to the legate in Syria or directly to the emperor. The events surrounding the procuratorship of Pontius Pilate reveal the pattern.

Pontius Pilate was installed as procurator in 26 CE, and his decrees soon provoked resentment among the Jews in Palestine.[1] He contravened standing Roman policy by allowing army standards bearing the insignia of the boar to parade through Jerusalem. Jews reacted in a peaceful demonstration at Pilate's headquarters in Caesarea. The depth of their resentment can be measured by Josephus's observation that Jews were prepared to die by the sword, rather than violate their religious law by ignoring the Roman standards. Pontius Pilate, fearing a major riot, removed the standards from Jerusalem. A second issue

---

1. Flavius Josephus, *The Great Roman–Jewish War: AD 66–70* (trans. William Whiston; rev. D.S. Margoliouth; Gloucester, MA: Peter Smith, 1970 [repr. of Harper Torchbook 1960 edn]), 2.174.

arose when the procurator confiscated money from the temple treasury to pay for the construction of an aqueduct. Again a peaceful demonstration was held, but this time Roman soldiers attacked, killing several demonstrators. Troubles continued to plague Pilate's inefficient and corrupt administration, with the result that he was recalled to Rome in 36 CE, the Jews rejoicing at his departure. As one incompetent procurator yielded to another, Roman–Jewish relations continued to decline, with predictable outcome.

In the year after Pilate's removal, Marullus was named procurator. During the four years of his administration, he found himself required to carry out an imperial decree that was guaranteed to put Jews and Romans at sword's point. The emperor Gaius Caligula, who fancied himself a god, stole a leaf from the book of Antiochus Epiphanes IV, and ordered the legate of Syria, Petronius, to place a statue of the emperor in the Jerusalem temple. The Jewish reaction was instant, but again non-violent, as Jewish leaders prevailed on Petronius to rescind the order.[1] Josephus notes that the incident was a potential cause for war.[1] Fortunately, Caligula died before the decree could be put into effect.

During the two decades from 26 to 44 CE, Roman offences against the Jewish community and its ritual law remained isolated incidents, departures from an imperial policy that was basically tolerant. It should also be remembered that the imperial government in Rome enacted special legislation not only to ensure religious freedom for Jews, but also to punish desecrators of the Jerusalem temple. Such desecration was considered a capital crime, even when a Roman legionnaire was involved. The emperor Tiberius, who enjoyed a long rule of 23 years (14–37 CE), was favourably inclined towards Jews, as was his predecessor, Augustus. The procurators whom they appointed to govern Judaea held office for many years, and this encouraged stability. Moreover, as Rhodes notes, the procurators, being of Italian origin, were not particularly biased in favour of the Greek communities in Palestine.[2] Until 44 CE, the actions of the procurators were never so harsh or stupid as to provoke violent Jewish reaction. All this was to change after 44 CE.

I shall begin by noting that after 44 CE the Jewish desert marauders,

---

1. Josephus, *Ant.* 18.302.
2. Rhodes, *Israel in Revolution*, p. 68.

the 'brigands' as Josephus calls them, began to gain control of the countryside, because the Roman procurators were unable to contain their activities. The result was the breakdown of legal order, a chaos in which villagers and townspeople lost respect for Roman authority, and also for the Jewish officials who could do little to stop the marauders.

From 44 to 66 CE a succession of Roman procurators, each seemingly worse than the other, undermined Roman–Jewish relations. In 48 CE, Cumnanus became procurator, and for the next four years engaged in a series of actions that would lead to armed conflict between Romans and Jews. According to Josephus, one day a Roman soldier made an obscene gesture on the roof of the temple portico, expressing the soldiers' contempt toward Jewish worship.[1] The Jews immediately demanded that Cumnanus punish the soldier. However, rather than complying, the procurator called out more troops to the temple. In fleeing the Roman soldiers, some Jews were trampled to death, thus becoming national heroes.

A second incident occurred when Roman soldiers pursuing Jewish brigands invaded Jewish villages and arrested several officials. In the encounter, a Roman soldier burned a copy of the Torah. The Jews, Josephus states, reacted 'as though it were their whole country which had been consumed by the fire', and again demanded that Cumnanus punish the soldier. In this instance fearing a riot, the procurator obliged by beheading the offender.[2]

The combination of chaos in the countryside, and weak procurators who could not or would not discipline Roman soldiers, had an effect on the stability of government in Jerusalem. In 51 CE a group of Jews on their way to Jerusalem for a festival were attacked by Samaritans. Cumnanus turned a deaf ear to their request to punish the attackers, and when they sought to administer their own punishment, they discovered that he had armed the Samaritans and turned Roman troops against the Jews. In the fight that followed, many Jews were killed. It was the first of much blood that would be spilled in the following years.

It is important to recognize that nowhere in Josephus's text is there evidence that Jews were planning or eager to fight Rome; but once

---

1. Josephus, *War* 2.223-227.
2. *War* 2.229-230.

pushed by the Roman military they were, for the first time, willing to defend themselves by force. Rhodes remarks that the Jewish action 'in itself was an assertion of liberty, tantamount to an act of war which involved a failure to recognize the existing Roman authorities. Once the Jews were armed and active, they were willing to fight against the Romans—and the direct rebellion was at hand.'[1]

It is worth remembering that only a year before the incident of the Jewish–Samaritan conflict, the Jews had been evicted from Rome because of fomenting disturbances. More disturbances continued in the Palestinian countryside, where Josephus says 'robbery and riots and insurrections' were common. Over the next fifteen years disorders mounted. The procurator Cumnanus was succeeded by the equally inept Felix (52–60 CE), to be followed by Festus (60–62 CE) and Albinos (62–64 CE). All were Greeks, less tolerant of Jewish law and customs than were the Italian procurators, and more sympathetic with the Syrian-Greek population of Palestine. In the latter part of the 50s and the early 60s, robbery, assassination, and rioting spread to Jerusalem. The Jewish *sicarii* made their appearance. Hatred of the Roman authorities and of the Jewish officials who collaborated with them was openly and violently expressed on the streets of Jerusalem.

Many Jews throughout the country interpreted the disorders as a sign that the realization of the messianic idea was imminent. The belief spread that Rome was reaching the end of its days. Soon the wicked would be punished, the righteous vindicated. Israel would be reunited and restored to its land, to live under the Davidic prince. Some groups, like the Essenes, were prepared to leave the messianic event in God's hands. However, the messianic hope undoubtedly had a different effect on the revolutionaries who sought to clear the way for God's Day of Judgment. Josephus is fairly silent on how messianism affected the Jewish revolutionaries, because he would not permit his readers to believe that they had any noble, religious, or idealistic reasons to take up arms against Rome.

War broke out during the procuratorship of Florus (64–66 CE), when disorders reached their height in the countryside. The general unrest was fed by the measures taken by the emperor Nero in Rome. One particular act deeply offended Palestinian Jews and convinced them they had little or no standing in the empire. A local conflict

1. Rhodes, *Israel in Revolution*, p. 72.

between Syrian and Jewish inhabitants of Caesarea over the administrative control of the city in 66 CE was decided by Nero in favour of the Syrians, thus putting Jews in an inferior legal and social position in the city. The Jewish community of Palestine feared that what happened in Caesarea could also happen in Jerusalem; the protection and the privileges which it had historically enjoyed in Palestine seemed to be evaporating. Now the high priests of the temple and wealthy aristocrats also began to turn against government authority. Among them was Josephus himself, a member of a most influential Jewish family linked to the Hasmonaean princes. Josephus would become a revolutionary general until he ultimately defected to Rome.

It is a mistake to assume that the Great Revolt was caused merely by the immediate incidents which sparked violent conflict. The deeper truth is that Jews were at war with Rome for some twenty years prior to the attempt of Florus to rob the temple treasury, thus triggering a violent conflict that lasted seven years. Rhodes makes us aware of social and economic conditions that contributed to the outbreak of the war.[1] The lower classes were crippled by high taxes, not only those collected by Roman authorities, but also those paid for the upkeep of the temple and its hierarchy. Large landowners exploited the peasants in order to pay their own heavy taxes to the government. Small landowners who could not pay their taxes risked losing their land to the government. 'The result', says Rhodes, 'was an abundance of fugitive slaves and miserable free working men.'[2] Many of these desperate souls turned to robbery, or relied on brigands to solve their problems, 'Robin Hood' fashion. Josephus mentions the famine of 48 CE which devastated the country.

The Jews were divided socially and economically long before the war turned the Jewish community violently against itself. Upper class Jews increased their wealth by acting as tax-collectors, positions purchased with bribes from the Romans. High priests, who took the temple fees, exploited ordinary priests. Rhodes states that 'since the wealthy had the most to lose by a war with Rome, the revolutionary cause was quite popular among lower classes who saw the rebellion not only as a struggle against the Romans, but also as an opportunity

---

1. Rhodes, *Israel in Revolution*, pp. 176-78.
2. Rhodes, *Israel in Revolution*, p. 81.

to gain revenge against the oppressive Jews of the upper class'.[1]

By the mid 60s Jerusalem and Palestine were in chaos. Contributing to the turmoil was the completion of the temple's construction which left some 18,000 workers unemployed. The high priests decided to use temple funds to re-employ many of the workers in a project of repaving the streets of Jerusalem in white stone. One can imagine, therefore, the consternation the priests felt when it was discovered that Florus had tried to rob the temple treasury.

Josephus leaves no doubt that the Jewish revolution was doomed from the outset because of internal quarrels. The internecine conflict among the Jewish factions began in early 67 during the period of the provisional government, at the end of the first year of the war, and continued even as Titus's troops were besieging Jerusalem. Yet is is probable that Rome would have crushed the rebellion no matter how well organized or united the rebels were. Josephus was not unaware of this, because his own decision to switch to the Roman side sometime after the zealot party had taken control of Jerusalem in 67–68 CE was influenced by a realistic assessment of the power of Rome.

There were, of course, Jewish 'pacifists' like Johanan ben Zakkai, who preferred to suffer indignities rather than take up arms. But they were a minority. The vast majority of Jews believed their fight was just, that God would grant them victory over the pagan Romans, and that the nation of Israel would once again know freedom in its own land. They mistakenly assumed that Nero was too busy with his own troubles to bother with a revolt in a distant land, and underestimated the willingness of Rome to fight for Palestine as a land-bridge between the rich provinces of Syria and Egypt. They expected that the Parthian nation to the east, a perpetual thorn in Rome's side, would capitalize on the Jewish revolt by launching an offensive of its own. The Parthians eventually did so, but too late to help the Jewish cause.

The revolutionary groups were five: the Sicarii; the force commanded by John of Giscala; a second force led by Simon bar Giora; the group identified as Idumaeans; and the fighters who called themselves Zealots. At some point in the four years before the Roman conquest of Jerusalem, each group made an alliance with one or more of the others to achieve control of the revolution. It is difficult to explain this internal conflict, except to say that it was a reflection of

---

1. Rhodes, *Israel in Revolution*, p. 81.

the extremely variegated character of Jewish society in the first century. Just as no one form of 'Judaism' was practised, so there was no one type of 'Jew'. Jews could only agree on their hatred of the Roman government and on the quest for the freedom of Israel. Beyond that they were a people deeply divided. We know this to be true, because no sooner was the temple seized by the revolutionary band led by Eleazar, enabling the resumption of the temple services, than the high priests were excluded from them. Thus, from the beginning, the rebellion against Rome contained elements of a Jewish civil war.

But the war against Rome proved a stronger force than the internal fights among the Jews. At a crucial point in the revolt, when the provisional government was formed under the leadership of Ananus the high priest, it seemed that he, with the support of other priests and moderate elements, would arrange a cease-fire and a political compromise with the Roman authorities. Recognizing this, the Zealot party was formed in the winter of 67–68 to combat the moderates and to continue the revolt. The assassination of Ananus spelled the end of compromise and sealed the fate of the Jewish nation, as Josephus noted with lament. After destroying the provisional government, the Zealots took control of Jerusalem in 68 CE, established their own government, and conducted a reign of terror against the 'wealthy and prominent'. For the next two years Jews fought each other in the city, while Vespasian, and then Titus, were methodically and effectively subduing Jewish strongholds in the countryside and laying plans for the siege of Jerusalem.

There were many calculations and miscalculations, but we cannot conclude, as Josephus did, that the Jewish revolutionaries fighting Rome acted basely, impiously, or were blinded by ambition. The opposite seems to be true. Roman government had become hateful in Jewish eyes, and Jews, trusting in God's providence as they always had, and having the successful Maccabaean revolt as precedent, took up arms against a vastly superior foe and lost a war. With hindsight we can say, as Josephus himself said sitting in Rome years after he quit his command as a general, that it would have been better for the Jewish nation if this war had never occurred. But to have said that is to fail to appreciate in full measure what the Jewish nation meant, religiously and politically.

Did nothing positive, creative, and lasting come of the Great Revolt? Did this conflict only inspire the Bar Kokhba fighters to launch an even more self-destructive attack on Roman imperial authority? Professor Harkabi believes that the Jewish rebels of the Great Revolt should have remembered Jeremiah's advice to King Zedekiah at the time of the Babylonian conquest: 'Serve Babylon, and live'.[1] Was that advice sound? Before answering the question we should not forget that the dangers facing Israel under Babylonian captivity were not nearly as great as those experienced under centuries of Greek and Roman rule. Jeremiah's Israel was not confronted by the actual danger of national extinction through cultural dissolution. When we consider that all other minority peoples living under Greek and Roman rule eventually made an accommodation with the culture of the rulers, it is astonishing to realize that only the Jews continued to resist actively, hoping for divine intervention to support their cause.

Why did the Jews resist? The answer is that they believed that Israel had to retain its integrity and freedom to be Israel, that is, God's covenant partner. In this respect the Great Revolt, like the Maccabaean struggle which preceded it and the Bar Kokhba rebellion which followed it, helped preserve a sense of Jewish national uniqueness. If we accept this judgment, we must recognize that the fighters of the 66–74 CE war made a creative and lasting contribution to Jewish history. No one stated that contribution better than Michael Avi-Yonah:

> If we regard Jewish history as a whole, we cannot deny that in a certain sense the Zealots were successful in their struggle. The destruction of the Temple and the elimination of Jewish statehood widened an already existing gulf between Judaism and its environment to such a degree that no conciliation in the fields of art and literature could bridge it. Judaism secluded itself within its own boundaries. It succeeded in detaching itself more or less completely from the common fate of the ancient world. If Israel has kept its national identity to this day, the only nation of antiquity to do so, and has survived the decline and fall of the ancient world, this is due in no small measure to the warriors of its two lost wars against Rome. From the point of view of Jewish nationality their desperate undertakings thus appear in a positive light, however much one can regret the amount of suffering caused to the community and to individuals.[2]

1. Harkabi, *The Bar Kochba Syndrome*, pp. 4-6.
2. Avi-Yonah, *The Jews under Roman and Byzantine Rule*, pp. 13-14.

THE IMPORT OF EARLY RABBINIC WRITINGS FOR AN UNDERSTANDING OF JUDAISM IN THE HELLENISTIC–ROMAN PERIOD

Gerald J. Blidstein

This paper will be divided into two parts. The first part will raise ideational issues that, in my view, emerge from the way certain rabbinic legal texts are constructed, or from the way the laws are formulated. The second part will make use of particular rabbinic texts in an attempt to derive from them an insight into the Jewish society of the Hellenistic–Roman period. I have chosen to focus on the fourth and fifth chapters in Mishnah tractate *Gittin* which deals with divorce. These chapters move beyond a narrow focus on divorce, and present a broad swath of rabbinic law and concerns that emerge associatively from the laws regarding divorce.

I

The ideational aspect may be further divided into narrow philological issues, and a broader consideration. I shall begin with the philology. The chapters on which I focus discuss at length rabbinic enactments; the verb applied to such enactments is *tikken* or *hitkin, letakken* or *lehatkin*, usually translated as 'to correct' or 'to set in order'.[1] The Mishnah gives the reasons for these enactments—in Danby's rendition, 'precautions for the general good'. That is a very loose translation of the Hebrew phrase *mipnei tikkun ha'olam* which is better rendered 'to order the world correctly'.[2]

---

1.   The verb *tikken, hitkin* is found only three times in the Bible, in Ecclesiastes, and appears several times in Ecclesiasticus. It is clearly a term which entered more common usage after the closure of the Hebrew canon.

2.   I doubt that *'olam* means *aeon* here; it probably means something more like

I am intrigued by the connection of this rabbinic expression to a prayer known as '*aleinu* which is probably of Second Commonwealth provenance. '*aleinu* contains a familiar phrase, *letakken 'olam bemalkhut shaddai*, 'to order the world so as to achieve the kingdom of heaven'. In the prayer, the achievement of the kingdom of heaven is God's task; but in the rabbinic phrase the ordering of the world becomes humanity's task. This may be symptomatic of the way the rabbis were appropriating terminology—in a very subtle and minor, but nonetheless significant, way. *malkhut shaddai* is, perhaps, God's task; but the human task or the task of the sages is to correct any small injustice within society, so as ultimately to achieve that kingdom of heaven.

The second point is somewhat broader. In chapters four and five of *Gittin* one finds the repeated refrain: this was enacted, or this was ordered, 'for the benefit of society'. The text manifests the rabbinic consciousness of actually making law, rather than a process of biblical exegesis that ultimately results in law. The rabbis are clearly saying that through their institutions and their courts they are fundamentally establishing how people and society are to behave, rather than arguing that this is what the Bible says.[1]

Of course, one can also find reams of rabbinic texts which are exegetical in character; I have obviously chosen texts that suit my purposes. However, the issue is not whether the rabbis teach biblical exegesis, or even what their self-awareness is when they do so—which in itself is a significant question with regard to the rabbinic mentality. Significance lies in the fact that legislation exists alongside exegesis, and that the rabbis are conscious and willing to label this activity explicitly as legislative.

Occasionally one can see the rabbis striking out in both directions at the same time, and one does not know whether to interpret this activity as evidence of fluidity and alternative models, or of tension and

society, i.e. 'to order society correctly'.

1.   Urbach has claimed that rabbinic legislation is older than exegesis, because it presumes an institutional base which was very well developed until the destruction of the Second Temple; only then does rabbinic society shift to exegesis. Other scholars argue that exegesis came first and only later did the rabbis move to legal enactment. That question is not at issue here. I think it is significant that we are dealing with neither inspiration nor inspired exegesis. The text clearly reflects rabbinic enactment based on institutional legal patterns and authority.

rabbinic need to backtrack into a model that may be considered more legitimate. To give one example, *m. Giṭ.* 4.3 contains the concise statement: 'Hillel ordained the *prosbul* for the ordering of society'. The *prosbul* cancelled the biblical remittance of debts during the sabbatical year. It was legislated because the biblical injunction that all debts be remitted in the seventh year made it very hard for the needy to obtain credit. Hillel realized that the remittance of debts was dysfunctional to society, and then ordained the *prosbul* as a device by which debts could be collected even after the sabbatical year.

The text describes *prosbul* as a piece of legislation—in Hebrew, *hillel hitkin*—and the reason given is *mipnei tikkun ha'olam.* However, the tannaitic Midrash to Deuteronomy describes the institution of *prosbul* and Hillel's activity not as an enactment, but as *midrash,* exegesis. One wonders whether those who put Hillel's pronouncement into a midrashic mold were not trying to say that something as radical as *prosbul* cannot be enacted legislatively by the sages, because it fundamentally undercuts a biblical institution, and that the rabbinic society can legitimately institute such a change only by deriving it from the biblical text. Thus, the fundamental question posed here is whether Jewish law is always an offshoot of biblical law, or is at times innovative legislation.

II

I should now like to move away from the world of thought of the rabbis and from their self-awareness, toward the actual areas of life with which they were concerned. In these two chapters of *Gittin* one discovers the full range of rabbinic enactments, which include areas that today would be called civil law. Marc Bloch[1] makes the point that one cannot claim to know how a society works by merely studying its laws, for the conflicts of daily life are not usually put before legal authorities but are settled in much more domestic ways. Nonetheless, I think one can get a flavour of the Second Commonwealth society by reading rabbinic legal material.

Obviously, those chapters in *Gittin* describe matters of marriage and divorce such as, for example, the payment of divorce settlements. However, one also finds questions dealing with manumission and the

---

1.   M. Bloch, *The Historian's Craft* (New York: Vintage Books, 1953).

financial obligations that remain after a slave has been freed, the ransoming of captives, the payment of debts, and so on. The text includes very little religious or cultic law, but considerable legislation dealing with civil issues concerning society's less fortunate elements—minors, imbeciles and slaves—that is, people who were on the fringes of the community in the legal sense. The rabbis often deal with problems caused by the consistent application of the legal system, which then leads society into impossible situations. The following examples will indicate how people living during the Second Commonwealth period sometimes behaved in terms of their legal obligations or rights.

First, an issue of divorce law which according to biblical and rabbinical tradition is in male hands: the husband writes the bill of divorce, or has it written and gives it to the wife. *M. Giṭ*. 4.1 describes a situation in which a man has written a bill of divorce and has had it delivered to his wife by an agent. His wife is clearly not living with him—which may be a significant fact and not merely a technicality. The husband then changes his mind and decides that he no longer wishes to proceed with the divorce. The text reads as follows: 'In former times, a man was allowed to bring together a court of three wherever he was, and cancel the *get* (bill of divorce)'. This describes an informal legal structure in which the man who changed his mind about a divorce would simply set up a court of three in order to cancel the bill of divorce although it was already on its way. Here is a situation in which a *get* that is no longer legally valid is being delivered to its recipient, who will receive it elsewhere and will be free to remarry and have children. The possible evils arising thereby are only too obvious: through no fault of her own, the woman will be producing 'bastards' (*mamzerim)* in terms of rabbinic law.

One may speculate that the situation of a husband who has a change of heart, and cancels the bill of divorce after having it written and sent on its way, is not as innocent as it may at first seem. We are dealing with a husband and wife who live at some distance from one another, and perhaps with a husband whom a rabbinic court has compelled to write a divorce—which was part of their authority in mishnaic times and possibly in an earlier period. It is likely that the husband whom a rabbinic court compelled to write a divorce was not sympathetic with the injunction, and might scurry off elsewhere to try to have the *get* annulled before it was delivered. The rabbis sought to close that loophole in the law, for the good of the woman or of the family.

The Mishnah informs us that Rabban Gamaliel the Elder ordained that men should not do this, as a precaution for the general good.[1] The Mishnah does not deal with the question of what would happen if one ignored Rabban Gamaliel's stricture, or whether he had the power to do anything about it. What is clear is the rabbinic statement that the exercise of the husband's legal power leads to no good societal result; and therefore, this legal right is either rescinded, or is strongly criticized.

Now, a second example from ch. 4:

> If a man was half-bondman and half-freeman he should labour one day for his master and one day for himself. Thus (holds) the School of Hillel. The School of Shammai said to them: He had ordered it well for his master but for him he had not ordered it well. He cannot marry a bondwoman since he is half-free, he cannot marry a free woman since he is half-bondman, being half owned by his master. May he never marry? Was the world not created for fruition and increase, as it is written: He created it not a waste; he formed it to be inhabited. But, as a precaution for the general good (*tikkun ha'olam*), they compel his master to set him free, and the bondman writes him a bond of indebtedness for half his value.

Here again the legal system creates a situation which is perfectly legitimate within law, within a society that endorses slavery, a slave can have two owners and one of them can set his 'half' free. Yet the legal situation is fundamentally intolerable in terms of the moral right of a slave to marry, the rabbinic societal norm being that one ought to be married and bring children into the world. Shammai expresses the more activist rabbinic stance, insisting that the master do something about it; Hillel says one cannot compel the master to do so. From a modernist (admittedly anachronistic) point of view, Shammai seems to be more in tune with human values. In the above case, the School of Hillel came around to Shammai's view. Such a situation might not have been an everyday occurrence, but it could arise in the Jewish society of the Second Commonwealth period, and the rabbis felt constrained to deal with it.

---

1.   The text refers to Rabban Gamaliel the Elder, who lived during the period of the Second Temple. However, there are reasons to question the correctness of this text.

The final example deals with a situation which has unfortunately become very concrete in contemporary Israeli society, this Mishnah being constantly cited as a ruling that ought to guide policy in similar situations. 'Captives should not be ransomed for more than their value, as a precaution for the general good' (*mipne tikkun ha'olam*) (*m. Gi.t.* 4.6). If captives are held by an enemy or, more commonly, by bandits, one does not ransom them for more than their market value, or for more than they would bring when sold into slavery if they were not Jews who could appeal to a Jewish community to ransom them. Ransoming of captives was a responsibility that the Jewish society assumed in both antiquity and mediaeval times; and for a variety of reasons the Jewish community was often faced with Jewish captives.

The Mishnah seems to imply that the ransom of Jewish captives for more than they are worth may become an inducement for the taking of such Jewish captives, and encourage banditry aimed directly at Jews. I have, however, historical as well as textual difficulties with this explanation. At face value, this poses an interesting moral question. The text confronts us with what is, after all, a moral duty and a moral good, namely to save somebody from distress at the best, and perhaps even from slavery and death. Yet this immediate good is rejected in the interest of the future good of the larger community.[1] This poses an interesting moral dilemma and is an example of the kind of consideration that would exercise the rabbis.

Let me now raise a question which issues almost directly from this last case. To what degree did the rabbis consider such issues among themselves, and to what degree were they in touch with a wider society? The number of sages mentioned by name in the talmudic literature is not very large; Albeck claims that from the third to the sixth century they total approximately 600. If this figure is broken down by century, and then by decade, one gets an average of fifteen sages per decade. Consequently, the question arises whether the rabbis were fundamentally a small group addressing another slightly larger group, or whether they were the guides of Jewish society in general.

The above text is framed in a way which leads to the assumption that, at least in terms of the authors' self-consciousness, they saw

---

1. It may be noted that Jewish communities by and large did not abide by this rather stringent rule.

themselves influencing the larger society. At times one is quite confounded by the ambition, almost the arrogance, revealed in that presumption. In this instance, the rabbis seem to assume that by setting limits to the ransom price paid for Jewish captives, they influence the behaviour of bandits on the open sea or the activities of the Roman armies, and believe that their enactment could have an impact on the general society.[1] They certainly assumed that a large number of Jews would abide by their enactment; otherwise it could have no effect at all!

Another example concerns an institution known in Hebrew by the non-Hebraic term *din sicaricon* (*m. Giṭ.* 5.6). While the origins of the term are not fully clear, it is apparent that the law related to the confiscation of Jewish lands by the Romans. The question faced by the rabbis and eventually by the Patriarch, was how to deal, through their legal system, with the confiscation of Jewish land by Roman authorities. The law went through three stages of development. First there was virtual non-recognition: a Jew who bought land from the Romans without first squaring the purchase with its original Jewish owner (i.e. paying for it), could not hold the land against the claim of that owner; rather, the first owner retained the title to the land. In the next stage, the Jew who bought the land from the Romans or was granted ownership by them, received title but had to pay a small sum to the original owner; the latter, however, was given the first right to repurchase it. In the third stage even this requirement was dropped.

One might suppose that this development was intended to ensure a certain degree of stability in land ownership; if someone buys land from the Roman government they are entitled to continue living on it. The Talmud, however, sees it in a different light. It claims that the rabbis wanted to safeguard stability so as to encourage Jews to buy land back from Romans, and thereby return it to Jewish ownership. As long as a Jew buying land from the Roman authorities had to consider the possibility that its original owner could appear at any time and legitimately demand its return, the likelihood of such land purchases would be diminished.

If this theory (which is presented in the Tosefta) is correct, it means that the rabbis assumed that their legislation not only had sufficient

---

1.   There is, of course, another explanation, namely, concern for the public treasury.

impact on the behaviour of people who were their followers, but would also affect the transferral of lands from Roman military control back to the Jewish society. This reflects a sense of social power. The rabbis assumed that they exercised sufficient control over enough people to influence patterns of property ownership throughout the land.

One further comment is in order here. It is very clear from the Mishnah that the rabbinic discussion is really concerned with relations among Jews. The legal problem posed is to what extent Jew A who bought a field from the Romans has to reimburse Jew B, the original owner. There is no attempt here to influence Jews in their behaviour towards the Romans. It is a given that Jews are wont to buy land from the Romans. The basic question, which continues to be discussed throughout mediaeval times, concerns the impact this legislation has on the inner workings of Jewish society. Even high-flown phrases such as 'the law of the kingdom is law' are, in fact, attempts to order the internal relations of the Jewish society rather than to order the relations of that society with its dominant or ruling host society.[1]

The final point which I would like to make concerns *m. Giṭ.* 5.8-9, which contains a lengthy list of enactments that are not motivated by *tikkun ha'olam,* 'the ordering of society', but apply what the Mishnah calls *darkei shalom*, 'ways of peace'. *M. Giṭ.* 9 contains a famous pronouncement on the relations of Gentiles and Israelites: 'Greetings are to be offered to Gentiles in the interest of peace'. The Baraita then expands upon this by saying: one gives charity to Gentiles along with Jews, in the interest of peace; one cares for non-Jewish sick along with Jewish sick, in the interest of peace; one buries non-Jewish dead along with Jewish dead, in the interest of peace.

A variety of interpretations have been applied to this Baraita. At times this explanation sounds somewhat apologetic or trivial; for example, Judaism recognizes peace as a value equalizing all humans. Other exegetes rationalize the list in cynical or pragmatic terms: Jews realize that if they are to live within a society which is in large measure Gentile, Jewish particular morality will have to bend a bit; therefore one has to behave decently to Gentiles just as one behaves decently to Jews.

---

1.   See G. Blidstein, 'The Function of "The Law of the Kingdom is Law" in the Medieval Jewish Community', *Jewish Journal of Sociology* 15 (1973), pp. 213-20.

I think that both of these interpretations take this particular list of guidelines out of its context. *M. Giṭ.* 5.8-9 deals with the social relationships of groups among whom tension often exists. The text begins with different Jewish societal strata: priests, Levites and Israelites; it then continues with specific categories such as deaf-mutes, imbeciles, and minors. The tensions that arise when such groups mingle in an organic society become the subject of rabbinic discussion. Next come the obvious tensions which exist between the *'amei ha'aretz*, the less observant peasant population, and the members of groups who meticulously abide by the biblical and rabbinic injunctions, as well as the tensions between those who abide stringently by the regulations of the sabbatical year and others who do not. Finally, one arrives at the tensions between Gentile and Jew. I think that this text is presenting a cross-section of social classes in the Second Commonwealth period that were prone to experience friction and hostility.

The rabbis are saying, with neither a universalistic nor a cynical vision, that if all these groups are to live together, someone has to establish regulations to ensure that certain decencies are maintained among them. I believe that this is, fundamentally, all that one can find in this text. The Mishnah obviously recognizes the existence of tensions that are ready to flare up; this is clear to any sociologist who reads the laws of *demai*, or the laws regulating the relations between the stringently observant *havurot* and the more lax *'amei ha'aretz* regarding their produce and their foods. There is also acknowledgment of the fact that tension may be sparked by even a minor incident, not to mention more serious matters. This concern is clearly evident in the rabbinic texts, and provides some small insight into the society to which they were addressing themselves.

LITERARY TYPOLOGIES AND BIBLICAL INTERPRETATION IN THE HELLENISTIC–ROMAN PERIOD*

Devorah Dimant

One of the most surprising aspects of the Qumran discoveries is the sheer number of unknown works of literature—some in Hebrew, some in Aramaic—which have come to light. At a single stroke, a whole new world of literature was resurrected from the caves of Qumran to give us a new and startling insight into Jewish literature of the Hellenistic–Roman period. We now realize that the literary works of this period which had previously come down to us were but a small fraction of a vast body of literature which had existed in Eretz Israel and perhaps in the diaspora as well. It is significant that the library of Qumran contained samples of almost all the literary genres already known, as well as some new ones. This not only sheds light on the various literary styles in which Jewish literature of that period was couched, but also enables us to understand it better.

Under the impact of the Qumran discoveries, and the increasing interest in literary criticism and hermeneutics, a gradual shift of focus is taking place: side by side with the steady output of traditional philological–historical studies, a growing number of works are being devoted to literary and structural analysis. This new trend in research is producing a more sensitive approach to the interpretative function of Jewish literature of the Hellenistic–Roman period, and additional works are studying the various modes of biblical interpretation current in that literature.

The reader who is even slightly familiar with the literary world of Judaism in the Hellenistic–Roman period, is struck by the centrality of

*For a full discussion and analysis serving as the basis for this paper, see my chapter 'Use and Interpretation of Mikra in the Apocrypha and Pseudepigrapha', in *Mikra* (ed. J.M. Mulder; Assen: van Gorcum, 1988), pp. 379-419.

the Hebrew Bible in post-biblical literature. One explanation is that this literature is not far removed in time from the later biblical books such as Qohelet and, especially, Daniel. In fact, the later canonical books are contemporary with the early apocryphal and pseudepigraphical works. This may, perhaps, account for the continuity of biblical forms and styles in one segment of post-biblical literature, and for the vitality and creativeness of biblical exegesis in other segments of this literature.

The area most fully researched in this respect is the New Testament, but more recently, studies have also been published on biblical interpretation in Philo's commentaries, the writings of Josephus, and rabbinic midrash. However, until now, these different biblical interpretations were studied separately, or at most sporadically compared with some other works. We have as yet no systematic collection of data nor any comprehensive methodological framework. This article cannot, therefore, provide a complete survey of the subject. It will be, perforce, programmatic and selective.

Current scholarship on the interpretation of biblical elements in various literatures tends to concentrate on the content of these elements and to neglect their function. It seems to me that the time has come to pay more attention to functional analysis, in order to increase our understanding of the post-biblical texts.

Biblical elements function in post-biblical literature in two main ways: one may be defined as expositional, the other as compositional. In its *expositional* function, the biblical element is presented explicitly and is interpreted as sacred text. The interpretation is usually effected by exegetical techniques and formal terminology. In its *compositional* function, the biblical element is integrated into the structure of the work; it is introduced without any formal marker. This non-explicit use of the biblical elements relies, for achieving the desired effect, on the understanding and active participation of the reader, who is assumed to have the necessary background of knowledge to detect the allusion.

These two basic modes of function, the expositional and the compositional, are operative in two different genres which exhibit distinctive styles, modes of expression, and terminology. The expositional function operates in genres which characteristically contain formal lemmata of the biblical text, to which exegetical comments are added. The lemmata, as well as the commentaries, are usually introduced by special, formal terms, so that the reader is made aware of their function.

To this type of genre belong the rabbinic midrashim, the Qumranic *pesharim*, and the commentaries on the Torah by Philo and other Hellenistic authors. Each of these literary genres aims at interpreting biblical texts. They all share three fundamental features: (1) a biblical quotation introduced by a special formula; (2) interpretation of the quotation, either explicitly formulated or implied by the context; and (3) the use of exegetical procedures to extract the desired meaning from the biblical text.

A good example of such a genre is to be found in the structure of a *pesher*. The *pesher* on Habakkuk, for instance, in commenting on Hab. 1.6, which alludes to a fearful, awesome nation of warriors, states:

> *The interpretation of it concerns* the Kittim; by the way of the level plain they come to smite and to loot the cities of the land, for *this is what it* [Scripture] *says*: 'To take possession of dwelling places not their own. Fearful and terrible are they. A claim to dignity goes out from them'. *The interpretation of it concerns* the Kittim, fear and dread of whom are upon all the nations. . .

We notice in this short passage the precise, distinctive terminology which introduces the biblical text and the interpretation which follows it. Similar patterns occur in the rabbinic midrash, the allegorical commentaries of Philo, and the explicit quotations found in the New Testament and the Apocrypha.

When comparing the various genres in which these biblical elements occur, it becomes clear that while they differ in form and ideological bias, they share the same exegetical methods and often evidence a common exegetical tradition. Thus, for instance, some of the exegetical rules used in the halakhic midrash ascribed to Hillel and to Yishmael, are also employed in the *pesharim*. The study of George J. Brooke[1] on 4QFlorilegium has recently provided additional examples, e.g. the use of the rule of *gezerah shavah*. Another interesting parallel is suggested by Philo's allegorical interpretations of the Torah, as compared with the allegorical interpretations found in the *pesharim* of certain passages in the Prophets. As I have said, a detailed comparison of Philo and the *pesharim* has yet to be undertaken.

---

1. G.J. Brooke, *Exegesis at Qumran: 4QFlorilegium in its Jewish Context* (JSOTSup, 29; Sheffield: JSOT Press, 1985).

But over and above specific connections and affinities between the various genres which employ the exegetical function, they share the common purpose of interpreting an authoritative, sacred text. Their shared problem is how to extract from the Bible a meaning that is applicable to a current situation. Toward this end they employ appropriate exegetical procedures.

An additional expositionary form has been generally neglected in scholarly research, namely, that of isolated explicit quotations. Such quotations appear in genres which normally use biblical elements in a compositional function, such as narratives, prayers, wisdom discourses, and testaments. They are found, *inter alia,* in the Apocrypha, the New Testament, and such sectarian writings as the *Rule of the Community* and the *Damascus Covenant*. These quotations possess all the features which characterize the genres using biblical elements in expositional function, and should be considered as another such genre. In the Apocrypha, explicit quotations of biblical text are quite rare, and appear mostly in discourses where they form part of the rhetorical argument. Interestingly, most of these discourses are prayers, whereas the biblical quotations are usually taken from speeches in the Torah, and quote laws or divine promises. Only in two cases do explicit biblical quotations (from the Prophets and Psalms) occur in narratives. The first is in Tob. 2.6 (quoting Amos 8.10), and the other is in 1 Macc. 7.16-17 (quoting Ps. 79.2-3). The choice of the Torah, the Prophets, and the Psalms as sources may be explained by the fact that they were already canonized, and could be interpreted as sacred texts.

I shall illustrate the complexity of the subject by looking more closely into one type of expositionary genre, namely the *pesharim* (commentaries). The *pesher* first came to be considered as a literary form in its own right following the discovery in Qumran of biblical commentaries written in distinctive style and in accordance with a special method. These commentaries aim at interpreting biblical prophecy in the light of current events in the life of the Qumranite commentary. In fact, the commentary of the *pesharim* consists in reading the current events into the biblical text by means of exegetical procedures. Entire works were found written in this manner, namely, running commentaries on biblical Prophets or Psalms. Commentaries also exist on selected verses. Most significantly, we also find *pesharim* on single verses, with the quoted verse followed by commentary.

These isolated *pesharim* constitute a special type of explicit quotation comparable to the explicit quotations in the Apocrypha.

One observes a particular affinity between the *pesharim*, certain explicit quotations in the Apocrypha (cf. Tob. 2.6 and 1 Macc. 7.16-17) and the so-called formula quotations in the Gospel of Matthew. All these are instances of biblical prophecies seen to have been fulfilled in subsequent historical events. For this purpose the Psalms are treated as prophecies of David. This correspondence suggests that while the *pesharim* reflect, in content, the particular ideology and aims of the Qumranite community, the genre itself was not invented by the Qumranites. The similarity of method in all these instances leads to the conclusion that the *pesher*, or a *pesher*-like method of interpretation, was widely used in various circles, for different purposes, during the Second Commonwealth Era. The Qumranic *pesharim* are only one instance of this method.

In all the genres which employ biblical elements in an expositional function, the elements are explicit, and are present in the surface of the text. It is no wonder, therefore, that most scholarly studies deal with these explicit elements. Examples of such studies are the Brooke monograph mentioned above, the great majority of discussions on biblical interpretation at Qumran (Elliger, Brownlee, Horgan, Nitzan),[1] and much of what has been written on the quotations in the New Testament.

The compositional mode of employing biblical elements is used as extensively as the expositional function. It is especially prevalent in the various genres of the Apocrypha and Pseudepigrapha—which are, basically, the genres of biblical literature itself: narrative, wisdom discourses, testaments and prayers. In all these literary forms biblical elements function compositionally. Unlike the use of biblical elements in the expositional mode, these elements are never explicitly signalled in the compositional mode, but rather are integrated into the fabric of the work as elements of style or form, or else serve as models.

At least three basic ways of integrating biblical elements may be

---

1.   Cf. K. Elliger, *Studien zum Habakkuk-kommentar vom Toten Meer* (Tübingen: Mohr, 1953); W.H. Brownlee, ed., *The Midrash Pesher of Habakkuk* (Missoula, MT: Scholars Press, 1979); M. Horgan, *Pesharim: Qumran Interpretations of Biblical Books* (CBQMS, 8; Washington, DC: Catholic Biblical Association, 1979); B. Nitzan, *Pesher Habakkuk* (Jerusalem: Bialik Institute, 1986).

discerned: first the incorporation of biblical texts into, the work; second, mere allusions to the biblical text; and third, the use of biblical, literary or thematic models.

The device of incorporating biblical texts is used extensively in the Apocrypha and Pseudepigrapha, and even in the Bible itself. It is a main feature in narrative works sometimes designated 'rewritten Bible', such as *Jubilees* and Josephus's *Antiquities*. These works are modelled on biblical stories, and their narrative sequence is composed mainly of stretches of running text taken from the corresponding biblical sources. This device is also used to reproduce specific 'biblical-like' situations in works less closely linked to scriptural texts.

Allusions or non-explicit quotations usually consist of hints at terms or motifs taken from recognizable biblical contexts. This device is widely used, chiefly in the Apocrypha and Pseudepigrapha. Thus, for instance, in the book of Tobit, Tobit is described in terms similar to those applied to Job in the Bible. In the Ethiopic *Enoch*, Enoch is described in the same terms as the seer Balaam.

These allusions and implicit quotations should, of course, be distinguished from the use of biblical expressions for purely stylistic purposes—a distinction not always easy to make. Generally speaking, the distinction may be defined as follows: both allusions and non-explicit quotations should be referable to an identifiable biblical text, which then becomes part of the structural and thematic pattern of the secondary work into which the reference is incorporated.

The use of biblical elements in the compositional manner described above does not, of course, exclude the presence of interpretative elements. In fact, each time a biblical element is employed in this way, a certain interpretation of it is implied, and is built into the extra-biblical work. The process of interpretation in the compositional mode is different from the overt exegesis of the expositional mode, but I believe that here too certain exegetical patterns—such as the equation of a biblical situation with a current one—are intended to achieve a reactualization of the biblical prototype. However, the issue has yet to be studied.

The use of non-explicit quotations and allusions is extensive and varied. The following examples will illustrate some of the techniques and problems involved. Non-explicit quotations and allusions in the narrative genres are particularly instructive. In narratives whose plot does not derive from the Bible, such as Tobit, Judith, 1 Maccabees and

2 Maccabees, biblical quotations and allusions are often worked into the story for a particular purpose. In one such instance, 1 Macc. 5.48, the return of Judah the Maccabee with the Jews of Gilead is described in words taken from Num. 20.17-20, 21.22, and Judg. 11.17-19, which depict Moses and the Israelites passing through the Land of the Emorites. This is clearly a non-explicit quotation compounded from several parallel biblical texts. By this method the author hints at an analogy between the return of Judah and the Gileadites, and the approach of the Israelites to the Land of Israel.

This device is most common in Greek works based on a Hebrew or Aramaic *Vorlage*, such as Tobit, Judith, and 1 Maccabees, which imitate biblical style. In works of Greek origin, for example 2 Maccabees, it is used to a lesser extent. In such writings, Hellenistic models are employed.

Pseudepigraphic narrative frameworks present a special problem. Most of the Pseudepigrapha is set in a narrative framework which provides explicit information about the hero, usually a biblical figure. This immediately sets the story in a specific and distinct biblical context. In this respect, pseudepigraphical frameworks belong to genres in which biblical elements function expositionally. At the same time these frameworks often contain non-explicit quotations, and allusions to biblical episodes which do not directly relate to the hero. A good example is the introduction to the *Testament of Enoch* in *1 En.* 91.1, which is patterned after the opening verses of the Blessing of Jacob in Genesis 49.

The latter example also illustrates the fact that various literary forms, such as the testament, the psalm, and the wisdom discourse, are often patterned after the corresponding biblical genres. For example, a testament usually follows the form of the *Testament of Jacob*, or the farewell discourse of Moses; a prayer is always modelled on some biblical prayer; and wisdom discourses are patterned after the biblical wisdom sayings ascribed to Solomon. In each of these cases the pattern is formed by means of allusions and non-explicit quotations from corresponding biblical passages.

Allusions and specific terms may also refer to thematic motifs. Thus, for instance, Tobit, one of the two main figures in the book of Tobit, is partly modelled on Job. This is achieved by reproducing both the thematic sequence and specific details of the Job story: the loss of his house and property, his illness, the mockery of his neighbours and the complaints of his wife.

These few examples are intended to give an idea of the complexity and variety of the phenomena under review. Moreover, we now know that this diversity was rooted in a widespread literary tradition. The Qumran scrolls contain ample evidence that various literary notions and forms existed side by side in the Covenanters' community. Works of midrashic and halakhic character appear alongside pseudepigraphic ones. This plurality of forms and methods indicates that they were in general use, and that they did not necessarily originate from a particular socioreligious group.

THE BOOK OF BEN SIRA:
IMPLICATIONS FOR JEWISH AND CHRISTIAN TRADITIONS

Maurice Gilbert

Ben Sira wrote his book in Hebrew at the beginning of the second century BCE in Jerusalem. The Greek translation was done, probably in Alexandria, by his grandson, during the last decades of the same century. For centuries, the book of Ben Sira was known only through versions in Greek, Latin and Syriac, produced mainly by Christians. These versions, however, present at least two different sorts of texts, of which one is shorter than the other.[1]

The Hebrew book of Ben Sira was current in ancient Judaism, but in time this Hebrew text disappeared. Only at the end of the last century was a great portion of it rediscovered in fragmentary manuscripts from the Cairo Genizah, and a few decades ago additional manuscripts were found at Qumran and Masada.[2] Today the text of Ben Sira is based principally on these Hebrew fragments, with the missing parts restored from the short Greek version. This holds true for the modern Hebrew editions of M.H. Segal and A.S. Artom, for instance,[3] and for the edition of A. Vaccari in Italian, L. Alonso

---

1. The best critical edition of the Greek version (the short text with the principal Greek additions) is that of J. Ziegler, *Sapientia Iesu Filii Sirach* (Septuaginta 12,2; Vandenhoek & Ruprecht: Göttingen, 1965).

2. The best edition of the Hebrew fragments is *The Book of Ben Sira. Text, Concordance, and an Analysis of the Vocabulary* (foreword by Z. Ben-Hayyim; Jerusalem, 1973). Recent complements are: A. Schreiber, 'A Leaf of the Fourth Manuscript of Ben Sira from the Geniza', *Magyar Koenyvszemle* 98 (1982), pp. 179-85; P.C. Beentjes, 'Some Misplaced Words in the Hebrew Manuscript C of the Book of Ben Sira', *Bib* 67 (1986), pp. 397-401; A.A. Di Lella, 'The Newly Discovered Sixth Manuscript of Ben Sira from the Cairo Geniza', *Bib* 69 (1988), pp. 226-38.

3. M.H. Segal, *Sefer Ben Sira haShalem* (Jerusalem, 2nd edn, 1958);

Schökel in Spanish, P.W. Skehan and A.A. Di Lella in English, G. Sauer in German, and A. Chouraqui in French.[1]

The following survey of the research carried out on the Ben Sira text will point to the relationship between its author and the Qumran community.

Qumran

In March 1952, two small Hebrew fragments of the book of Ben Sira were discovered in the second Qumran cave and were given the siglum 2Q18. Only the second fragment was identified with certainty as Sir. 6.20-31, with the help of MS A discovered at the end of the last century in Cairo.[2]

These discoveries made it evident that the Hebrew text of Ben Sira was still read in the main Jewish community during the second half of the first century BCE and at Qumran during the first century CE. It also became apparent that the texts found during the last century in Cairo were not retroversions, but were, in fact, copies of the original Hebrew text. And, finally, it became clear that the Greek version, produced by the grandson of Ben Sira, was closer to the original Hebrew text than MS A of Cairo where the latter differs from the Greek version. (The text of Sir. 6.23-24, 26 is extant in Hebrew in Qumran, and in Greek, but is absent from MS A of Cairo.)

In 1956, a revision of Sir. 51.13-19, 30 was found in the Psalms scroll from Cave 11 (11QPs^a), among several other psalmodic compositions interspersed between the biblical Psalms 101–151.[3] Two points need to be made concerning this text.

A.S. Artom, *Ben Sira* (Tel Aviv: Yavne, 1963).

1.   A. Vaccari, *I libri poetici della Bibbia* (Rome, 1925), pp. 331-408; L. Alonso Schökel, *Eclesiastico* (Los Libros Sagrados 8.1; Madrid, 1968); P.W. Skehan and A.A. Di Lella, in *The Wisdom of Ben Sira* (AB, 39; New York, 1987); G. Sauer, *Jesus Sirach (Ben Sira)* (JSHRZ 3.5; Gütersloh, 1981); A. Chouraqui, *L'univers de la Bible*, VII (Paris, 1984), pp. 303-31.

2.   M. Baillet, *Les 'petites grottes' de Qumran* (DJD, 3; Oxford: Clarendon Press, 1962), Texts 75-77, Plates xv, 18.

3.   J. Sanders, *The Psalms Scroll of Qumran Cave 11 (11QPs^a)* (DJD, 4; Oxford: Clarendon Press, 1965), Texts 79-85, Plates xiii-xiv.

1. It confirms G. Bickell's intuitive supposition that Sir. 51.13ff. is an alphabetic or acrostic poem.[1] The parallel text found in MS B of Cairo is a retroversion from the Syriac, as I. Levi has already suggested.[2] Despite differences, the Greek version is closer to the Qumran text than is the Syriac version.[3]

2. Against the opinion of J.A. Sanders, the majority of scholars agree that 11QPs[a] is a collection of liturgical texts.[4] Therefore the insertion of Sir. 51.13ff. among canonical Psalms has no bearing on its canonical or quasi-canonical status, and it need not be separated from the book of Ben Sira. It could well have been an original part of the book, perhaps serving as its conclusion, similar to the alphabetic composition at the end of the book of Proverbs (Prov. 31.10-31).

Masada

In 1965, Y. Yadin found at Masada fragments of Sir. 39.27-32 and 40.10–44.17, written at the beginning of the first century BCE.[5] Even if it is accepted that some members of the Qumran community were at

---

1. G. Bickell, 'Ein alphabetisches Lied Jesus Sirachs', *ZKT* 6 (1882), pp. 319-33.

2. *L'Ecclésiastique ou la sagesse de Jésus, fils de Sira* (Bibliothèque de l'Ecole des Hautes Etudes, Sciences religieuses, 10.2; Paris, 1901), pp. xxi-xxvii.

3. This is also the opinion of M. Delcor, 'Le texte hébreu du cantique de Siracide LI, 13 et ss. et les anciennes versions', *Textus* 6 (1968), esp. pp. 39-40.

4. S. Talmon, *'Pisqah Be'emsa Pasuq* and 11QPs[a], *Textus* 5 (1966), pp. 11-21; M.H. Goshen-Gottstein, 'The Psalms Scroll (11QPs[a]): A Problem of Canon and Text', *Textus* 5 (1966), pp. 22-33; P.W. Skehan, 'Qumran and Old Testament Criticism', in *Qumran, sa piété, sa théologie et son milieu* (ed. M. Delcor; BETL, 46; Gembloux, 1978), pp. 163-82; M.R. Lehmann, '11QPs[a] and Ben Sira', *RevQ* 11.42 (1983), pp. 239-51; see the discussion of the issue by G.H. Wilson, 'The Qumran Psalms Scroll Reconsidered: Analysis of the Debate', *CBQ* 47 (1985), pp. 624-42.

5. Y. Yadin, *The Ben Sira Scroll from Masada* (Jerusalem: IES, 1965); J.T. Milik, 'Un fragment mal placé dans l'édition du Siracide de Masada', *Bib* 47 (1966), pp. 425-26; J.M. Baumgarten, 'Some Notes on the Ben Sira Scroll from Masada', *JQR* 57 (1968), pp. 323-27; J. Strugnell, 'Notes and Queries on the Ben Sira Scroll from Masada', *EI* 9 (1969), pp. 109-19.

Masada before its destruction in 73 CE,[1] nothing definite can be said about a relation between this new text of Ben Sira and Qumran.

The discovery probably proves that Ben Sira was read in Hebrew not only by the Qumranites, but also by others. This would explain the presence of quotations from Ben Sira in early rabbinic writings.

Nevertheless, the text found at Masada proves, even more than the fragments found at Qumran, that the Cairo manuscripts are copies of the Hebrew original and are not a retroversion from the Greek. It also testifies to the reliability of Cairo MS B. Moreover, it shows that the Hebrew text rendered in Greek by Ben Sira's grandson was very similar to the text found at Masada.

Thus the Qumran finds confirm the quality of the short Greek version and the textual authenticity of the Hebrew manuscripts found in Cairo. Furthermore, we now know beyond doubt that Ben Sira was read in Hebrew at Qumran, at Masada, and elsewhere.

Quotations in Ancient Jewish Sources

One of the most recent studies on the use of Ben Sira in ancient Jewish sources is that of S.Z. Leiman.[2] I quote his conclusions:

> The book of Ben Sira was venerated by the Tannaim and Amoraim. The rabbis, cognizant of its late authorship, did not accord it biblical status (i.e. include it among the inspired canonical books). It was expounded by Tannaim and Amoraim, which indicates that it was numbered among the uninspired canonical books. When sectarian groups included Ben Sira in their biblical canon, R. Akiba banned the book. When the threat to normative Judaism subsided, the book of Ben Sira was once again considered an uninspired canonical book, and was freely expounded, especially in

1. Y. Yadin, *Masada, Herod's Fortress and the Zealots Last Stand* (Jerusalem, Tel Aviv: Steimatzky, 1966), p. 174; E. Wilson, *The Dead Sea Scrolls 1947–1969* (London: Oxford University Press, 1969), p. 210; R. de Vaux, *Archaeology and the Dead Sea Scrolls* (Schweich Lectures, 1959; London, 1973), pp. 121-22; E.M. Laperrousaz, 'Qumran. III. La secte. A. Histoire', *DBSup*, IX (1978), p. 789.

2. S.Z. Leiman, *The Canonization of Hebrew Scripture: The Talmudic and Midrashic Evidence* (Transactions, 47; Hamden, CN: Published for the Conneticut Academy of Arts and Sciences by Archon Books, 1976), pp. 92-102 (102). Also M. Haran, 'Problems of the Canonization of Scripture', *Tarbiz* 25 (1955–56), pp. 245-71 (Hebrew, with English abstract); P. Rüger, 'Le Siracide: un livre à la frontière du canon', in *Le canon de l'Ancien Testament, sa formation et son histoire* (ed. J.-D. Kaestli and O. Wermelinger; Geneva: Labor et Fides, 1984), pp. 47-69.

Palestine. With the introduction of the Talmud into the academies, the study of the book of Ben Sira was neglected, and eventually ceased entirely.

We still have to face two questions concerning the text of Ben Sira to which we do not yet have definite answers.

1. The rabbinic quotations from that book generally are not literal. Segal reasons that the rabbis quoted the text by memory.[1] According to M.R. Lehmann, literalness was not required; the quotations were adapted to suit the later context because the book of Ben Sira was not a biblical book.[2] Which theory should we follow?

2. Were the quotations taken from a complete edition of Ben Sira without any additions? Or did the rabbis quote a florilegium?

Jerome and Ben Sira

In Jerome's preface to his translation of Proverbs–Qohelet–Canticles (written in 398 CE), he states that he had found a manuscript entitled 'Proverbs' which contained the Hebrew text of Ben Sira. In this manuscript the book of Ben Sira was followed by Qohelet and Canticles.[3] Several issues arise out of this information:

1. Where was this copy of Ben Sira found? Is it possible that a Jew showed it to Jerome? According to Leiman,[4] R. Joseph (290–320 CE) seems to have had a Hebrew copy of Ben Sira with some Aramaic additions. Thus it is possible that, during the fourth century, copies were still in the possession of some Jews. We know that Jerome was in contact with Jews, especially while preparing to translate Qohelet; Baranina was one of them.[5] But is it feasible that in the fourth century a

---

1. M.H. Segal, 'The Evolution of the Hebrew Text of Ben Sira', *JQR* 25 (1934–35), esp. pp. 135-36.

2. M.R. Lehmann, '11QPs and Ben Sira', *RevQ* 11 (1983), pp. 242-46.

3. See *Libri Salomonis id est Proverbia Ecclesiastes Canticum Canticorum* (Biblia Sacra iuxta latinam vulgatam versionem ad codicum fidem; Rome, 1957), p. 4.

4. Leiman, *The Canonization*, p. 101.

5. See G. Bardy, 'Saint Jérôme et ses maîtres hébreux', *RBén* 46 (1934),

Jew had a manuscript in which Ben Sira in Hebrew preceded the canonical texts of Qohelet and Canticles? A positive answer seems doubtful to me.

2.   If this copy of Ben Sira did not come from a Jew, could we suggest that Jerome saw it in Caesarea in the library of Origen?[1] This is not impossible. We must bear in mind that Origen had a copy of a Greek Psalter which he used as the 'Sexta' in his Hexapla. Concerning this Psalter he wrote a comment, discovered by Mercati at the beginning of the twentieth century, in which he briefly noted that at the time of Caracalla (211–217 CE) several books in Hebrew and in Greek were found (by whom, we do not know) near Jericho, stored in a jar.[2] Some scholars presume that this was the first discovery of scrolls which may have originated from Qumran. It is not impossible that at Qumran a manuscript was current which included Ben Sira in Hebrew, together with Qohelet and Canticles, and which could possibly be compared with 11QPs[a].

3.   The title of the Hebrew Book of Ben Sira seen by Jerome was 'Proverbs', *meshalim*. The first page of the Hebrew text of Ben Sira is no longer extant, but the subscription in Cairo's MS B does not bear the title *meshalim*. Leiman, however, notes that a commentary to *Sanhedrin* found in the Cairo Genizah mentions *meshalim* as the title of the book of Ben Sira.[3] Can we assume that this was the title of the book in the Cairo manuscript? It is impossible to provide a definite answer. However, if the answer were positive, this could also have been the title of the book at Qumran. In this way, a connection may be drawn, through Origen, between Jerome and the manuscripts discovered at the time of Caracalla.

4.   It is certain that Jerome never used the Hebrew text of Ben Sira. He refused to provide a new Latin translation of that

pp. 145-64.

1.   Concerning Jerome and Origen's library, see F. Cavallera, *Saint Jérome, sa vie et son oeuvre* (Louvain–Paris, 1922), II, pp. 88-89.

2.   R. de Vaux, *RB* 56 (1949), pp. 236, 592; P.E. Kahle, *The Cairo Geniza* (Oxford: Blackwell, 1959), pp. 240-45; S. Jellicoe, *The Septuagint and Modern Study* (Oxford: Clarendon Press, 1968), pp. 118-20.

3.   *The Canonization*, pp. 98, 185 n. 459.

book. Even when he quoted Ben Sira in his works (eighty times), he usually made his own translation in Latin from the short Greek version, as I explain elsewhere.[1]

The Cairo Genizah and Qumran

It is generally accepted today that the manuscripts of Ben Sira found in the Cairo Genizah are copies of texts which were discovered a few years before 800 CE in a cave near Jericho. That discovery may have brought Qumran works to the knowledge of the Karaites. Among these scripts was the Hebrew text of Ben Sira, which became known to others as well—for instance, to Saadya Gaon (882–942 CE).[2]

The tenth- and eleventh-century Cairo manuscripts of Ben Sira offer three different kinds of texts:

1. Some present each verse in a line divided in two stichs. The best is MS B, which also contains marginal corrections. Two others of the same kind are not as well written; these are MS E, and the fragment recently published by A. Schreiber as part of MS D (I would prefer to call it F).[3] The presentation of the text there is similar to that of 2Q18 and to that of the Masada finds.

2. Like 11QPs[a], MSS A and D present the text in continuous form.

3. MS C is a florilegium, also in continuous writing. It contains only eighty verses. But does this indeed come from Qumran, or is it a Karaite production? We are unable to answer this question.

The study of P. Rüger indicates that the Cairo manuscripts of Ben Sira point to the existence of two different text traditions. One, shorter and more original, is mainly preserved in MS B and corresponds to the short Greek version. The other, extant in MS A, contains

---

1. 'Jérome et Ben Sira', *Le Muséon* 100 (1987), pp. 109-20.

2. Kahle, *The Cairo Geniza*, p. 25; A.A. Di Lella, 'Qumran and the Geniza Fragments of Sirach', *CBQ* 24 (1962), pp. 245-67, and *The Hebrew Text of Sirach: A Text-Critical and Historical Study* (Studies in Classical Literature, 1; The Hague, 1966).

3. See Schreiber, 'A Leaf of the Fourth Manuscript of Ben Sira'.

many additions and double readings, which may have parallels in the Syriac version.[1]

According to Rüger, the second edition of the Hebrew text of Ben Sira was prepared between 50 and 150 CE. However, if the Cairo manuscripts are copies of Qumran manuscripts or of the texts which underlie them, could we not say that this expanded text of Ben Sira was already extant before the destruction of Qumran in 68 CE? P.W. Skehan proposed to date this secondary text to around 80–60 BCE.[2]

The Additions to the Ben Sira Text and Qumran

The Cairo manuscripts, especially MS A, along with the long Greek, the Latin and the Syriac versions, contain many additions which are not in the short Greek version. A small number of the additions in Latin and in Syriac are probably of Christian origin. In his edition of the *Sacra Parallela* text of Ben Sira, O. Wahl points to some additions in Greek which had been known previously only in the Latin version.[3] According to G.L. Prato, some additions in Greek are of Greek origin, stemming from the Alexandrian school of Aristobulos.[4] Today, however, it is generally accepted that the majority of the additions are of Hebrew origin.

These facts suggest that the expanded text of Ben Sira grew little by little. We must not imagine only one official second edition, revised and expanded, but rather a long process of expansion. Not being acknowledged as a biblical book in Judaism, the text of the book of Ben Sira could freely incorporate doublets and additions, which were not necessarily transmitted in all manuscripts and all versions. The expanded text of Ben Sira, therefore, is multiform.

Two main theories attempt to explain the Hebrew origin of these additions:

1. *Text und Textform im hebräischen Sirach* (BZAW, 112; Berlin, 1970).
2. See his review of Rüger, 'Text and Textform', *Bib* 52 (1971), p. 274.
3. O. Wahl, *Der Sirach-Text der Sacra Parallela* (Forschung zur Bibel, 16; Wurzburg, 1974); M. Gilbert, 'L'Ecclésiastique: quel texte? quelle authorité?', *RB* 94 (1987), p. 249 n. 37.
4. 'La lumière, interpreté de la sagesse dans la tradition textuelle de Ben Sira', in *La sagesse de l'Ancien Testament* (ed. M. Gilbert; Gembloux–Leuven, 1979), pp. 317-46.

1. According to A. Hart, followed by Oesterley and recently by the French ecumenical translation, the expanded text was prepared by the Pharisees.[1] Today, however, this theory has to be revised, because the arguments put forward by Hart are mainly based on Greek sources (Philo, Josephus and Paul).

2. C. Kearns studied the eschatological dimensions of the expanded text, and his conclusion was that these additions were made by the Essenes.[2] But today, being better acquainted with Qumran literature, we must again raise the question regarding the possible Hebrew origin of other additions as well. For instance, in the early Christian composition *The Two Ways*—which was written at the end of the first century CE but has a Jewish origin or basis and, according to J.P. Audet,[3] may be linked with Qumran—we find two passages, *Didache* 1.6 and 4.5, which bring to mind the expanded text of Ben Sira.

Where Do We Go from Here?

The renewal of interest in the book of Ben Sira seems to be less related to the question of its exclusion or inclusion in one or another canon of Scriptures than to textual problems. Research into the ancient history of Judaism and Christianity continues to bear on the question of canonicity. In reference to Judaism, the explanation given by Leiman differs from those given by M. Haran and P. Rüger. With reference to Christianity, we have only general views which concern the authority of the so-called 'deutero-canonical' or 'apocryphal' book at the time of the Church Fathers.

The real problem, as I have said, is primarily a textual one. As long

---

1. A. Hart, *Ecclesiasticus* (Cambridge, 1909), pp. 272-320; W.O.E. Oesterley, in *The Apocrypha and Pseudepigrapha of the Old Testament*. I. *The Apocrypha* (ed. R.H. Charles; Oxford, 1913), pp. 282-87; *Traduction oecuménique de la Bible, Ancien Testament* (Paris, 1975), p. 2109.

2. C. Kearns, *The Expanded Text of Ecclesiasticus. Its Teaching on Future Life as a Clue to its Origin* (Rome, 1951 [unpublished]), and 'Ecclesiasticus', *A New Catholic Commentary on Holy Scripture* (London, 1969), pp. 546-50.

3. J.-P. Audet, *La Didaché. Instruction des Apôtres*. (*EB* Paris, 1958), pp. 158-60, 276-80; P.W. Skehan, 'Didache 1,6 and Sirach 12,1', *Bib* 44 (1963), pp. 533-36.

as the Hebrew text of Ben Sira remains incomplete—even the critical edition of the fragments, announced ten years ago by Rüger, has not yet been published—research on the issue will be severely hampered. In the meantime, three fields of study may be suggested:

1. We need a more complete collection of ancient Jewish quotations from Ben Sira, with a critical analysis of their text. The lists provided by Schechter,[1] Cowley–Neubauer,[2] Segal[3] and others[4] are important. But, following Segal's work, a textual comparison with the Hebrew fragments and with the ancient versions should be continued. One important question in this regard is which text the rabbis quoted: was it the original Hebrew of Ben Sira, or the expanded text?

2. A second study could be concerned with the additions—their origin, their content and their transmission. The comparison with Qumran literature, partly initiated by Kearns, should be enlarged.[5]

3. A third line of research should concern the original Hebrew text of Ben Sira, of which the short Greek version is a good witness, even if it is not perfect. It will also be useful to continue the comparison between Ben Sira and Qumran.[6]

The preparation of these studies could interest academic institutions concerned with philology and linguistics, history of texts, the Bible,

1. S. Schechter, 'The Quotations from Ecclesiasticus in Rabbinic Literature', *JQR* 3 (1891), pp. 682-706.

2. A.E. Cowley and A. Neubauer, *The Original Hebrew of a Portion of Ecclesiasticus* (Oxford, 1897), pp. xix-xxx.

3. M.H. Segal, 'The Evolution of the Hebrew Text of Ben Sira', *JQR* 25 (1934–35), pp. 133-40, and *Sefer Ben Sira haShalem* (Jerusalem, 2nd edn, 1958), pp. 37-42.

4. S. Lieberman, 'Ben Sira à la lumière du Yerouchalmi', *REJ* 97 (1934), pp. 50-57; Lehmann, '11QPs^a and Ben Sira'.

5. See M. Philonenko, 'Sur une interpolation essénisante dans le Siracide (6, 15-16)', *Orientalia Suecana* 33–35 (1984–86), pp. 317-21.

6. See, for instance, M.R Lehmann, 'Ben Sira and the Qumran Literature', *RevQ* 3 (1961–62), pp. 103-16; J. Carmignac, 'Les rapports entre l'Ecclésiastique et Qumran', *RevQ* 3 (1961–62), pp. 209-18; M.R Lehmann, 'Ben Sira and the Dead Sea Documents', *Tarbiz* 39 (1969–70), pp. 232-47 (Hebrew; English abstract), and '11QPs^a and Ben Sira', pp. 239-51. See also J. Carmignac, 'L'infinitif absolu chez Ben Sira et à Qumran', *RevQ* 12.46 (1986), pp. 251-61.

oriental studies, ancient Judaism and early Christianity, apocryphal literature, patristic literature, and theology. Where Ben Sira is presented academically on the undergraduate level, it is possible to explore relations to Qumran literature, not only because of issues pertaining to the transmission of the text, but also because of possible contacts in matters of content.

PART II

QUMRAN BETWEEN JUDAISM AND CHRISTIANITY

THE QUMRAN SCROLLS:
A REPORT ON WORK IN PROGRESS

John Strugnell

This report is written from the point of view of a general historian who analyses whatever types of data, literary or non-literary, may be pertinent to particular historical questions. The choice of the information used depends on availability and relevance, and on the particular expertise a given scholar will have in one ancillary field or the other. There is, of course, no special virtue inherent in studying epigraphy, ceramics, or any particular area of knowledge, and certainly there is no virtue in neglecting intentionally any of these research disciplines.

With regard to the study of Jewish literature of the period, from Alexander to Bar Kokhba, we are well provided with general surveys and introductions, especially in English.[1] Work is now primarily required in the more detailed exegesis of the texts, and in their correction. One must also keep in mind the broader question of the importance of the discovery of the Qumran literature within the wider

1. See P.M. Fraser, *Ptolemaic Alexandria* (Oxford: Clarendon Press, 1972), and *Jewish Writings of the Second Temple Period* (ed. M. Stone; CRINT, 2.2; Assen/Philadelphia: Van Gorcum/Fortress Press, 1984); J.J. Collins, *Between Athens and Jerusalem* (New York: Crossroad, 1983), and *The Apocalyptic Imagination* (New York: Crossroad, 1984); G.W.E. Nickelsburg, *Jewish Literature between the Bible and the Mishnah* (Philadelphia: Fortress Press, 1981); E. Schürer, *History of the Jewish People in the Age of Jesus Christ* (rev. by F. Millar and G. Vermes; Edinburgh: T.& T. Clark, 1986), esp. vol. III, 1; J.H. Charlesworth, *The Old Testament Pseudepigrapha*, I–II (New York: Doubleday, 1983–85). One should not neglect the relevant articles in *Encyclopaedia Judaica*. Some material in Hebrew, e.g. J. Guttman, *Hasifrut Hahelenistit* (2 vols.; Jerusalem: Mosad Bialik, 1958, 1963), deserves translation. On material in German, cf. the incomplete series *Jüdische Schriften aus hellenistischer-römischer Zeit* (Gütersloh: Gerd Mohn, 1973–). The material in Spanish, in Alejandro Díez Macho, *Apocrifos del Antiguo Testamento*, I (Madrid: Ediciones Cristianidad, 1984) is interesting but somewhat less extensive.

history of Jewish literature. We have at last found Hebrew and Aramaic texts from a community which hitherto we knew almost solely from Jewish-Greek literature. We now know this community far better, not only in its numerous details and its overarching structure, but especially insofar as we can now read its texts in the original languages, and can develop a 'feel' for the style of the community's life that is not affected by the possible 'treachery' of the translator. With this help, we may even hope to overcome the problem of the identity or differences between the Qumranites and Essenes, and to understand rationally the differences between the Greek and Semitic descriptions of these communities, namely, how the same community could be depicted by Greek sources as ascetic, while the Hebrew sources present it as living a life where priestly obligations were extended to all members.

I shall review what has been done, and is being done, by my colleagues and myself on those MSS kept in the Rockefeller Museum, Jerusalem, for whose publication we are responsible. I will leave to one side the various projects under the auspices of the Shrine of the Book, which involve other Qumranic materials from various finds and purchases—from the *Oṣar Hamegillot Hagenuzot* to the Temple Scroll. Nor will I deal with their treasures of Second Revolt material from the Judaean Desert; this material will be published in tandem with the publication of our group's material from the same places. Obviously, I am not underestimating the importance of these materials, but I would like to confine this report to what has been, or will be, published in the Clarendon Press series DJD (Discoveries in the Judaean Desert) or, in preliminary form, in other volumes *hors série*.

DJD was set up initially under the auspices of the Jordanian Government and the Palestine Archaeological Museum (now called the Rockefeller Museum) to publish the principal finds of the 1950s from the Judaean Desert, i.e. the excavations and surveys of the region, together with manuscript material from Caves 1–11 at Qumran (Caves 4 and 11 being the richest ones), together with other documents from Murabba'at and Mird, and further material purchased from clandestine excavators who had found them in the general region of Wadi Seiyal—a region later excavated in a more systematic and legal fashion by Y. Yadin and his colleagues.

By the summer of 1986, seven volumes had appeared in the main series of DJD, containing the finds from 1 Qumran, Murabba'at, 2–3 and 5–10 Qumran; one volume on Cave 11; and three on matter from Cave 4. Outside the series, eight volumes have appeared: a preliminary edition of an early revision of the Septuagint of the Minor Prophets, edited by D. Barthélemy (Leiden: Brill, 1963); A. Grohmann's edition of the earliest Arabic materials from Mird;[1] the Dutch edition of the *Targum of Job* by A.S. van der Woude (1971); J.T. Milik's edition of the *Fragments of Enoch*;[2] D.N. Freedman's edition of 11Q Leviticus (1985); C. Newsom's edition of the *Songs of the Sabbath Sacrifice*;[3] E. Schuller's editions of some 100 fragments of non-canonical psalters;[4] and J. Sanderson's introduction to her edition of the very long and very important, almost Samaritan, text.[5]

How slow should all this activity be considered—fifteen volumes in twenty-five years? It can, I think, be compared favourably with the edition of any comparable collection of numerous and badly damaged fragments (e.g. the Oxyrhynchus Papyri). Research and printing have frequently been slowed down for several reasons, such as the cessation, after 1960, of Mr. Rockefeller's financial aid to the project, the wars of 1956 and 1967, and the change of status of the museum where the fragments have been stored and on which the edition has depended. Yet we hope, with reasonable confidence, that as the various editors approach the completion of their sections, the twenty or so outstanding volumes scheduled to appear in the series and *hors série* will be ready for the printers within ten to twelve years.

To plan to produce twenty volumes in twelve years is not too unrealistic, though admittedly it took us thirty-five years to produce the first fifteen. Modern developments in publishing may, however, allow some acceleration. For instance, the computer and laser printer may enable us to eliminate the typesetting process which often added two years to the production of each volume. Such an attempt is being made with one volume, but because such works are diabolically difficult to typeset, it remains to be seen whether the new techniques

1.   *Arabische Chronologie. Arabische Papyruskunde...* (Leiden: Brill, 1976).

2.   *The Books of Enoch: Aramaic Fragments of Qumran Cave 4* (Oxford: Clarendon Press, 1976).

3.   Missoula, MT: Scholars Press, 1985.

4.   *Non-Canonical Psalms from Qumran: A Pseudepigraphic Collection* (HSS 28; Atlanta, GA: Scholars Press, 1986).

5.   *An Exodus Scroll from Qumran, 4QpaleoExod^m and the Samaritan Tradition* (HSS 30; Atlanta, GA: Scholars Press, 1983).

will effect savings in time. We also try to use microfiches instead of large plates for the photographic illustration of the volumes. If we can do that, we can substantially lower the price, vastly improve the quality of the reproduction and, again, accelerate the printing schedule. Finally, several of the original editors have delegated to other scholars a certain amount of the work originally assigned to them; this new group will finish the work in collaboration with the original editors or under their supervision. We are in the process of constituting a sizeable corps of such valued collaborators. This may also accelerate the process of publication.

I have listed the publications up to 1985, when the 11Q Leviticus manuscript was published by D.N. Freedman and his colleague K.A. Mathews. At the end of 1985, a large volume, the first fruits of the above-mentioned process of delegation, appeared. One of my doctoral students, Dr Carol Newsom, working under my close direction, produced a 500-page book on the *Songs of the Sabbath Sacrifice*. This interesting set of hymns has been published by Scholars Press in a preliminary fashion, *hors série*, in the Harvard Semitic Studies. The primary purpose was to elicit commentary from scholars all over the world, so that, after five or ten years, this publication can be incorporated in a revised form into the appropriate volume of the DJD series.

Let me explain the importance of the work. It is composed of thirteen hymns, attested by over eight fragmentary manuscripts. These are spread over the first thirteen Sabbaths of the year, structured as a continuous whole; they deal with God in his heavenly temple, with detailed Hekalot-style descriptions—transposed into the form of hymns. In my opinion, it constitutes a significant contribution to the question of whether there was any form of mysticism in the Judaism of Qumran. I would certainly suggest that these hymns were recited in order to project oneself into the heavenly court—not by a literal ascension, but by fashioning one's mind into the attitudes appropriate for the heavenly court. It is fairly clear that this tradition was highly developed at Qumran, though it probably had existed in Israel even earlier. Ezekiel knows of it, and it may well be that there was an esoteric set of 'mysteries' even in the time of the First Temple. It is intriguing to find occasional references in this Qumranic work to the vision of heaven in Exodus, or to note in the descriptions of heaven as a temple surviving elements which perhaps fit the Bronze Age rather than the Iron Age.

With these fragments of seven or eight manuscripts, we have been able to reconstruct the work in its totality, not fixing every word of the text, but establishing the order of the fragments and of the topics being discussed. Although the *Songs of the Sabbath Sacrifice* looks like Essene sectarian literature (and, indeed, fragments of it were found in both the fourth and the eleventh caves at Qumran), one large fragment was also discovered at Masada. C. Newsom and the late Y. Yadin worked on the Masada fragment, and published it jointly,[1] so that the former could then incorporate it into her complete edition of all the surviving fragments. There was, perhaps, no formal decision on 'canonicity' at Qumran but, if one considers which works were extensively read and authoritative there (such questions are also posed in studies of the Christian canon in its early days), it may be suggested that a work that was copied in eight or ten manuscripts would have to be called 'canonical' or 'regulative', for if not, one would have to call Jeremiah or several of the Ketubim 'non-canonical', because they were copied far less frequently.

The Harvard Semitic Studies series has published another portion of my lot of MSS, which I had delegated to my doctorand Eileen Schuller; she has edited five plates of fragments coming from two manuscripts of a non-canonical psalter (1987). By 'non-canonical psalter', I mean that this work is composed of psalms in biblical style, which sometimes approximate those we find in the Bible, but are not to be found there. There is nothing about them that is Qumranic in theology, and the thesis of E. Schuller is that these fragments probably come from another, non-Davidic, psalter. They have authors assigned to them, 'of Manasseh', 'of Moses the Man of God', and similar titles, though not 'of David'. They seem to be floating psalms, a part of the Israelite or Judahite corpus of religious poetry, collected perhaps during the Persian or even the early Hellenistic period, but in any case almost certainly of post-exilic times. This material will appear in a preliminary edition, like that of the *Songs of the Sabbath Sacrifice*.

The next recently published item of interest (again, in a preliminary form outside the DJD series) is a group of the documents from Wadi Daliyeh. These documents are latecomers to the Dead Sea scrolls corpus; they hail from caves about twenty very dry miles away from

---

1.   C. Newsom and Y. Yadin, 'The Masada Fragment of the Qumran "Songs of the Sabbath Sacrifice"', *IEJ* 34 (1984), pp. 77-88.

the Qumran region, in some of the most desolate territory I have ever encountered. In the 1960s, these caves produced a lot of papyri from about the year 330 CE. The documents seem to come from archives carried away by Samarians fleeing before Alexander or his generals. The Samarians were caught in the caves and killed there; the archives remained there until their recent discovery. They are not sectarian literature, but are more like the archives from Murabba'at, the family documents of people who had taken refuge in the wilderness. They are not very instructive, or at least not very edifying—being mainly the archives of a Samarian who traded in Edomite slave girls—though from them one now knows an immense amount about the legal forms to use when selling or buying an Edomite slave girl in 330 CE! In this case, F.M. Cross worked out the basic formulary of these slave contracts, and passed the group of them on to one of his doctorands, D. Gropp. The full edition of this type of document formed the topic of his thesis, and will eventually be published.

Now back to items more Qumranic in interest. I and my colleague Elisha Qimron of Ben-Gurion University are preparing a preliminary presentation of the complete text of a work existing in six copies (again, it must have had a certain 'canonical' or authoritative value),[1] which seems to be a letter or a treatise containing rulings on questions of purity, addressed by the leader of one group to another group's leader and his followers. It is written in a form of proto-Mishnaic Hebrew, not in Qumran's typical biblicizing Hebrew; indeed, it stands at the beginnings of literary composition in Mishnaic Hebrew. Its main importance, of course, lies in the type of legal rulings that it contains, namely, the halakhic element. As a result of much study, and with help from a goodly number of other scholars in Israel and elsewhere who are expert in early halakhah (a field in which I have no great competence of my own), we have come to the conclusion that this work 4QMMT (or 4Q *Miqṣat Ma'asei Torah*, so called from the phrase by which it describes itself) was written to defend halakhot that we would normally call 'Sadducaean', or to oppose halakhot that we usually call Pharisaic. Was this group whose legal writings formed a large part of the Qumran library also known as 'Sadducees' or 'Sadokites'? What did the pious men of Qumran have to do with the

---

1. A preliminary presentation of the document was published in the *Acts* of the Israel Exploration Society Congress of 1983.

'wine, women and song' type of Sadducees that we know from popular books? In the literature from around the turn of the Eras, however, the term 'Sadducee' was used in two completely different ways, sometimes referring to the 'Hellenizing' Sadducees, and at other times to a group of conservative priestly legalists who would not accept the Pharisaic updating or mitigation of the Law.

4QMMT is being prepared for publication in an extensive though still preliminary edition; thus it too will become available for discussion for some five to ten years, so that we can thereafter put out a second edition of it in DJD in something much closer to a final form.[1]

The next work to go to the printer is a certain body of the 4Q biblical manuscripts. When my colleague Msgr Skehan died, he left the edition of the manuscripts assigned to him in a good state of readiness. An American scholar, Eugene Ulrich, has been bringing Skehan's work up to date, checking readings, etc. He will publish one volume containing the Septuagint MSS, about twenty Isaiah MSS, and several palaeo-Hebrew MSS, one of which is an extensively preserved manuscript of Exodus. This last item is of vast interest because it contains what must be called a Samarian text, differing from that recension at only those few points where scholars have already suspected sectarian Samarian modification (e.g. different phrases used with reference to the site of the sanctuary, whether Yahweh is *going to* choose it, or whether he *has already* chosen it). Those few clearly Samaritan readings are not in the 4Q manuscript, but most other variant readings of the Samaritan text are found therein. The MS represents perfectly what Cross used to call the Palestinian text type, as opposed to the Masoretic and the Septuagint types. We also find this text type in other manuscripts of the second century BCE, but this particular MS from Qumran is very important because the text type is attested consistently through forty columns. (This does not mean that one can just unroll the scroll and there would be forty columns; alas, there would only be small fragments from which each of the forty columns can be partially reconstructed.)

---

1.   The sigla for the MSS of 4QMMT, i.e. 4Q394–399, say something about the size of the 4Q archive. The highest numbered siglum is something like 4Q590, implying that there are 590 manuscripts of which characterizable fragments have survived. Some of these, of course, are totally insignificant but identifiable fragments of some known (e.g. biblical) work—but most are more extensive pieces.

Before publishing the Qumran biblical MSS, we hope to come out with E. Tov's re-edition of the Seiyal MS of the minor prophets in Greek, a very interesting missing link in the history of the Septuagint. D. Barthélemy, its first editor, did not have time to work on its definitive edition, and asked E. Tov, of the Hebrew University, to take his place. The book will include an interesting study of the translation technique from Hebrew into Greek.

We hope to submit to the printer in the near future the second of the four or five major biblical volumes, containing principally MSS of the Pentateuch. It will include about fifty plates, and will be the first volume in which Cross will publish, with colleagues and students as collaborators and delegates, materials assigned to him. I also hope to have ready a volume with the first thirty of the plates for whose publication I have been responsible. Thereafter, we shall proceed with the publication of volumes planned according to a list (with dates) which I have submitted to the Director of the Department of Antiquities and Museums of Israel. But by then, the element of prophecy becomes larger and predictions less reliable.

When all this material is published, what unique contributions will it make to the study of the Qumran sect and its literature? Let us disregard for a moment the study of the text of the Bible; Qumran has already made its contributions there, and we do not expect many more novelties. I also suggest that for the time being we disregard the Apocrypha. We now have, in Hebrew or in Aramaic, apocryphal and pseudepigraphical works that we once knew only in Latin or Greek translation, or in some other language of the Eastern Church. Let me, therefore, substitute another question: what are the peculiarly dark ages that we would like to have illuminated? I suggest that there are two. The first is the Persian period from 530 to 330 BCE, of which we have been learning more, thanks to archaeological discoveries.[1] One

---

1.   There are four first-rate recent 'guidebooks' to various aspects of the Persian period. One is the *Cambridge History of Judaism. I. The Persian Period* (ed. W.D. Davies and L. Finkelstein; Cambridge: Cambridge University Press, 1984). Another is E. Stern, *The Material Culture of the Land of the Bible in the Persian Period* (Warminster: Aris & Phillips; Jerusalem: Israel Exploration Society, 1982), on the archaeological remains of the Persian period. While these may be minimal, the period has become far less of a dark age than it was before Stern published his book. Two very fine books on the Persian Empire are useful, though they look at Jerusalem and Judaism only from the point of view of the centre of the empire: the *Cambridge*

would certainly welcome finds of more books from that age. We may have rediscovered a psalter of the Persian period (mentioned above); it may be that Tobit should be put at the very end of the Persian period. But such details are not going to contribute too much. In general, the community of Qumran emerged too late to provide much illumination of that period, and it is other circumstances which are making that dark age lighter.

Another period where we might hope for illumination is the real dark age from 330 to 190 BCE, the Ptolemaic era in the history of Judaea and Judaism. Here we have very little scholarly monographic literature, and a few contemporary ancient texts: Ben Sira, some *Enoch* texts and, at the very end of the period, some texts of the early stages of the biblical book of Daniel. If these are dark ages literarily, they are also especially dark ages archaeologically; there is not much in the way of finds that we can date to the Ptolemaic period. This is a point, though, at which we might reasonably expect to find help from Qumran—at least if that community stands in continuity with any strand of Judaism of the immediately preceding Ptolemaic period. While the sect as an organization starts sometime around 150 BCE, it may have carried on the religious traditions of some preceding streams in Judaism.

It is important to ask systematically which of the non-biblical works found at Qumran were 'Qumranic' or stem from pre-Qumranic Judaism.[1] From the latter category we can obviously exclude as sectarian those works that mention the Teacher of Righteousness, those that use sectarian organizational terminology, and the *pesharim* that explain the Bible in the light of events in the life of the sect. But we will have to pose the question in reference to some other works that have in the past been considered as sectarian literature. The nucleus of

Ancient History of Iran has published its second volume on the Achaemenids (Cambridge: Cambridge University Press, 1985), and Richard N. Frye has published, *The History of Ancient Iran* (Handbuch für Altertumswissenschaft 3.7; München: Beck, 1984).

1.   If they are from the same period as the Qumran sect, one may still question whether they bear any relation to the sect itself. It is true that sects tend to have nothing to do with the works of rival groups, so it is not likely that any works found in the Qumran library were written by their opponents. Nevertheless, it is worth envisioning the possibility that these are writings of adversaries that were kept by the Qumranites for polemic purposes.

the legal code in the *Damascus Document* might conceivably go back to a prior period. The earlier sections of the book of *Enoch* are clearly a product of the late fourth or third century BCE. Does this point to some organizational or ideological affinity, something in the 'family tree' of the Qumran sect, that went back to (sectarian) predecessors who produced the books of *Enoch*? Qumran had the early *Testament of Levi* in its original form. It also had the *Temple Scroll* which could well—if I may express my own peculiar heterodoxy—go back to 250 BCE and not to the later dates that Yadin assigned to it. There is a collection of prayers for the various days of the week called *divrei hamme'orot*, written in a style of Hebrew and of theology that reminds me irrepressibly of Daniel 9, Ezra 9 and Nehemiah 9—those pietistic prayers that some scholars associate with the Hasidim. Again, there is at least one major apocalypse, the *Vision of the New Jerusalem*, which is in all probability pre-Maccabaean. In this work the seer is taken by an angel through the roads and buildings of the city, sees the dimensions of it, and observes the Temple's practices—obviously an apocalypse fashioned on the same pattern as Ezekiel 40–48. For these works, early dates are now far more frequently proposed or are even demonstrable.

We will have to raise the possibility of an earlier dating of other works as additional texts from Qumran are published. I think, for instance, of several apocryphal works of Moses, which have nothing Qumranic in their contents, or of the *Songs of Joshua* which were treated at Qumran as canonical, with their own exegetical tradition forming about them c. 100 BCE. However, books do not become canonical so fast, and it is therefore probable that these works are pre-Qumran in origin; they certainly should not be construed as giving us information about the death of Simon Maccabaeus, or the like.

We are already well-informed about the subsequent Maccabaean, Hasmonaean, Herodian, and Procuratorial periods. We have acquired more details from Qumran, but there are no real lacunae in our knowledge here, except in the presentation of the ideologies of the period. We now get at least one ideology presenting itself in its own terms and language, and in contemporary documents (cf. the *Serek*—the *Manual of Discipline*, and the *Hodayot*—the *Thanksgiving Songs*). This picture is further clarified by works like the already mentioned *Miqṣat Ma'asei Torah*, the recently announced 'letter' (or, better, 'treatise') which the teacher of Qumran (probably) addressed to his opponents. In this work we find interesting facts about the life of the community, but almost no new 'historical' information. I think also of the large work, the *Songs of the Sabbath Sacrifice*, which shows that the Qumran Covenanters were not just an apocalyptic group, but also partly a mystical one.

For the other blank period in Jewish history, the years between the two Revolts, we do not expect to get much light from Qumran, for obvious chronological reasons. However, illumination can be expected if we exploit the six complete Jewish works from that dark age to which historians scarcely refer—*4 Ezra*, *2 Baruch*, *3 Baruch*, the *Apocalypse of Abraham*, the *Paralipomena of Jeremiah*, and (one must not forget it) the Apocalypse of John in the New Testament. These works provide the complete ideology of rival groups questioning why God destroyed the Temple, and discussing whether it should be rebuilt. A different kind of help is available from archives of the Second Revolt, represented by finds from Wadi Murabba'at and from the caves around Naḥal Ḥever. These will be published by the Shrine of the Book and our group, and may well provide further data about the organizational and economic life of the Jewish people. However, relatively little information about their ideologies can be expected to be disclosed by these discoveries.

Let me now turn to certain criticisms that have been raised about the work that my colleagues and I are doing. Complaints have been aired that our group has wrongly chosen to produce long commentaries, thus slowing the work of editing the texts themselves. This, in fact, is not the case; even those of us who do write somewhat long commentaries, think that they are producing the most meagre and schematic ones imaginable. In fact, the length must depend on which particular work is being edited. The Isaiah scroll does not need much of a commentary, but if you have fragments of a work that is hitherto unknown, you must provide a certain amount of commentary if any sense at all is to be made of it. And between these two poles, there is a certain freedom of praxis.

Are my colleagues and I slow? Perhaps we are in some ways, though making some allowance for our peculiar circumstances, if you compare our task with the only similar project that I know in the world—the publication of the Oxyrhynchus papyri—we are proceeding at roughly the same pace, and they have been working twice as long!

Instead of complaining about our slowness, I would suggest that scholars devote themselves to a careful reading of the books that have already been published. We produce edition after edition of MSS and fragments, and scarcely anyone bothers to study them carefully and to suggest improvements. Our editions are not perfect (the scrolls say that perfection belongs not to man); we may make blunders—some small, others large—but no one corrects them. Let me mention two examples; I wrote a lengthy review of the volume prepared by J.M. Allegro (*DJD*, V), advancing the understanding of certain texts to the point that several one- or two-page items were ready for detailed commentary in an article or monograph. But the challenge was not picked up, and no one has yet written any of those desirable commentaries. Again, Menahem Kister identified three Qumran fragments as certainly belonging to a manuscript of the *Book of Jubilees*.[1] They are fairly large fragments, each of about four lines with some three words per line, and fit together very nicely. And where were they? They had already been published in a volume that came out in 1968, but were there ascribed to another hand. The fact that until now the true nature of those fragments was not recognized indicates that no one can have been working very hard on them, though I may boast of having hinted at the problem in a review.

To give another example: over twenty years ago, complete photographs of 4QDeuteronomy were published, and there is even a brief discussion of the MS by H. Stegemann; yet I know of no one who has pointed out, let alone discussed, the possibly very important readings which the MS contains. Further: in the volume published by Baillet there are three major works, of about eight plates each, which can be reconstructed far more fully than Baillet has done, and each is ripe for a detailed discussion.

During the earlier days of Qumran studies in the late 1950s, when he was preparing his publication of *DJD*, II (Murabba'at), Milik was the first to decipher the Jewish cursive. One or two others have since learned to do so, and now we have a somewhat larger corpus. While the script is still not easy to decipher, it can be done. Milik left for other scholars a picture of one complete, undeciphered, papyrus; after nearly thirty years, no one has published a decipherment of it.

---

1. The material was published by M. Kister, 'Newly-Identified Fragments of the Book of Jubilees: Jub. 23:21-23, 30-31', *RevQ* 48 (1987), pp. 529-36.

I therefore close this report with the suggestion that there is enough work to do—not only for me but also for you.

HEBREW BIBLICAL MANUSCRIPTS FROM THE JUDAEAN DESERT: THEIR CONTRIBUTION TO TEXTUAL CRITICISM*

Emanuel Tov

Background

Over forty years (1948–1987) of discoveries and publications of texts have passed since the first scrolls were found by chance near the Dead Sea. The initial finds were followed by official archaeological expeditions to various places in the Judaean Desert between 1949 and 1965. The most northern spot in this area where biblical texts have been found is Qumran, the most southern Masada; and in between are Wadi Murabbaʿat (18 km south of Qumran), Naḥal Ḥever (Wadi Khabra) and Naḥal Ṣeʾelim (Wadi h Seiyal).[1]

Forty years of research on the texts from the Judaean Desert area are documented in bibliographies by LaSor, Burchard, Yizhar, Jongeling, Fitzmyer, and in the recent updating by Koester and Schürer–Vermes–Millar–Goodman.[2] A glance at these bibliographies

---

*This is an abridged and revised version of an article published in *JSS* 39 (1988), pp. 5-37. Thanks are expressed to H. Stegemann (referred to as H.S.), J.L. Strugnell, E. Ulrich (E.U.) and G. Vermes for remarks on an earlier version of this article, and to S. Talmon for his remarks on the present version. The designation of the scrolls follows Fitzmyer, who also provides exact bibliographic references. Texts which have not been published in a final or preliminary form with accompanying photographs are designated with an asterisk.

1.   P.W. Skehan, 'Qumran and Old Testament Criticism', in *Qumran. Sa piété, sa théologie et son milieu* (BETL, 66; Paris: Duculot; Leuven: Leuven University Press, 1978), p. 167, also mentions a Psalms fragment from Ein Gedi (?).

2.   W.S. LaSor, *Bibliography of the Dead Sea Scrolls 1948–1957* (Pasadena: Fuller Theological Seminary, 1958); C. Buchard, *Bibliographie zu den Handschriften vom Toten Meer*, I, II (Berlin: Alfred Töpelmann, 2nd edn, 1965 [1959]); M. Yizhar, *Bibliography of Hebrew Publications on the Dead Sea Scrolls, 1948–1964* (Cambridge, MA: Harvard University Press, 1967); B. Jongeling, *A Classified*

evidences the interest aroused by the texts.

Forty years of mixed feelings about the biblical texts have passed. At first there was much excitement about the ancient manuscripts, one thousand years older than any other then known biblical document—the Nash papyrus, which is actually not a biblical text.[1] At a second stage there was some, even much, disappointment, as scholars asked themselves what had been learned from the biblical texts that was not known beforehand. To find the Masoretic Text (MT) in the Judaean Desert was not particularly exciting since that textual tradition was known from later sources as well, and it could be surmised that it had also existed in Palestine at the time of the Second Temple. The non-Masoretic texts, on the other hand, were a novelty. However, it was often claimed that most of them contain so many secondary readings in comparison with MT that they do not add much to our knowledge of the 'original' biblical text. Such evaluations were generally founded on 1QIsa[a],[2] which too often served as a basis for the characterization of all the Qumran biblical manuscripts.

Indeed, it is rightly claimed that, relative to the wealth of material from the Judaean Desert, the number of Qumran texts adding substantially to our knowledge of the presumed original biblical text is small. Furthermore, many Qumran scrolls contain unusual spellings as well as a host of secondary readings. The reason for the negative judgment on the value of the Qumran texts is thus understandable. At the same time, evidence pointing to a positive view of the scrolls, necessitated by some of the important texts, was often not readily available. Texts[3]

Bibliography of the Finds in the Desert of Judah 1958–1969 (STDJ, 7; Leiden: Brill, 1971); J.A. Fitzmyer, SJ, *The Dead Sea Scrolls: Major Publications and Tools for Study* (SBLSBS, 8; Missoula, MT: Scholars Press, 3rd edn, 1990 [1975]); C. Koester, 'A Qumran Bibliography 1974–1984', *BTB* 15 (1985), pp. 110-20; E. Schürer, G. Vermes, F. Millar, M. Goodman, *The History of the Jewish People in the Age of Jesus Christ*, III.1 (Edinburgh: T. & T. Clark, 1986), pp. 380-469.

1.   S.A. Cook, 'A Pre-Massoretic Biblical Papyrus', *PSBA* 25 (1903), pp. 34-56; F.C. Burkitt, 'The Hebrew Papyrus of the Ten Commandments', *JQR* 15 (1903), pp. 392-408, and *JQR* 16 (1904), pp. 559-61.

2.   For a negative evaluation of this scroll, see a series of six articles by H.M. Orlinsky in 1950–54, starting with 'Studies in the St Mark's Isaiah Scroll', *JBL* 69 (1950), pp. 149ff. Likewise, see E.Y. Kutscher, *The Language and Linguistic Background of the Isaiah Scroll (1QIsa[a])* (Leiden: Brill, 1974), pp. 89-95.

3.   For references to the publications of these texts, see Fitzmyer, *The Dead Sea Scrolls*. For the text of Joshua, see in the meantime R.G. Boling, *Joshua* (AB;

such as 4QDeut^q, 4QpJosh^{a,b}* 4QJudg^a*, 4QSam^a, and 4QJer^b were analysed or described relatively late after their discovery, or still remain unpublished, so the impact of the research was delayed, or was not felt at all.

In the light of these varied reactions it is important to define what kind of information we are looking for in the Qumran texts. Our judgment should not be influenced by the number of presumed original readings in the texts which are not of the MT family. Our objectives should be much broader and refer to the overall contribution of the texts to the study of the Hebrew Bible, to our understanding of the transmission of the biblical text, to textual criticism in general, and at times also to literary criticism. In all these areas the scrolls have indeed advanced textual scholarship more than any other discovery in recent centuries. They have also enabled us to understand better the nature of the sources known before 1974—in the first place MT, but also the Samaritan Pentateuch and LXX. Furthermore, the scrolls have provided us with a wealth of new textual data. Accordingly, we should still apply to the new texts the same superlatives and express the same enthusiasm shown when the scrolls were first found.

The Qumran biblical MSS have taught us no longer to posit MT at the centre of our textual thinking. If, in spite of this, they are still compared with MT, this is due to a scholarly convention derived from the central status of that text in Judaism and its availability in good editions. Obviously, comparison with MT can be misleading, as, for example, when a proto-Samaritan text (see below) is compared with MT, while it should actually be compared with the Samaritan Pentateuch. However, if we are constantly aware of the limitations of these procedures, we should nevertheless be able to describe the textual status of the scrolls correctly, as has been done in the past by Cross, Talmon, Skehan, and Ulrich.[1]

Garden City, NY: Doubleday, 1982), p. 110 (the end of ch. 8 differs much from all other sources), and for the text of Judges, Boling, *Judges* (AB; Garden City, NY: Doubleday, 1975), p. 40 (the fragment of Judg. 6.3-13 lacks v. 7a and possibly all of vv. 7-10).

1.   F.M. Cross, Jr, 'The Contribution of the Qumran Discoveries to the Study of the Biblical Text', *IEJ* 16 (1966), pp. 81-95; S. Talmon, 'The Old Testament Text', in *The Cambridge History of the Bible*, I (ed. P.R. Ackroyd and C.F. Evans; Cambridge: Cambridge University Press, 1970), pp. 159-99; see also F.M. Cross and S. Talmon, *Qumran and the History of the Biblical Text* (Cambridge, MA: Harvard

The finds from the Judaean Desert pertain to a long period, from the middle of the third century BCE to the beginning of the second century CE. We must therefore explore to what extent these texts are characteristic of the entire Palestinian tradition. It is possible that they typify only some groups that left the scrolls for posterity in the desert, namely, the Qumran Covenanters, the patriots of Masada, and the companions of Bar Kokhba. In that case, we should realize that the scribal and textual traditions embedded in them may not be distinctive of other groups and localities. However, this concern is unwarranted. It now seems likely that many, if not most, of the texts found in this region were copied in other parts of Palestine, and can be viewed as Palestinian texts. More specifically, it is likely that the scrolls found in Naḥal Ḥever and Wadi Murabba'at were probably not copied at those sites, although some found at Masada could have been copied there. The situation is different in respect to Qumran, since at least some biblical texts displaying the characteristic Qumran orthography and language were written locally, while others were copied elsewhere.[1] In the light of this situation, the biblical scrolls found in the Judaean Desert are relevant to our understanding of the state of the text of the Bible in Palestine as a whole, from the third century BCE until the second century CE.

Not all the evidence is available or accessible at this stage, but enough is known for an evaluation of the situation to be made. Obviously, however, some of the statements will have to be modified in the light of future publications.

Chronological Framework

The archaeological setting of most of the manuscript finds is quite clear, since various objects were discovered in the caves together with the scrolls. The remains at Khirbet Qumran apparently point to the period between 150 BCE and 68 CE, although the upper limit is less

University Press, 1975) (hereinafter *QHBT*), pp. 1-41; P.W. Skehan, 'Qumran. IV. Littérature de Qumran: A. Textes bibliques', in *Supplément au Dictionnaire de la Bible*, IX (Paris, 1978), pp. 805-28; E. Ulrich, 'Horizons of Old Testament Textual Research at the Thirteenth Anniversary of Qumran Cave 4', *CBQ* 46 (1984), pp. 613-36.

1. See E. Tov, 'The Orthography and Language of the Hebrew Scrolls Found at Qumran and the Origin of these Scrolls', *Textus* 13 (1986), pp. 31-57 and the discussion below.

certain. This applies as well to the pottery found in the caves, which has much in common with the finds at Khirbet Qumran.[1] While the *terminus ad quem* for the Qumran scrolls is 68 CE—for this purpose we disregard a short period of occupation of the ruins around 130 CE—the *terminus a quo* cannot be unequivocally established. It is, of course, earlier, since the Qumran settlers would have brought with them much older scrolls.[2]

For Masada, the *terminus ad quem* is 73 CE and for Naḥal Ḥever and Wadi Murabba'at, 132–135 CE (the Bar Kokhba revolt). The *terminus a quo* for Wadi Murabba'at is 42–43 CE,[3] while for the other two loci no such *terminus* can be determined.

Even though the Qumran biblical MSS are ancient, most are far removed from the time of the original compositions. However, two Daniel MSS (4QDan^{c,e}*), probably written between 125 and 100 BCE, are not more than sixty years removed from the date of composition of the book.

Nature of the Collections of Texts

Except for the Qumran finds, the *Sitz im Leben* of the text clusters discovered in the Judaean Desert poses no special problems. The groups who left remains in Naḥal Ḥever, Wadi Murabba'at, and at Masada possessed, *inter alia,* biblical manuscripts. The location where texts were found at Masada does not reveal much about the nature of this collection. It should be noted that the fragments of Deuteronomy and Ezekiel were found under the floor of the synagogue in what may

---

1. See R. de Vaux, *Archaeology and the Dead Sea Scrolls* (London: Oxford University Press, 1973), pp. 53-57, also *DJD*, Vl (1977), pp. 15-22; E.-M. Laperrousaz, *Qoumrân. l'établissement essénien des bords de la Mer Morte. Histoire et archéologie du site* (Paris: Picard, 1976), pp. 156ff.

2. The oldest texts are 4QExod^f* ascribed to 250 BCE by D.N. Freedman, 'The Massoretic Text and the Qumran Scrolls: A Study in Orthography', *Textus* 2 (1962), p. 93; 4QSam^b ascribed to the second half of the 3rd century BCE, and 4QJer^a* ascribed to 200 BCE by F.M. Cross, 'The Oldest Manuscripts from Qumran', *JBL* 74 (1955), pp. 147-72; 4QXII^a and 4QQoh^a (third century BCE). See also the detailed discussion (referring also to 4QPs^a) in F.M. Cross, 'The Development of the Jewish Scripts', in *The Bible and the Ancient Near East. Essays in Honor of W.F. Albright* (ed. G.E. Wright; New York: Doubleday, 1965), pp. 132-202.

3. See R. de Vaux, *DJD*, II (1961), p. 47.

have been a *genizah*. All these fragments, it should be remembered, reflect the proto-Masoretic text.

It is much more difficult to assess the nature of the collections of MSS found at Qumran, especially as they were situated in eleven different caves, and were written in Hebrew (in two different scripts), in Aramaic, and in Greek. So far, no solid criteria have been suggested for distinguishing between the contents of the various caves, but some of the following data may be relevant. If my own analysis of the Hebrew Qumran texts is correct, most caves contain imported as well as locally written scrolls. Cave 3 holds mainly local manuscripts. Three other caves (5, 6, 8) present a mixture of imported biblical scrolls and sectarian non-biblical writings. Most caves have yielded Aramaic texts, on whose origin we have not speculated. Greek documents were found only in Caves 4 and 7; the latter contained Greek texts alone. Scrolls written in palaeo-Hebrew were discovered in Caves 1, 2, 4, 6, 11. Well-preserved MSS were revealed only in Caves 1 and 11. Hebrew papyrus fragments (biblical and non-biblical) were found in small quantities in Caves 1 and 9, and more copiously in Caves 4 and 6. *Tefillin* and *mezuzot* were retrieved in large numbers only from Cave 4, while isolated finds came from Caves 1, 5 and 8. Only Caves 1 and 3 held large numbers of jars probably used for storing scrolls; but it is not known which scrolls were stored in them. Scribal marks were mainly discovered in the (large) texts from Cave 1 (see below). Tabs of leather used as fastenings for scrolls were found only in Caves 4 and 8.[1] Finally, the palaeographical dates ascribed to the texts do not provide the means to distinguish between the contents of the different caves (with the exception of Cave 7 containing only Greek documents). The main problem is posed by the major depositories of texts in Caves 1, 4 and 11, which display a variety of languages, scripts, orthographical systems, and topics, and, for the biblical texts, diversity of textual character.

It is even harder to decide on the nature of the overall collection. This, in turn, has repercussions on the analysis of the individual texts. Several caves were used as (temporary) dwellings.[2] The suggestion

---

1.   See J. Carswell, *DJD*, VI (Oxford: Clarendon Press, 1977), pp. 23-28.

2.   According to J.T. Milik's detailed description in *Ten Years of Discovery in the Wilderness of Judaea* (SBT, 26; London: SCM Press, 1959), pp. 20-21, most caves served as cells for hermits who left their domestic utensils there. Caves 1 and

that they served as some kind of *genizah* (thus Del Medico[1]) is not plausible. Nor can one plausibly accept the view which denies any connection between the texts and the Qumran community or the suggestion that the scrolls were brought to Qumran from somewhere else, perhaps from the Temple library (thus Rengstorf, Kutscher and Golb[2]). The archaeological links between the ruins and the caves, as well as the geographical proximity between the caves (especially Cave 4) and the settlement at Qumran are simply too strong to disassociate them. Thus, the only possible explanation of the presence of the texts in the caves is that at a time of crisis the Covenanters brought the scrolls there for safety, and that some of the community lived there for a time.[3] The collection thus reflects the books possessed by the Covenanters. Whether or not the entire collection, or only the contents of Cave 4, should be called a 'library' is probably no more than a semantic question. The employment of that term is not problematic if by 'library' one refers to all the books which the community owned or stored, without implying that they used them or agreed with their contents.[4]

3, on the other hand, would only have been used as hiding places.

1.   H.E. Del Medico, *L'énigme des manuscrits de la Mer Morte* (Paris: Librairie Plon, 1957); ET, *The Riddle of the Scrolls* (London: Burke, 1958). Against this possibility see especially R. de Vaux, *DJD*, VI (Oxford: Clarendon Press,1977), p. 22 n. 1.

2.   K.H. Rengstorf, *Hirbet Qumran und die Bibliothek vom Toten Meer* (Studia Delitzschiana, 5; Stuttgart: Kohlhammer, 1960); Kutscher, *The Language and Linguistic Background of the Isaiah Scroll*, pp. 89-95; N. Golb, 'The Problem of Origin and Identification of the Dead Sea Scrolls', *PAPS* 124 (1980), pp. 1-24.

3.   According to Milik, in *Ten Years of Discovery*, the palaeographical (late) date of some of the Cave 4 scrolls indicates that the texts were stored there close to the time of the Roman attack.

4.   The enormous number of MSS (biblical and non-biblical) found in Qumran (823 according to a count in 1985—see H. Stegemann, 'Some Aspects of Eschatology in Texts from the Qumran Community and in the Teachings of Jesus', in *Biblical Archaeology Today* [Jerusalem: Israel Exploration Society, 1985], p. 421 n. 4) offers no clue for the solution of this problem. The actual number of MSS was even larger, as indicated by the number of leather fastenings of scrolls whose contents have not been preserved. See J. Carswell in *DJD*, VI (Oxford: Clarendon Press, 1977), p. 24.

Provenance of the Texts

The question of the provenance of the Qumran MSS has already been mentioned briefly. If all the scrolls were not brought there by outsiders, as some scholars believe, at least some were certainly imported, while others would have been written on the spot, possibly in the so-called 'scriptorium'.[1] However, no criteria have been suggested for distinguishing between these two groups, with the exception of those proposed in my study. The main criterion refers to a difference between two types of orthography and language. One group of texts—produced by a scribal school, probably at Qumran—is recognizable by several distinct features; the other group—of probably imported texts—lacks these characteristics. (It is important to stress that the scribal conventions used in the writing of biblical texts do not differ from those applied in the writing of non-biblical texts.) Beyond those criteria, already discussed in my article, five further distinguishing features which mark the works of the Qumran scribal school are advanced here. These five criteria have a cumulative force and enable us to determine the origin of even small fragments.

1. The first criterion pertains to orthography and language. The sectarian writings of the Qumran community are written in the special 'Qumran' orthography and language briefly described below, which will henceforth be called the 'Qumran system'. It is probable that only the Qumran sect wrote in this way.[2] Whatever views one may have on the nature of this peculiar orthography and language, the fact remains that two (and not more) systems of writing can be recognized in the

1.   The Qumran ostracon containing an abecedary and representing a scribal exercise may indicate that the scribes were trained on the spot. For a good photograph, see J. Allegro, *The People of the Dead Sea Scrolls* (London: Routledge & Kegan Paul, 1959), p. 183. This applies also to another writing exercise from Cave 4; see J. Naveh, 'A Medical Document or a Writing Exercise? The So Called 4Q Therapeia', *IEJ* 36 (1986), pp. 52-55. Other writing exercises, all containing at least part of the alphabet, have been found in Murabba'at, some on leather (Mur 10B, 11), others on sherds (Mur 73, 78–80).

2.   In his study of the scribal character of the major works of Cave 1, M. Martin (*The Scribal Character of the Dead Sea Scrolls* [Bibliothèque du Muséon, 44; Louvain: Publications Universitaires, 1958], p. 684) intuitively felt that 1QIsa^b differed so much from the other texts that its copyist could not have belonged to the same scribal school which produced the other texts that he studied. The latter are all written in the Qumran orthography and language, while 1QIsa^b lacks these characteristics.

Qumran scrolls, and that the Covenanters' compositions are written exclusively according to the so-called 'Qumran system'. This conclusion has a bearing on the biblical texts. It implies that MSS such as 1QIsa[a] and 4QSam[c], characterized by the same orthographical-linguistic system, were copied by Qumran scribes, while MSS not written in this system were imported.[1] In this context it should be pointed out that only two scribes can be identified as having written more than one scroll, and these were copyists of sectarian compositions. The above analysis does not refer to Aramaic works. To the best of my knowledge, there are no demonstrably sectarian documents among them, and it is possible that all were imported.

2. With the exception of the 'parenthesis' in 11QpaleoLev, one instance of cancellation dots in 4QJer[a]*, and the *paragraphos* in the Aramaic 4QTestLev[a],[2] scribal marks of any kind are found only in the Hebrew manuscripts written in the 'Qumran system', especially in the scrolls from Cave 1.[3] This applies to the signs at the ends of lines or in the space between columns, which are similar to, but much bigger than, the letter x. They appear in 1QpHab, 1QH, 1QS, 1QIsa[a], 11QTemple[b],[4] and in a different way in 4QCatena[a] (177) and 4QCryptic (186). A horizontal line with or without a curving line bending to the left, similar to the *paragraphos* in Greek (secular and biblical) and Aramaic documents (in Qumran: 4QTestLev[a]), is found

---

1.   This assumption is supported by another. Palaeographers tells us that the earliest Qumran texts are biblical; see F.M. Cross, *Scrolls from the Wilderness of the Dead Sea* (Claremont, CA: School of Theology at Claremont, 1977), p. 5. Indeed, it stands to reason that the early settlers would have brought biblical texts with them, while their sectarian compositions could have been written on the spot.

2.   M. Baillet, the editor of '2QDeut[a]' in *DJD*, III (Oxford: Clarendon Press, 1962), noted an apostrophe after Deut. 1.8, but this sign, not known from other texts, occurs at the edge of the fragment and its real nature is not at all clear. Note further the writing in red letters of two lines at the beginning of a new section in 2QPs (fragmentary) and 4QNum[b]* (see *DJD*, III, p. 70), also known from Egyptian texts and the Deir Alla inscription.

3.   Another exception refers to a text found outside Qumran, viz. MasSir (II 8, 24; III 18), containing stylized forms of the 'paragraphos'.

4.   See the Rockefeller photograph 43.975 presented as plates 36* and 37* in Y. Yadin, *The Temple Scroll* (Jerusalem: Israel Exploration Society, Hebrew University, Shrine of the Book, 1977; ET London: Weidenfeld and Nicolson, 1983), parallel to columns XIX-XX and XXI.

in 1QIsa[a] and in many non-biblical texts.[1] Likewise, cancellation dots figure in similar list of sources.[2] Other signs, not all of them comprehensible, are attested only in texts written in the 'Qumran system': 1QIsa[a], 1QS, 4QDibHam[a] (504), 4QSir[b] (511). Especially remarkable is the resemblance of 1QIsa[a] and 1QS in the use of unusual scribal signs.[3] By extension we should also mention the habit of writing the divine name with four dots: 1QIsa[a] (corrector), 4QSam[c], 1QS, 4QTest (175), 4QTanh (176); and the placing of a 'colon' before the Tetragrammaton (in the Assyrian script) in 4Q364*.[4]

It is noteworthy that these scribal marks are employed only in some MSS written in the 'Qumran system'—especially in the 'large' texts from Cave 1. It is therefore possible that they were used by only a segment of the Qumran scribal school.[5] This group seems to have been more conversant with the scribal habits of Hellenistic Egypt than were scribes outside Qumran. If the strange occurrences of an *aleph* at the ends of the lines in 1QpHab 2.5, 6 reflect the 'x' sign, misunderstood as *aleph* (H.S.), we should probably consider this copy as stemming from the second generation of a scribal school.

3. The use of initial-medial letters in final positions is another characteristic of the texts written in the 'Qumran system'. This applies to three scrolls studied in detail by Siegel (1QIsa[a], 4QTest [175], 11QPs[a]),[6] as well as to a large group of other texts.[7] We cannot

1. 1QpHab, 1QMyst (27), 1QS, 1QS[a,b], 4QpIsa[c], 4QTestim (175), 4Q502 ('rituel de mariage'), 503 (daily prayers), 4QDibHam[a] (504), 509 (PrFêtes[c]), 512 ('rituel de purification').

2. 1QIsa[a], 1QS, 1QM, 1QH, 1QpHab, 4QCatena[a] (177) 1.15, 4Q365* ('biblical paraphrase'), 11QTemple 45.18. See also the aforementioned instance of such dots in 4QJer[a]*.

3. Cf. the charts in M. Burrows, *The Dead Sea Scrolls of St Mark's Monastery* (New Haven: American Oriental Society, 1950), XVI with plates V, VII, IX of 1QS.

4. 'Biblical paraphrase', similar to 4Q158 (*DJD*, V). See J.P. Siegel, 'The Employment of Palaeo-Hebrew Characters for the Divine Names at Qumran in the Light of Tannaitic Sources', *HUCA* 42 (1971), pp. 159-72, esp. 171 n. 41.

5. It is not impossible that these texts reflect one of the periods of the activity of the Qumran scribal school as suggested by J.M. Oesch, 'The Division of Texts in the Qumran Manuscripts', in *Proceedings of the Eighth World Congress of Jewish Studies*, Division A (Jerusalem: Magnes, 1982), pp. 99-104. Oesch speaks about the period between 125 and 75 BCE.

6. J.P. Siegel, *The Scribes of Qumran. Studies in the Early History of Jewish Scribal Customs, with Special Reference to the Qumran Biblical Scrolls and to the*

simply say that those scribes did not properly distinguish between final and initial-medial forms of letters, because this non-distinction is fairly regular.

4. The best preserved texts are written in the 'Qumran system'. This may point to a difference in the material used by the Qumranites as against scribes outside of Qumran. Cave 1, in particular, furnished long scrolls which are all written in the 'Qumran system': 1QIsa[a], 1QM, 1QH, 1QS and 1QpHab. Other sectarian texts from Cave 1 have been preserved in fragments; but *all* the 'non-Qumranic' scrolls from this cave (except for 1QIsa[b]), are fragmentary. Is it a mere coincidence that the best preserved texts from Qumran, including the longest surviving scroll, 11QTemple, are all written in the 'Qumran system'? Some Cave 1 texts may have been stored in the jars that contained scrolls, according to the testimony of their Bedouin discoverers, as recorded by de Vaux.[1] Such an assumption would apply only to a few texts from Cave 1, but not to the Temple Scroll.[2] It is, of course, equally possible that the material on which these particular texts were written was more durable than that of the others.[3] The same applies to the threads used for stitching the sheets together to form a scroll. The great majority of threads were preserved in texts written in the 'Qumran system',[4] and they are thicker and whiter than

---

Tannaitic Traditions of Massekheth Soferim (PhD dissertation; Brandeis University, Waltham, MA, 1972), pp. 111-82, esp. 113.

7.   The research was carried out on the basis of a list of reverse order forms prepared by the Israel Academy of the Hebrew Language (courtesy of E. Qimron) referring to all non-biblical scrolls published up to 1975. Some texts contained only initial-medial forms in final position, while most of the scrolls contained a mixture of forms in final position. All these texts are written in the 'Qumran system': 1QH, 1QS, 1QM, 1QDibMos, 1Q25(?), 1QpHab, 1QpSoph, 4QFlor (174), 4QTanh (176), 4QCatena[a] (177), 4QpHos[a], 4QpPs[a], 4QpIsa[c], 4QDibHam[a] (504).

1.   *DJD*, I (Oxford: Clarendon Press, 1955), pp. 12-13.

2.   Unless of course, some of these jars disappeared at the time of their discovery (observation by F.M. Cross, Jr).

3.   The skins were probably prepared in Qumran itself; as suggested by de Vaux, *Archaeology and the Dead Sea Scrolls*, pp. 79-82, such installations may have been preserved. Mrs E. Chazon has pointed out that the scrolls brought from outside possibly deteriorated to a greater extent as a result of having been exposed to harsher climatic elements.

4.   1QIsa[a], 4Q185, 4QCryptic (186), 4QLam (501), 4QDibHam[a] (504), 4QpHos[b], 4QpIsa[c], 5Q11 ('règle de la communauté'), 13 ('une règle de la secte'),

the few found in imported texts: 1QPs, 4QpaleoExod[m]*, 4QDeut[q], 4QJer[c]*, 4Q381.[1] This list is not complete and this issue, too, must await detailed examination.

5. A further characteristic of texts in the 'Qumran system' pertains to the writing of the divine names *'l(hym)* and *yhwh*, sometimes in conjunction with another divine name and together with prefixes, in palaeo-Hebrew characters,[2] in texts written in the Assyrian script. This practice is evidenced in the *pesharim* (1QpMic, 1QpZeph, 1QpHab, 4QpPs[a]* [together with 4Q183[3]], 4QpIsa[a]) and other sectarian writings (1QH, 1QH[b] [1Q35], 1QMyst [27], 4QAgesCreat [180], 6QD [CD], 6QHym [18]), and also in a few biblical texts (2QExod[b], 4QIsa[c4]) and a collection of biblical and non-biblical Psalms (11QPs[a])—often inconsistently, and certainly not in all works belonging to a given group (note, e.g., 4QpNah). Furthermore, this scribal practice is found in biblical texts which on orthographical grounds (because of their fragmentary nature) cannot be included in this category: 1QPs[b], 3QLam, 3Q14 (an undetermined fragment) and 11QLev. Siegel sees in this custom a desire to 'insure that under no conditions would the (holy) Name be erased'.[5] In this matter, the Qumran scribal custom reflects the spirit of the rabbinic law in *j. Meg.* 1.9 (71d).

The above analysis has shown that information of different sorts can be combined in order to determine the 'Qumranic' origin of a text: orthography, morphology, the use of scribal marks, the use of initial-medial letters in a final position, the writing of the divine names in palaeo-Hebrew characters, and possibly also the material used. Some

11QPs[a], 11QTemple.

1. E.M. Schuller, *Non-Canonical Psalms from Qumran: Pseudepigraphic Collection* (HSS, 28; Atlanta: Scholars Press, 1986).

2. For a complete list of the evidence, see K.A. Mathews, 'The Background of the Paleo-Hebrew Texts at Qumran', in *The Word of the Lord Shall Go Forth* (ed. C. Meyers and M. O'Connor; Winona Lake, IN: Eisenbrauns, 1983), pp. 549-68, esp. 561-62. See further P.W. Skehan, 'The Divine Name at Qumran, in the Masada Scroll, and in the Septuagint', *Bulletin IOSCS* 13 (1980), pp. 14-44.

3. For the identity of the two texts, see J. Strugnell, 'Notes en marge du volume V des "Discoveries in the Judaean Desert of Jordan"', *RevQ* 7 (1970), p. 263 and plate III.

4. According to the detailed description of P.W. Skehan, 'The Text of Isaiah at Qumran', *CBQ* 17 (1955), pp. 158-63, this scroll contains all the characteristics of the 'Qumran system'.

5. See 'The Employment of Paleo-Hebrew Characters', p. 169, rsp. 166-67.

of these criteria pertain to characteristic habits of the Qumran scribes (the writing of the divine names?); but others are found also outside Qumran, such as the *puncta extraordinaria* and the writing of *hem* with initial-medial *mem* in MT Neh. 2.13.

The evidence presented here points to the existence of a Qumran scribal school, but not necessarily to the existence of only one such school. In principle, it may be posited that the presumably imported compositions, according to my thesis, were also copied at Qumran, but by a different group of scribes. However, such an assumption cannot be upheld since other factors indicate that the scrolls were written prior to the settlement in Qumran and were brought there by (the founding?) members. Besides, the Qumran scribes needed imported prototypes as *Vorlagen* for their own texts. Furthermore, it does not seem likely that they wrote in two different systems, since no sectarian writings have been preserved in a non-Qumranic spelling and language. But my main argument is of a different character. As will be stressed at the end of this paper, there is a difference of approach from one group of biblical texts to another. The scrolls written in Qumran orthography and language display a tendency to modernize the biblical Hebrew spelling and language. This indicates a free handling of the biblical text, as do the frequent contextual changes, and the many mistakes and untidy corrections.

Many scrolls in the 'Qumran system' are written sloppily, not in the handsome handwriting of most presumably imported scrolls which do not as a rule exhibit this free approach to the biblical text. The so-called proto-Masoretic manuscripts are conservative both in spelling and content. The same may be said of other imported scrolls, except for the so-called proto-Samaritan MSS. Without speculating on the origin of the two scribal customs which reflect a different socioreligious environment, it is unlikely that two such different approaches would have been practised in one locality.[1] Nor is it likely that one

---

1. On the basis of the halakhic writings of the Qumranites, Y. Zussman claimed (lecture of June 24, 1987) that they were stringent in their halakhic decisions. Since this approach is not visible in the copying of the biblical writings, it appears that the concept of the holiness of the transmission of biblical writings did not exist in the Qumran community. (See also the careless writing of the *mezuzot* and *tefillin,* both those written in the 'Qumran system' and the rest.) On the other hand, this evidence should not be used against my claim that the special system of orthography and language is Qumranic, since all sectarian compositions are written in this system.

community would have created texts as different as these, simultaneously or at different periods (note that scrolls of both groups are assigned to the whole period of settlement at Qumran). At the same time, having been created, the texts could have co-existed peacefully in Qumran—a topic to which I shall return later.

The combination of criteria for identifying the origin of the texts found in Qumran helps in establishing a list of scrolls which belong to one or another group.[1] When compared with the putative dating of the texts on palaeographical grounds, it appears that for the early period of scribal activity (250–150 BCE [pre-Hasmonaean or archaic]) we find only imported scrolls at Qumran. These dates fit the archaeological evidence which points to the middle of the second century BCE (or somewhat earlier) as the beginning of the settlement at Qumran. The scrolls dated earlier are not written in the 'Qumran system', indicating that they were probably brought there by the (first) settlers. Other scrolls were probably brought to Qumran throughout the period of settlement, or else at one given time. The dates given to texts in the 'Qumran system' on palaeographical grounds also fit this framework, since for other reasons all have been tied to the period of settlement at Qumran. Most biblical texts written in the 'Qumran system' are assigned to the period between 50 BCE and 68 CE (one to 50–68 CE), the last years of the sectarian settlement (4QIsa^{c}*),[2] and a few to an earlier stage (4QSam^{c} [100–75 BCE], 1QIsa^{a} [125–100 BCE], 4QPs^{a}*

---

1. The following (still partial) list of biblical texts does not distinguish between the different degrees of probability governing the assignment of texts to one of the two groups. An earlier version of this list was published in Tov, 'Orthography and Language'.

Scrolls written in the Qumran orthography and language: 1QDeut^{a}, 1QIsa^{a}, 2QExod^{a,b}, 2QNum^{b}, 2QDeut^{b,c}, 2QJer, 3QLam, 4QDeut^{k,m}*, 4QSam^{c}, 4QIsa^{c}, 4QHos, 4QPs^{a,e,f,n,s}*4QQoh^{a}, 4QLam^{a}*, 4QDan^{b}*, 11QLev. Biblical paraphrases: 4Q158, 4Q364*, 4Q365*, 4QPs^{f}, 11QTemple, 11QPs^{a,b}, 11QPsAp^{a}.

Biblical texts not written in the Qumran orthography: 1QGen, 1QExod, 1QpaleoLev, 1QpaleoNum, 1QDeut^{b}, 1QJud, 1QSam, 1QIsa^{b}, 1QPs^{a,b}, 1QPs44, 1QDan^{a,b}, 2QGen, 2QpaleoLev, 2QNum^{a}, 2QPs, 2QJob, 2QRuth^{a,b}, 4QExod^{f}, 4QpaleoExod^{1,m}*, 4QDeut^{a,c,d,e,f,g,h,j,n,q}*, 4QJos^{a,b}*, 4QSam^{a,b}, 4QIsa^{a}, 4QJer^{a,b,c}*, 4QEz^{a,b} (see J. Lust, *BETL* 74 [1986], pp. 90-100), 4QPs^{b,c,d,k,l,q}*, 4QPs89*, 4QpaleoJob^{c}*, 4QDan^{a,c}*, 5QDeut, 5QLam^{a,b}, 4QPs119, 6QpaleoGen, 6QpaleoLev, 6QKings, 6QCant, 6QDan, 8QGen, 8QPs, 11QpaleoLev, 11QEz. Biblical paraphrases: 4Q366*, 4Q367*.

2. See Skehan, 'Qumran IV', p. 811.

and 4QQoh[a] [both: 150 BCE]).[1] Likewise, most non-biblical texts written in the 'Qumran system' are dated to between 50 BCE and 50 CE, and some to an earlier period ranging from 150 BCE (4QDibHam[a]) to 100–75 BCE: 1QS, 4QM[d], 4Q499, 500, 502, 503, 504, and 509.

External Data on the Biblical Texts

The first issue to be treated is the question of which books have turned up in the Judaean Desert. Although the actual preservation of certain scrolls is coincidental, at least some minimal conclusions may be permitted. Excavations at Masada have produced texts of Exodus (?),[2] Leviticus (two copies), Deuteronomy, Ezekiel, and Psalms;[3] in Naḥal Ḥever: Genesis, Numbers, and Psalms;[4] and in Wadi Murabba'at: Genesis, Exodus, Numbers, Deuteronomy, Isaiah, and Minor Prophets.[5] The preponderance of Pentateuchal texts is noteworthy.

As for Qumran, in 1965 Skehan listed 172 different scrolls,[6] with some of the Pentateuchal texts containing two books.[7] In 1978 he listed and described all the texts of Isaiah and Psalms. Several scrolls probably contained only sections of books (4QDeut[q] presumably contained only Deuteronomy 32 [note the empty column after that chapter

---

1. For the Psalms scroll, see Skehan, 'Qumran IV', p. 815. For the Qoheleth scroll, see J. Muilenburg, 'A Qoheleth Scroll from Qumran', *BASOR* 135 (1954), pp. 20-28.

2. See P. Wernberg-Møller, 'The Exodus Fragment from Massada', *VT* 10 (1960), pp. 229-30 (based on *The Times* of Feb. 16, 1960).

3. See Y. Yadin, *Masada, Herod's Fortress and the Zealots' Last Stand* (Haifa: Steimatzky, 1966), pp. 168-89. In his earlier account, *Masada, First Season of Excavations, 1963–1965* (Jerusalem: Israel Exploration Society, 1965 [Hebrew]), p. 11 = *IEJ* 15 (1965), pp. 103ff. P. 104 also mentions a scroll of Genesis, but this may well be the same text described as *Jubilees* on p. 179 of the 1966 volume.

4. See Fitzmyer, *The Dead Sea Scrolls*, p. 46.

5. *DJD*, II (Oxford: Clarendon Press, 1961).

6. P.W. Skehan, 'The Biblical Scrolls from Qumran and the Text of the Old Testament', *BA* 28 (1965), pp. 87-100 = *QHBT*, pp. 264-77.

7. The relevant evidence (see below) has not yet been published. In the meantime see Skehan, 'The Biblical Scrolls', p. 265. Four blank lines have been preserved before the text of 4QpaleoExod[l*] as well as the last words of Genesis. The fragments of Mur1 probably reflect a scroll containing both Genesis and Exodus, and possibly also Numbers, but this evidence refers to a later period (note the long columns of 48–50 lines).

and the small column block]; several scrolls held no more than an anthology of Psalms). The recognition of what constitutes a separate scroll is mainly based on an analysis of the handwriting. This reasoning, however, may lead to imprecise conclusions, since fragments of the same book in different handwritings could have belonged to the same scroll (in 1QH, for example, the change of scribe took place in the middle of column XI). The actual number of scrolls could therefore be slightly smaller. The updated numbers—according to Strugnell (June 1989)—of the biblical texts discovered in Cave 4 alone (including those written in palaeo-Hebrew) give a good impression of the overall proportions of the books.

For Genesis, there are 11 (one includes Exodus: 4QGen–Exod^b*); for Exodus, 12 (one includes Genesis: 4QpaleoExod^l* [E.U.]); for Leviticus, 4; for Numbers, 2 (one continues from Leviticus: 4QLev^a–Num^a*). For Deuteronomy, there are 19; Joshua, 2; Judges, 2; Samuel, 3; Kings, 1; Isaiah, 20 (22?); Jeremiah, 3; Ezekiel, 3; Minor Prophets, 7; Psalms, 20; Job, 3; Proverbs, 2; Ruth, 2; Song, 3; Qoheleth, 2; Lamentations, 1; Daniel, 5; Ezra, 1; Chronicles, 1. Excluded from this list are the biblical texts contained in *mezuzot* and *tefillin*, many of which have been found in the area.[1]

All the books of the Hebrew canon are represented at Qumran, with the exception of Esther. Little notice should be paid to that omission due to the brevity of the book. If only one small fragment remains of 1–2 Chronicles (4Q118*), it is not surprising that the much smaller book of Esther has not been found at all. Note also that no fragment of Nehemiah has been preserved. (Ezra is represented at Qumran.)

It is noteworthy that the biblical books have been preserved at Qumran in different quantities. The list of texts from Cave 4 indicates that the three books most frequently represented are Deuteronomy (19 copies), Psalms (20 copies), and Isaiah (20 [22?] copies). All other books except for Genesis (11 copies) have turned up in much smaller numbers. This proportion may well point to the Qumran Covenanters as the owners of the scrolls, though not necessarily as their copyists, for in the sectarian writings of the Qumranites Deuteronomy, Isaiah, and Psalms are the most frequently quoted biblical books.[2]

---

1.   See especially, *DJD*, VI (Oxford: Clarendon Press, 1977).

2.   E.g. J. Carmignac, 'Les citations de l'ancien testament dans "La guerre des fils de lumière contre les fils de ténèbres"', *RB* 63 (1956), pp. 375-90;

Furthermore, the style of several sectarian prose works is based on Deuteronomy, that of many hymnic works on Psalms (taken as a 'prophetic' book [cf. 4QpPs]), while the prophecies of Isaiah played a prominent part in the thinking of the sect.

Closely connected with this issue is the question of canon. It is not clear whether the texts found at Qumran actually reflect the authoritative books of the people who deposited the scrolls, as suggested by several scholars. Since the excavations have unearthed not only biblical and sectarian works, but also 'apocryphal' books such as Tobit, Ben Sira, and the Epistle of Jeremiah, as well as such 'pseudepigrapha' as *Jubilees*, *Enoch*, and the *Testaments of the Twelve Patriarchs*, scholars sometimes speak of an open-ended canon in which there was room for works which we would now call 'non-canonical'.[1] This description would also apply to the finds at Masada where, in addition to biblical and (Qumran) sectarian works, a Ben Sira scroll and a copy of *Jubilees* (?) have been discovered. However, so little is known about the circumstances surrounding the depositing of the scrolls in Qumran and Masada that the evidence may be irrelevant and misleading. I therefore conclude that the evidence to be derived from the biblical scrolls concerning the authoritative books of the Qumran Covenanters and the patriots of Masada is very limited. It would be more relevant to examine the *pesharim* and the biblical citations in the sectarian writings, such as the reference to Daniel in 4QFlor (E.U.).

As for biblical translations, Aramaic targums of Leviticus have been identified in Cave 4 (4Q156 [nature uncertain]), and of Job in Caves 4 and 11.[2] The Greek Bible is represented by 8HevgrXII and by the following Qumran fragments, all from the Pentateuch: pap7QLXXExod, 4QLXXLev[a], pap4QLXXLev[b]*, 4QLXXNum, 4QLXXDeut, and probably also 7Q3–19.[3] Aramaic was known at

P. Wernberg-Møller, 'The Contribution of the *Hodayot* to Biblical Textual Criticism', *Textus* 4 (1964), pp. 133-75, esp. 173-75.

1.   E.g. Skehan, 'Qumran IV', p. 819.

2.   For 4Q156 and 4Q157 (Job) see *DJD*, VI (1977); for details on 11QtgJob see Fitzmyer, *The Dead Sea Scrolls*, p. 36.

3.   P.W. Skehan, 'The Qumran Manuscripts and Textual Criticism', *VTSup* 4 (1957), pp. 157-59 (4QLXXLev[a]); P.W. Skehan, '4QLXXNum: A Pre-Christian Reworking of the Septuagint', *HTR* 70 (1977), pp. 39-50, and *VTSup* 4 (1957), pp. 155-57; E. Ulrich, 'The Greek Manuscripts of the Pentateuch from Qumran, Including Newly-Identified Fragments of Deuteronomy (4QLXXDeut)', in *De*

Qumran, as is evident both from the many Aramaic works found there and the influence of that language on the scribe of 1QIsaᵃ. Greek must have been familiar to the people who left the texts at Naḥal Ḥever since other Greek documents were found there as well.[1] As for Qumran, the finds of Greek documents in Caves 4 and 7[2] render it likely that some of the settlers at Qumran were able to read these texts, but knowledge of that language among all the Qumranites cannot be assessed. It appears that all the Greek and Aramaic works found in Qumran have been 'imported'.

Qumran has yielded twelve biblical scrolls written in palaeo-Hebrew script: two copies of Genesis, two of Exodus, four of Leviticus, one of Numbers, two of Deuteronomy, and one of Job.[3] Three other fragments from Cave 4 contain non-biblical works, and an unidentified palaeo-Hebrew work has been retrieved from Masada. Evidently, the palaeo-Hebrew script was preserved for the writing of 'early' biblical books, among which the presence of Job is worth noting. Some scholars believe that the use of this script reflects a revival of palaeo-Hebrew, but this would require the unlikely assumption that the texts were copied from scrolls written in the Assyrian script. It is more reasonable to posit a continuous tradition of writing in Hebrew, even after the Assyrian script has been introduced.[4]

Septuaginta. Studies in Honour of J.W. Wevers on his Sixty-Fifth Birthday (ed. A. Pietersma and C. Cox; Missisauga; Ont.: Benben, 1984), pp. 71-82; further publications by Ulrich are still in the press. The Greek fragments from Cave 7 probably derive from the LXX as well: see C.H. Roberts, 'On Some Presumed Papyrus Fragments of the NT from Qumran', *JTS* ns 23 (1972), pp. 321-24: A.C. Urban, 'Observaciones sobre ciertos papiros de la cueva 7 de Qumran', *RB* 8 (1973), pp. 16-19. According to J. O'Callaghan, *Los papiros griegos de la cueva 7 de Qumran* (BAC, 353; 1974), these fragments represent the New Testament, but this view has not been accepted by other scholars. See further, A R.C. Leaney, 'Greek Manuscripts from the Judean Desert', in *Studies in New Testament Language and Text* (ed. J.K. Elliott; Leiden: Brill, 1976), pp. 283-300. On the other hand, O'Callaghan's views have been accepted by C.P. Thiede, *Die älteste Evangelien Handschrift?* (Wuppertal: Brockhaus, 1986).

    1.   See Fitzmyer, *The Dead Sea Scrolls*, pp. 85-88.
    2.   *DJD*, III (Oxford: Clarendon Press, 1962), pp. 142-46.
    3.   1QpaleoLev, 1QpaleoNum, 2QpaleoLev, 4QpaleoGen¹, 4QpaleoExod^{1,m*}, 4QpaleoDeut^{r,s*}, 4QpaleoJob^{c*}, 6QpaleoGen, 6QpaleoLev, 11QpaleoLev.
    4.   See Cross, 'The Oldest Manuscripts', p. 189 n. 4, and R.S. Hanson,

The palaeo-Hebrew texts could have been produced at Qumran;[1] note the palaeo-Hebrew writing, although of a different nature, in 4QCryptic (186) written in the 'Qumran system', as well as the writing of the palaeo-Hebrew divine names.[2] However, it is more likely that, together with other texts, they were imported. Knowledge of palaeo-Hebrew does not imply that the Qumran scribes would have written complete works in that script. Moreover, the orthography, linguistic structure, and scribal conventions of the palaeo-Hebrew scrolls differ completely from the texts written in the 'Qumran system'.

Contribution to Biblical Scholarship

The main areas in which the Qumran finds have enriched our knowledge are: (1) the transmission of the biblical text; (2) the content of the newly found texts; (3) the textual variety of the manuscripts from the Judaean Desert; and (4) the approach to the biblical text in Qumran and Palestine as a whole during the Second Temple period. These four areas are closely connected.

The Transmission of the Biblical Text

The newly found texts provide a vast amount of technical data pertaining to ancient scrolls and scribal conventions. Although several aspects of these issues have been discussed in the works of Kuhl, Martin, Oesch, Siegel, and Stegemann,[3] major studies are still needed in an

'Jewish Palaeography and its Bearing on Text Critical Studies', in *Magnalia Dei. The Mighty Acts of God. Essays in Memory of G.E. Wright* (ed. F.M. Cross, W.E. Lemke, P.D. Miller; New York: Doubleday, 1976).

1. See Mathews, 'The Background of the Paleo-Hebrew Texts at Qumran', pp. 549-68, esp. 561-62.

2. See Skehan, 'The Divine Name at Qumran, in the Masada Scroll, and in the Septuagint', pp. 14-44.

3. C. Kuhl, 'Schreibereigentümlichkeiten: Bemerkungen zur Jesajarolle (DSI^a)', *VT* 2 (1952), pp. 307-33; Martin, *The Scribal Character of the Dead Sea Scrolls*; J.M. Oesch, *Petucha und Setuma. Untersuchungen zu einer überlieferten Gliederung im hebräischen Text des AT* (OBO, 27; Göttingen: Vandenhoeck & Ruprecht, 1979), and 'The Division of Texts'; Siegel, 'The Employment of Paleo-Hebrew Characters'; H. Stegemann, 'Methods for the Reconstruction of Scrolls from Scattered Fragments', in *Archaeology and History in the Dead Sea Scrolls* (ed. L.H. Schiffman; JSPSup, 8; Sheffield: JSOT Press, 1990).

area which has been explored much less extensively than the textual status of the new discoveries. Study of the scribal habits is an integral part of the description of the transmission history of the biblical text. At the same time, it may enable us to establish connections between individual Qumran texts, biblical and non-biblical, between Jewish and non-Jewish scribal traditions, and to arrive at conclusions on matters of authorship and origin.

Within this framework, the following areas have been studied, or deserve to be analysed: the form of the scroll, materials, fastenings of the scrolls, length of individual sheets, methods used in combining sheets, number of columns per sheet and their measurements, ruling and other markings, and patching. Elements of the scribal conventions that should be considered are: script, orthography, correction systems, stichometric arrangement, paragraphing, word division and *scriptio continua*.

The Content of the Newly Found Texts

Obviously, the content of the documents has received most critical attention, for it touches upon the study of textual transmission, even if details agree exactly with MT or differ 'only' in matters of orthography. Attention is aroused when individual readings agree with sources known previously, mainly the Samaritan Pentateuch and the LXX; in the latter case, the reliability of the reconstruction of Hebrew variants from the Greek translation is enhanced. But the texts have provoked most interest when providing previously unknown readings, irrespective of their being considered inferior to or an improvement upon known readings. Official publications of the scrolls and the subsequent literature discuss these readings in the context of the textual criticism of the Bible, and of literary criticism as well.

Textual Variety among the Manuscripts from the Judaean Desert

All the texts found outside Qumran, that is, in Naḥal Ḥever, Wadi Murabbaʿat and at Masada,[1] are proto-Masoretic. Occasionally they differ in orthography and in minute details of content, but one remains impressed by the basic identity of MT and a long text such as Mur 12. Although this text was from the outset very close to MT, it

1. For Wadi Murabbaʿat, see *DJD*, II (1961), and for Naḥal Ḥever see the references in Fitzmyer, *The Dead Sea Scrolls*, p. 85.

also contains nine corrections toward MT (eight supra-linear additions and one erasure), and one correction away from MT. This textual unity refers to the period until 73 CE for Masada, and to 132–135 CE for Naḥal Ḥever and Wadi Murabbaʿat.

As opposed to the textual unity found in these three localities, Qumran presents a picture of textual variety in each cave, as well as in the group of caves as a whole. The variety is usually described in terms of proximity to texts known before the Qumran discoveries. This descriptive method is a mere convention, derived from the accident that for several centuries scholars knew the mediaeval copies of MT, the Samaritan Pentateuch, and LXX, but no earlier texts. Because of this somewhat unusual situation, the referents of the data are usually cited in reverse order, so to speak. When all the texts have been published it will be possible to depict this relationship correctly, but even at this stage it is already clear that the proximity of the proto-Masoretic texts to the later MT should not be stressed, but rather that of MT to the earlier sources; not the proximity of the proto-Samaritan witnesses to the later Samaritan Pentateuch, but that of the latter to the former. In this way, it will be easier to understand how MT developed from earlier texts which we now call proto-Masoretic, and how the Samaritan Pentateuch was created from texts which we now identify as proto-Samaritan.

Let us turn to a description of the recently discovered documents according to their textual character, and not according to the sequence of the biblical books. The textual variety characterizing the complete collection did not necessarily exist for each individual book, and appears to relate to the hazards of the textual transmission. That is, scribes who changed the nature of a given text (book) by expanding, shortening, or rewriting, by changing the orthography or adding certain linguistic features, did not occupy themselves consistently with certain biblical books. For this reason, a textual development known from one book should not be similarly posited for all biblical books.

Although no predictions regarding the contents of the Qumran caves could have been made, it was actually no surprise to find in them proto-Masoretic texts, although their frequency is remarkable. Many Qumran texts, of which the earliest (4QExod[f]*) has been ascribed to 250 BCE, are (almost) identical with MT. This group includes all the palaeo-Hebrew texts except for 11QpaleoLev and

4QpaleoExod[m], as well as many others in the Assyrian script.[1] Although they are all very close to MT, one of them also reflects what looks like (inconsistent) correction towards MT: 4QJer[a], ascribed by Cross to 200–175 BCE.[2] Because of its length and proximity to MT, special mention should be made of 1QIsa[b], dated to between 30 BCE and 70 CE.[3]

The LXX translation was prepared in Egypt from Hebrew sources still unknown. It was therefore a pleasant surprise to find at Qumran Hebrew texts containing individual readings known from that translation. However, although many such texts agree occasionally with the LXX, only one is sufficiently close to be considered as related to the Hebrew *Vorlage* of that version.[4] Like the LXX, 4QJer[b,d] is much shorter than MT and reflects a different sequence of verses and probably also of chapters.[5] These differences between MT on the one hand and 4QJer[b,d] and the LXX on the other are considered recensional, as they reflect different stages of the development of the Hebrew book.[6]

Like several other texts, 5QDeut agrees a few times with the LXX against some witnesses, and with MT and the Samaritan Pentateuch against the others. This text is special, however, in that it contains four supra-linear corrections agreeing with the LXX.[7] Unfortunately,

---

1. For the palaeo-Hebrew texts, see p. 122 n. 3. See further 1QGen, 1QExod, 1QDeut[b], 1QJud, 1QSam, 1QIsa[b], 1QPs[a,b], 1QPs44, 1QDan[a,b], 2QGen, 2QExod[a,b], 2QNum[a], 2QPs, 2QJob, 2QRuth[a,b], 4QExod[f*], 4QDeut[a,c,d,e,f,g,h,j,l,n,q*], 4QSam[b], 4QIsa[a*], 4QJer[a,c*], 4QPs[b,c,d,q*], 4QPs89, 4QDan[a,c*], 5QLam[a,b], 6QKgs, 6QCant, 6QDan, 8QGen, 8QPs, 11QLev, 11QEzek.

2. Cross, 'The Oldest Manuscripts', p. 137, lines 3, 5 and commentary.

3. Cross, 'The Oldest Manuscripts', p. 179.

4. Other Hebrew texts were described as 'Septuagintal' as well, but in our view the evidence is too scanty: 2QDeut[c] (see *DJD*, III [Oxford: Clarendon Press, 1962], p. 61); 4QExod[a*] (see F.M. Cross, *The Ancient Library of Qumran and Modern Biblical Studies* [New York: Doubleday, 1961–62], p. 184; R.W. Klein, *Textual Criticism of the Old Testament* [Philadelphia: Fortress Press, 1974]; pp. 13-15); 4QDeut[q] (P.W. Skehan, 'A Fragment of the "Song of Moses" (Deut. 32) from Qumran', *BASOR* 136 [1954], pp. 12-15). See further below.

5. For a preliminary publication, see J.G. Janzen, *Studies in the Text of Jeremiah* (HSM, 6; Cambridge, MA: Harvard University Press, 1973), pp. 174-81.

6. See E. Tov, 'Some Aspects of the Textual and Literary History of the Book of Jeremiah', in *Le livre de Jérémie* (ed. P.M. Bogaert; BETL, 54; Leuven: Peeters–Leuven University Press, 1981), pp. 145-67.

7. See Milik's notes in *DJD*, V (Oxford: Clarendon Press, 1968), pp. 169-71.

because of its fragmentary nature, it is not clear whether the complete scroll was corrected towards the Hebrew text underlying the LXX. Likewise, 4QSam[a] often agrees with the LXX, either with the main tradition or the Lucianic text;[1] but it also often disagrees with those textual traditions. Furthermore, it contains many non-aligned readings and cannot, in consequence, be classified as closely related to the LXX. However, the exact relation of both 4QSam[a] and 4QSam[b] to the LXX has yet to be determined after the full publication of the texts.

Another pleasant surprise was the discovery in Qumran of a relatively large group of texts related to the Samaritan Pentateuch, written in the palaeo-Hebrew (4QpaleoExod[m]*) and Assyrian script (the other sources). These texts are now named 'proto-Samaritan', as the sectarian Samaritan Pentateuch was presumably based on a non-sectarian text like these.[2] In a way, the existence of these texts at Qumran advanced scholarship more than the discovery of proto-Masoretic texts, or of scrolls related to the LXX, since the proto-Masoretic texts are known from MT, and philological expertise would have guided us in reconstructing the latter from the LXX. But we would never have been able to recreate proto-Samaritan texts by removing the sectarian readings from the Samaritan Pentateuch for the best preserved proto-Samaritan source, 4QpaleoExod[m]*,[3] also differs in other matters from

1.   See especially the article by F.M. Cross, 'A New Qumran Biblical Fragment Related to the Original Hebrew Underlying the Septuagint', *BASOR* 132 (1953), pp. 15-26; E. Ulrich, *The Qumran Text of Samuel and Josephus* (HSM, 19; Missoula, MT: Scholars Press, 1978), as well as many additional articles. For evaluation, see E. Tov, 'Determining the Relationship between the Qumran Scrolls and the LXX: Some Methodological Issues', in *The Hebrew and Greek Texts of Samuel, 1980 Proceedings IOSCS: Vienna* (ed. E. Tov; Jerusalem: Akademon, 1980), pp. 45-67.

2.   There is no support for the view of M. Baillet that these proto-Samaritan texts, as well other Exodus scrolls containing occasional agreements with the Samaritan Pentateuch, actually reflect Samaritan texts: 'Le texte samaritain de l'Exode dans les manuscrits de Qumran', in *Hommages à André Dupont-Sommer* (ed. A. Caquot and M. Philonenko; Paris: Librairie d'Amérique et d'Orient, Adrien-Maisonneuve, 1971), pp. 363-81. The known proto-Samaritan sources do not contain any sectarian readings. For the reasons why 4QpaleoExod[m]* could not have included the Samaritan Tenth Commandment, see P.W. Skehan, 'Qumran and the Present State of Old Testament Text Studies: The Masoretic Text', *JBL* 78 (1959), pp. 22-23.

3.   A photograph of col. XXXIX together with a transcription has been published by Skehan, 'Exodus in the Samaritan Recension from Qumran', *JBL* 74

the Samaritan Pentateuch. Its spelling is more full, and it lacks the other distinguishing mark of the Samaritan Pentateuch, viz. its Samaritan phonetic features. It shares with the Samaritan Pentateuch its linguistic simplifications, harmonizations in small matters, as well as non-characteristic readings, yet it also differs in many details in these areas.[1] Moreover, it contains various readings not known from other sources. These features are also found in the other proto-Samaritan sources. It has been surmised by recent generations of scholars that the Samaritan Pentateuch was composed of two different layers, but the exact nature of these two layers has only now been clarified. The second, 'Samaritan', layer is thin, and can be 'peeled off' rather easily.

Because of these differences between the proto-Samaritan sources and the Samaritan Pentateuch, it should be stressed that the large harmonistic pluses and the additions from Deuteronomy in Exodus and Numbers (and in one case, vice versa) suffice to prove the special character of the proto-Samaritan texts. In 4QpaleoExod[m]*, these harmonistic features are well represented, especially in the explicit execution of the divine commands to Moses and Aaron, who were to warn Pharaoh before each plague. A second proto-Samaritan source, 4Q158 ('biblical paraphrase'),[2] has added in the Sinai pericope in Exodus parts of the parallel account in Deut. 5.24-31 as well as the divine command to install a prophet (Deut. 18.18-22). In this it is like the Samaritan Pentateuch. This source also contains the performance

---

(1955), pp. 182-87. Columns I and II have been published without transcription in the article by Skehan, 'Qumran IV'. The character of this scroll is discussed in detail by J.E. Sanderson, *An Exodus Scroll from Qumran. 4QpaleoExod[m] and the Samaritan Tradition* (HSS, 30; Atlanta: Scholars Press, 1986), p. 223.

1.   In the three published columns (see previous note), see especially the full spelling of *'hrwn and wy'wmr*, reminiscent of the full Qumran orthography. Note also an occasional agreement with the characyteristic Qumran language (*m'dh* quoted by Sanderson, *An Exodus Scroll from Qumran*, p. 40). These spellings, however, are exceptional for the Exodus scroll. For small harmonizations of the Samaritan Pentateuch not found in the Exodus scroll, see in the published section 6.27, 30; 7.2, and for a linguistic simplification not shared with the scroll see 7.4.

2.   Published by J. Allegro in *DJD*, V (Oxford: Clarendon Press, 1968), on which see the detailed notes and additional reconstructions by J. Strugnell, 'Notes en marge du volume V'. See also the detailed discussion of this text in E. Tov, 'The Nature and Background of Harmonizations in Biblical Manuscripts', *JSOT* 31 (1985), pp. 3-29.

of the command of Deut. 5.30, a detail not shared with the other witnesses of the biblical text. These data are relevant in spite of the fact that 4Q158 is not a regular biblical text, but consists of a combination of biblical texts interspersed with midrashic exegesis.

Another 'biblical paraphrase', 4Q364*, also contains major harmonizing additions shared with the Samaritan Pentateuch.[1] 4QNum^b* reportedly also contains major harmonizing pluses from Deuteronomy in Numbers, again shared with the Samaritan Pentateuch.[2] The sequence of the scriptural passages in 4QTest (175) corresponds with the Samaritan Pentateuch.[3] Finally, 4QDeut^n ('All Souls') adds, like the Samaritan Pentateuch, the text of Exod. 20.11 after Deut. 5.15. All these texts thus form a typologically similar group, related in character yet sometimes different in content, distinguished mainly by harmonizing additions reflecting a free editorial approach. Just as these texts relate to each other, the Samaritan Pentateuch is akin to all of them, although that text is somewhat remote from them because of its subsequent ideological and phonetic developments.

The greatest surprise of the Qumran discoveries derives from texts maintaining an independent status, not particularly close to MT, LXX or the Samaritan Pentateuch. Such texts may contain many agreements with those three sources, but at the same time they significantly disagree with them. Of greater importance, they contain a large number of readings not shared with the three sources. They are thus independent.

It has now been recognized that the textual variety in Qumran can no longer be described in terms of the tripartite division of the textual witnesses customary before 1947.[4] According to the old-fashioned concepts with which most scholars still work, all the Qumran texts can somehow be fitted into the tripartite picture of the MT, LXX and Samaritan Pentateuch, in the case of the Pentateuch, and under a different name in the other books of the Bible. However, several

---

1. E.g. Jacob's dream after Gen. 30.36 (= 31.11-13). 4Q364* agrees in several details with 4Q158 against MT.

2. See Cross, *The Ancient Library of Qumran*, p. 186.

3. Exod. 20.18 (= Deut. 5.25-25; 18.18-19); Num. 24.15-17; Deut. 33.8-11; Josh. 6.26. Also in the Samaritan Pentateuch the first two mentioned passages are added after Exod. 20.18.

4. See E. Tov, 'A Modern Textual Outlook Based on the Qumran Scrolls', *HUCA* 53 (1982), pp. 11-27.

Qumran texts do not fit within such a framework, and must be considered as sources *additional* to those known before. Of these, I mention here 2QDeut[c], 4QDeut[a*,q], 4QJos[a*], 4QSam[a], 5QKgs, 11QpaleoLev.[1]

It should be added, parenthetically, that in determining the textual character of a writing, the paleo-Hebrew script apparently plays no special role. 4QpalaeoExod[m] is a proto-Samaritan text, 11QpaleoLev is independent, while all the other palaeo-Hebrew documents are proto-Masoretic.

Qumran thus displays a picture of textual variety, including many proto-Masoretic texts, several proto-Samaritan texts, a number of independent scrolls, and one text agreeing with the *Vorlage* of the LXX. If the aforementioned description is correct, all of these texts were imported to the community. Within this variety, one further group must be taken into consideration, viz. the texts written in the 'Qumran system'. These comprise a separate class characterized by matters of orthography and language, and not of content.

For any given biblical book, a number of different texts, as described above, could have existed. It is not impossible that a greater textual diversity developed for some books than for others, but this cannot be determined because of the current fragmentary state of our knowledge.

Approach to the Biblical Text at Qumran and in Palestine as a whole during the Second Temple Period

I now turn to an analysis of the approach to the biblical text in the Second Temple period, paying special attention to differences between the various texts. The first part of this analysis focuses on the textual

---

1.   On the independent nature of the Leviticus scroll, see E. Tov, 'The Textual Character of 11QPaleoLev', in *Shnaton* 3 (Jerusalem–Tel Aviv, 1978–79), pp. 238-44 [Hebrew]; K.A. Mathews, 'The Leviticus Scroll (11QpaleoLev) and the Text of the Hebrew Bible', *CBQ* 48 (1986), pp. 171-207. On 4QDeut[q] see Skehan, 'A Fragment of the Song of Moses', and P.-M. Bogaert, 'Les trois rédactions conservées et la forme originale de l'envoi du Cantique de Moïse (Dt 32,43)', in *Das Deuteronomium: Entstehung, Gestalt und Botschaft*, BETL 68 (1985), pp. 329-40. On 4QSam[a], see the statistics in E. Tov (p. 124 n. 1). On 4QJosh[a*], see Boling, *Joshua*. The statistics for the other texts mentioned here are provided in the article mentioned in the preceding note, pp. 21-22.

situation at Qumran, from the middle of the third century BCE until 68 CE. At a second stage we turn to a discussion of the overall textual situation in that period in Palestine.

Probably the majority of scholars assume that all Qumran texts reflect the outlook of the Qumran community. If that is true, the texts found there reflect a broadness of mind in matters of canon and an acceptance of textual variety, for the collections contain not only sectarian and biblical books, but also various extracanonical works, now called Apocrypha and Pseudepigrapha. Furthermore, the caves provide biblical scrolls on leather as well as papyrus, in palaeo-Hebrew as well as the Assyrian script, and even in translation (Aramaic, Greek). However, the clearest evidence of the presumed open-mindedness of the community is the existence of many different texts, as described above. Both the texts written in Qumran and those that were imported show varying approaches to the biblical text.

Taking as our point of departure that these texts reflect the thinking of the sectarians, we must enquire into their *Sitz im Leben* within the Qumran community. On a practical level, openness to textual variety would appear in the indiscriminatory use of the texts in daily life; the sectarians were not Bible scholars, and the differences in content, orthography and textual approach may not have disturbed them. But it is equally possible that the Qumranites used the scrolls in different circumstances. In that case, they would have chosen a certain type of text for the official reading of the Bible, and another one for study purposes, both communal and individual. It is also possible (H.S.) that new members of the community brought with them their private scrolls which were stored in the 'library' of the community and were not used actively.

Alternatively, the various readings could correspond to different attitudes toward the biblical text in the course of several generations, with scrolls of one textual character preferred in a given period. This assumption can be discarded as far as the distinction between local and imported scrolls is concerned, since palaeographical considerations lead us to believe that both types of scrolls derived from the whole period of the sect's settlement at Qumran.

All these reflections concerning the Qumranites' openness to questions of canon and text are mere speculation. After all, nothing is known of the circumstances surrounding the deposition of the texts. Further, we do not understand the character of the collections found in Qumran, nor why they were placed there. More important in the present context, we do not really know whether all the texts found in Qumran were used actively by the community at some stage of its history. If most of the texts remained locked in a 'library', and if the sectarians used only one group of texts in their daily life, we cannot speak of their openness to matters of canon and to textual diversity. Considerable freedom is visible in the creation of scrolls written in the 'Qumran system', but this is not equivalent to acceptance of the variety of texts found in the Qumran caves. If my theory distinguishing between the different origins of the Qumran texts is not correct, we know absolutely nothing of the background of the scrolls. If, on the other hand, it is realistic, we are enabled to distinguish between the scrolls copied at Qumran and the imported scrolls. But this distinction does not allow us to determine the status of the imported texts in the community.

The only hint pointing to the Qumranites' approach to the imported and local texts might be found in their use of these texts in their own writings. There are indications that the Qumranites preferred to quote from the local scrolls written in the 'Qumran system'. This assumption derives from a parallel between 1QDeut[a] and 11QTemple,[1] possible parallels between 1QIsa[a] and 4QDibHam[a] (504).[2] However, this is a question which still needs to be studied in detail. Other relevant information may come from the quantitative relation between the scrolls written in the 'Qumran system' and the imported scrolls. According to the present state of knowledge, there were more imported than local scrolls in Qumran; but these data are merely provisional.[3]

While the Covenanters' approach to the texts discovered in Qumran cannot be determined, some minimal conclusions can be drawn concerning the state of the text in Palestine. Based on the determination

---

1.   1QDeut[a] reads in Deut. 13.5: *l' lwhykmh tlkwn w' wtw t'b wdwn*. The same reading is reflected in 11QTemple LIV 14. Instead, MT and the Samaritan Pentateuch read *tlkw* and place *t'bdw* at the end of the verse. In analysing these parallels as well as the ones mentioned below, one should take into consideration the fact that the palaeographical dates of these compositions do not allow for such conclusions. The parallels may thus refer to an earlier copy of the biblical texts.

2.   Note the correspondence in small details between 4QDibHam[a] (504) and 1QIsa[a] in 48.17-18 (brought to my attention by Mrs E. Chazon).

3.   See the temporary list cited above (p. 115 n. 1).

that some of the texts found in Qumran originated elsewhere, we may deduce that Palestine was characterized by textual diversity. This diversity had not been documented earlier, although it could have been surmised before 1947, and in any event was more extensive than expected.

The proportional distribution of the texts from Qumran may give some indication of the degree to which the various texts were accepted in Palestine; but again we are left with questions. Does the large number of proto-Masoretic texts point to a wide acceptance of this textual tradition outside Qumran in the Second Temple period? The one place for which such an assumption is valid is Masada, where all the biblical evidence antedating 73 CE reflects MT. How large was the group of proto-Samaritan texts, and what was their geographical distribution? Finally, were there other texts in Palestine similar to those written in the 'Qumran system'?

The Qumran discoveries have disclosed important details about the three sources around which textual discussions evolved before 1947—MT, the Samaritan Pentateuch, LXX.[1] We now know that these sources do not constitute the three pillars of the biblical text, nor are they the archetypal representatives of three textual recensions of that text, as had been claimed by most scholars. The myth of this tripartite division of the textual witnesses now belongs to the past, for the simple reason that in each book of the Bible evidenced in Qumran we are now faced with many more than three textual entities. We should no longer try to fit the Qumran texts into this imaginary framework, created because the MT, Samaritan Pentateuch and LXX were the only preserved textual sources. In addition to these, we now know of various independent texts, as well as texts written in the 'Qumran system'.

Due to be cast aside, too, is the scholarly terminology applied to the textual sources: the three 'main' entities have usually been named 'recensions' or 'text-types'. However, in my view, a recension or text-type should contain certain typological characteristics (e.g. short, long, full of glosses), but these can only be substantiated for the proto-Samaritan texts and the Samaritan Pentateuch.[2] In consequence, this

---

1. See Tov, 'A Modern Textual Outlook Based on the Qumran Scrolls', pp. 11-27.

2. These typological features include harmonizing additions from Deuteronomy in Exodus and Numbers, as well as others within individual stories, and the frequent

terminology is inappropriate. Instead, it is preferable to use a neutral term for the textual witnesses: they should be called 'texts'. Even if this suggestion sounds simple, within the scholarly world it is a novelty.

The Qumran texts have thus brought about two changes in our perception, one positing an almost endless number of texts for the individual biblical books, and the other concerning the terminology used for the textual witnesses (texts). However, this view should not lead us to forget certain facts. The variety of texts in the Second Temple period may have been great, but among these texts were certain groups created by an approach common to several scribes. One such group consists of the texts written in the 'Qumran system'; another is that of the proto-Samaritan texts. These two groups are rather tight, even though there are minor or major differences in orthography and content. A third, closer, group is that of the proto-Masoretic texts. Therefore, we must recognize that together with a number of unrelated texts, groups of texts were created (of which three are known thus far) due to socioreligious and other reasons, as has often been stressed by Talmon.[1] Some of these had a greater distribution than others, perhaps because the individuals behind them were more influential than others. (This formulation suggests that finding a large number of similar texts implies a socioreligious motivation and not necessarily quality.)

Because of the importance of the proto-Masoretic texts, serious thought must be given to the possibility that other texts were adapted to this textual tradition. So far, no such 'adapted' texts of a different background have been found. Corrections toward the form of MT in proto-Masoretic texts, as known from mediaeval MSS, do not prove this procedure; in most cases these are mere corrections of mistakes, even though 4QJer[a]* and Mur12 also contain corrections of synonymous words, which could point to a systematic procedure of correction. Other texts sometimes agree with MT, but more frequently the corrections bring the text into disagreement with it (4QSam[c], 11QPs[a], and especially 1QIsa[a]). It must therefore be concluded that most of these corrections have been made without regard to MT.[2]

---

occurrence of 'secondary' readings.

1. See Talmon, 'The Old Testament Text', p. 198.
2. I should also note the aforementioned corrections in 5QDeut towards a

All the documents found at other sites in the Judaean Desert that were written before 73 CE (Masada) or 135 (Naḥal Ḥever, Wadi Murabbaʿat) reflect a proto-Masoretic text. This situation is usually described in scholarship as the victory of MT (often, Masoretic recension or text-type) over the other recensions or text-types. However, caution is in order since this was probably a result of historical accident, as stressed by Albrektson.[1] Most of the religious groups which perpetuated the different biblical texts simply ceased to exist after the destruction of the Second Temple. The Pharisees were the sole surviving group that had influence; thus the only texts to be expected after 70 CE are proto-Masoretic.

Beyond the textual variety reflected in the finds from the Judaean Desert one recognizes two different approaches to the biblical text. A 'free' approach to the text of the Bible is visible in the texts introducing the 'Qumran system' of orthography and language as well as contextual changes. These texts were written in careless handwriting with many mistakes. The free approach is similarly reflected in the proto-Samaritan texts with their extensive editorial rewriting. At the same time, as far as we can ascertain, these texts did not allow for sectarian readings.[2] At the other extreme is a 'conservative' stand visible in the proto-Masoretic texts, in the one scroll close to the Hebrew *Vorlage* of the LXX, 4QJer[b] (and others?), and in the Qumran texts characterized as 'independent'. None of these texts displays major interventions in orthography, and hence they are relatively defective, as MT. The conservatism of these texts is also seen in the relative absence of secondary readings such as those described here. At the same time, the differences among these sources do not undermine their description as 'conservative', since the concept of a universally accepted text had not been created.

Hebrew text reflected by the LXX.

1.   B. Albrektson, 'Reflections on the Emergence of a Standard Text of the Hebrew Bible', *VTSup* 29 (1978), pp. 49-65.

2.   The few sectarian readings in the biblical lemmas in 1QpHab should be disregarded in this context, as the *pesher* itself is sectarian.

QUMRAN AND RABBINIC HALAKHAH

Lawrence H. Schiffman

A fundamental problem in the history of Judaism is the prehistory of rabbinic halakhah. That corpus of Jewish ritual and civil law clearly evolved not only out of biblical tradition, but also out of a complex historical process in which certain forms of exegesis fused with ancient customary law and later decrees and enactments, to produce the system of thought and law which serves as the basis of the Mishnah. This system becomes the basis of talmudic tradition in the Land of Israel and in Babylonia, and of subsequent Jewish life.

Until very recently, an informational gap of hundreds of years existed between the biblical sources and the early history of Jewish law in the rabbinic period. Even when sources such as the *Book of Jubilees* and the *Zadokite Fragments* which pertain to that 'dark age' of documentation began to become available, a lack of perspective made it difficult to judge the true relevance of those texts for the history of the halakhah. Indeed, our predecessors in the *Wissenschaft des Judentums* were easily misled into arranging sources in chronological order, on the assumption that there was a linear development from the stricter, 'older' halakhah to a more lenient version which supposedly was in evidence in tannaitic sources.

The discovery of the Dead Sea scrolls, and the publication of a good part of the legal materials from this corpus, has made possible a radical restructuring of our positions on these matters. It is now possible to paint a much clearer picture of the way the system of Jewish law enshrined in rabbinic halakhah developed. These new perspectives are also essential for understanding the background of the divergence between Judaism and Christianity.

I should emphasize that the results of research into the Jewish legal materials found in the Dead Sea scrolls have not yet shown significant impact on the more recent surveys of the field. Nor has this complex of issues yet found a place in the curricula of most institutions of learning. In the present context I can only attempt to sketch the basic conclusions which the new discoveries suggest and highlight their significance for teaching and research.

Centrality of Jewish Law in the Second Temple Period

It is essential for an understanding of the issues and developments in the Second Temple period to realize that Jewish law was at the heart of the manifold controversies which then beset Judaism. Basic issues regarding the Temple and its cult, the ritual calendar, ritual purity and impurity, and similar matters caused a part of the Jewish population of the Second Temple period to constitute themselves into what have come to be called 'sects'. Admittedly, these controversies involved the intellectual and religious elite for the most part; the wider population seems not to have taken part in them, and evidence points to widespread observance of the basic provisions of Jewish law, in some form, among the common people.

I should call attention to a feature of these controversies between representatives of various groups or sects which is often overlooked. The bulk of the observances and laws of Judaism seems to have been shared by all. The controversies pertained to certain specifics of observance of the law. To take a simple example: the Essenes mentioned by Josephus, the *havurah* described in tannaitic sources, the Sadducees, and the sect that produced the Dead Sea scrolls all followed a similar set of purity restrictions regarding food. They disagreed, though, on certain specific details. Only by fully realizing the centrality of Jewish law in Judaism of the Hellenistic–Roman period, and by understanding that the disagreements must be viewed against the background of a commonly accepted basic tradition, can we properly evaluate pre-rabbinic Judaism and its importance for the understanding of later tannaitic and amoraic teachings.

The Sources

It is now clear that the Qumran scrolls provide us with information not only about the Dead Sea Covenanters, identified by many scholars with the Essenes, but about a much wider variety of groups within the Judaism of that period. The following brief survey of the pertinent writings and the views which they illumine is necessarily based on the published materials. Substantial manuscript material from Qumran still awaits publication, and its appearance may require a reassessment of various points.

First and foremost, the scrolls inform us about the views on Jewish law of the sectarians who bequeathed us the library in the Qumran caves. The *Zadokite Fragments* enlighten us about their stance on a wide variety of matters pertaining to Sabbath, oaths and vows, purity and impurity, the laws of courts and testimony. The fact that these legal *serakhim* (lists of rules) are preceded in that work by admonitions to remain faithful to the teachings of the sect, and by an account of its rise, intimately links this text with the community of Qumran.

The *Megillat Ha-Serakhim* (*Rule Scroll*) contains the sect's rulings on membership and initiation, penalties and punishments, and various other offences. The messianic *Serekh Ha-'Edah* reflects the sectarians' aspirations for the end-of-days which, we must emphasize, is expected to be primarily a period of perfection and purity, a fulfillment of Jewish law in the life of the individual and the community. Even the *War Scroll* contains legal regulations regarding the manner in which the purity of the camp is to be maintained, detailing various rites and rituals, and enumerating the laws of conscription. In addition, various smaller texts, such as those entitled 'Ordinances', reveal the particular views of the sect on matters of Jewish law.

Somewhat different are the materials in the *Temple Scroll*. This document outlines the author's (or redactor's) dreams for a perfect sanctuary and government, for the sanctity of the land of Israel, the people of Israel, and the worship of Israel's God. This document does not reflect the teachings of the Qumran Covenanters, but rather those of some allied or similar group which may also have been closely connected with the Sadducees. The author sees the sacrificial worship and the government of Israel as requiring reform. He has essentially produced a polemic against the Hasmonaean Temple and kingship. This is not a messianic text. Redacted in the late second or early first century BCE, the scroll sets out an ideal society, a pre-messianic vision for a perfect Israel in the present age.

The *Miqsat Ma'asei Torah* (4QMMT) seems in certain ways to be related to the *Temple Scroll*. At the same time, it exhibits certain divergences. Most interesting is the fact that the text sets out a variety of laws preceded by the assertion that the addressee of this 'letter' takes a view which is in opposition to that of the text's author. Several Pharisee–Sadducee disputes recorded in tannaitic literature are referred to in the 'letter', with the author taking the view of the Sadducees and attributing to the Jerusalem establishment the view assigned by the tannaim to the Pharisees. This text raises anew the question of the relationship of the Qumran sect to the Zadokite (or Sadducaean) priesthood, especially in the aftermath of the Maccabaean takeover of the high priesthood. Further, it lends credence to the tannaitic assertion that the Pharisees actually were able to bring about adherence to their views in the Jerusalem Temple, and weakens the arguments of scholars who cast doubts upon that claim. In any case, it is clear that the final publication of this document will radically change our understanding of the history of Jewish law. Most important, this document illumines the views of a variety of groups, not just those of the so-called Qumran sect.

The fragments of *Jubilees* found in the caves were most probably not penned there and do not suggest that the work was authored by a member of the Qumran sect. But the publication of the *Jubilees* material from Qumran will help us better understand the important collection of laws found in that book. The *tefillin* exhibit two patterns which were current at the time—one similar to that of the later tannaim and one apparently typical of the sectarians. The same is the case with the *mezuzot*. The Qumran texts have helped us greatly to understand the calendar of *Jubilees*, *Enoch*, and that of the sect. But it is clear that some texts, such as the liturgical texts from Cave 4, do not use this calendar. Thus, we must now begin to ask if those latter materials stem in fact from the Covenanters, or if they were simply part of the collection which they had assembled.

This brief survey of 'halakhic' materials from the Qumran corpus indicates that these texts relate not only to the Covenanters, but to other groups as well. Some texts are certainly those of allied groups whose materials were of sufficient interest to the sectarians of Qumran to be included in their library. With the publication and analysis of the remaining material, we should gradually learn much about Jewish law as understood by the Qumranites as well as by other groups of Jews in the Second Temple period.

The 'Theology' of the Law

Second Temple Judaism was intensely concerned with the question of how to incorporate the extra-biblical traditions and teachings into the legal system, and how to justify them theologically. Despite the fact that in antiquity and late antiquity there was little theoretical theological inquiry in Judaism (except in the Hellenistic Diaspora), issues of theology were of central importance and often lay behind other more clearly expressed disputes.

All Jewish groups in the Second Temple period endeavoured to assimilate extra-biblical teachings into their way of life. The detailed examination of the writings of the Qumran sect has led us to determine that they did so through the concept of *nigleh* ('revealed') and *nistar* ('hidden'). That which was 'revealed' was the simple meaning of Scripture, and the commandments that were readily apparent from the text. These were known to all Jews. But only the members of the sect possessed the 'hidden' knowledge, discovered through what they saw as inspired biblical exegesis on the part of their leaders. Tradition is regarded as having no authority, since all Israel has gone astray and the true way was rediscovered by the 'Teacher' alone. The laws which emerged from this concept were eventually composed in *serakhim*, lists of sectarian rules. These were then redacted into such collections as the *Zadokite Fragments* (*Damascus Document*) or the less strictly organized 'Ordinances' (4Q159, 513, 514). These rules, and the interpretations upon which they were based, served to clarify the application of the Law of the Torah to the life of the group, and to enable its members to live in accord with the 'revealed' Torah in the present, pre-messianic age.

We do not have Pharisaic texts from this period. But we can sketch the approach of this group in general lines, by utilizing later accounts in the New Testament, the writings of Josephus, and reports in the even later tannaitic corpus. The Pharisees possessed teachings 'handed down by the fathers', and 'unwritten law'. These included various legal traditions of great antiquity as well as interpretations of biblical texts. Indeed, the Pharisees were known as expounders of the Torah, and seem to have excelled in the adaptation and application of the laws of the Pentateuch to their own circumstances and times. Somewhat later, their successors, the tannaim (teachers of the Mishnah) would develop the notion that God had revealed these traditions to Moses on Sinai as a second Torah. The Rabbis asserted that God had given two Torahs to Israel, the written and the oral. For the rabbis, this view essentially elevated the *torah shebe'al peh* to a sanctity and authority equal to that of the *torah shebiktab*. The available evidence does not suffice to ascribe such an assertion to the Pharisees themselves, and the sources do not allow us to make definite pronouncements in this matter.

The Sadducaean approach has yet to be properly investigated. The general claim that the Sadducees were strict literalists represents a misunderstanding of their concepts, often predicated on late rabbinic sources and on a parallel misunderstanding of the mediaeval Karaite movement. The Sadducees apparently recognized only the written law as authoritative, although they admitted the need to interpret it. Their exegesis attempted to adhere as closely as possible to the plain meaning of Scripture (*peshat* in later rabbinic terminology).

Against this background we can better understand the views of the author of the *Temple Scroll*. He seeks to assimilate extra-biblical traditions by the contention that his new, rewritten Torah properly expresses the will of God as revealed in the original document. He asserts that the correct meaning of the divine revelation at Sinai, which apparently was left vague in the canonical Torah, is to be found in the *Temple Scroll*. It follows that, like the sectarians of Qumran, he has no dual Torah concept. But, unlike that group, he does not accept the notion of a continuous, inspired revelation through biblical exegesis. He recognizes only a one-time revelation, at Sinai, and in this respect he agrees with the later tannaim. However, the one-time revelation as conceived by the tannaim is of two Torahs, while for the author of the *Temple Scroll* it is of a single Torah, whose true contents are expressed in the scroll which he authored or redacted.

The scrolls provide a window into the theological divergence in the Judaism of the Hellenistic–Roman period. With such fundamental differences of opinion regarding the very basis of Jewish law, it is no wonder that the various groups arrived at different halakhic rulings. The scrolls testify in various ways to the vitality of the debate regarding the theoretical basis of the law, the exegesis applied to it, and to the specific decisions reached by the several groups.

The Background and History of Rabbinic Halakhah

The methodological considerations outlined above, and the new data that have emerged from the study of the Dead Sea scrolls, have revolutionized our understanding of the early history of post-biblical Judaism. At the same time, advances in talmudic studies have served to heighten the importance of reconstructing the background and early history of rabbinic Judaism. While the treatment of the specific details regarding individual laws must remain outside the scope of this essay, the general observations that follow are based on the careful investigation of many such legal issues, as part of our ongoing study of the legal materials in the Dead Sea corpus.

First and foremost, it must be emphasized that this research has led to the conclusion that the extent of discontinuity between Second Temple and tannaitic sources is much less pronounced than appears to be the case. We do not seek to deny the historical development which lies behind tannaitic tradition. However, we can often determine that the view propounded in tannaitic sources either mirrors a position held by the Pharisees or some other group in Second Temple times, or that it reflects a reaction to a view known to have been held then by some group. Tannaitic tradition may also evince a historical deviation from such a view, or even reflect an outright and direct polemic against it. In many cases, we have absolutely no evidence for a position espoused by the Pharisees, despite the fact that we do have tannaitic traditions which pertain to an issue under scrutiny. While we cannot assume offhand that those traditions go back to pre-destruction materials, we can assert that the halakhic and exegetical issues to which the view apparently seeks to respond were indeed dealt with in Second Temple sources.

The Qumran material has yielded new evidence regarding the question of Pharisaic domination of the halakhic process in the Temple during the Hasmonaean period—a matter which is generally regarded as being unlikely. 4Q *Miqṣat Ma‘asei Torah* appears to imply that, at least in certain matters, the Temple procedures followed views attributed in tannaitic sources to the Pharisees, rather than those attributed to the Sadducees. We must now seriously reckon with the possibility of Pharisaic leadership in Second Temple halakhah, and accordingly reevaluate historical questions pertaining to the changing fortunes of the Pharisaic party in Hasmonaean times. The existence of Pharisaic leadership in this period would help us to understand the rapid ascendancy of that group in the aftermath of the revolt. Again, continuity seems to outweigh discontinuity.

Another area of significance is that of literary form. There can be no question that in the period after the destruction of the Second Temple, the tannaim made great strides in the organization and presentation of literary materials they had inherited or composed. As yet, we cannot point to any materials of Pharisaic origin which had already been redacted in Second Temple times. But in one area it is now possible to make some observations. There has been consistent debate among scholars of early Judaism concerning the relationship and history of the literary forms of midrash that presents the law as derived from the biblical text, and of mishnah that presents abstract, apodictic law. The Dead Sea corpus shows evidence of both literary genres, although it cannot be ascertained whether they coexisted in any one group. The *Zadokite Fragments* represent a technique of redacting clusters of apodictic laws according to subject matter, similar to the method of the mishnah. In contrast, the *Temple Scroll* is an example of legal matters tied intimately to the biblical text; but that work is not really a midrash since the laws are mostly couched in the language of the biblical *Vorlage*. This is also the case in the earliest examples of *midrash halakhah* in Ezra and Nehemiah, and may typify the incipient stages in the history of halakhic midrash.

Finally, I must call attention to the contents of the halakhic system. The writings of various groups, found in the caves of Qumran, indicate the shared notion that all aspects of life should be sanctified by specific religious practices. While debates ensued in Second Temple times and in post-70 CE tannaitic sources regarding the specifics by which this way of life should be regulated, the beginnings of a prayer service, *tefillin* and *mezuzot*, Torah study, and civil law were clearly central issues by the Hasmonaean period. It was the task of the tannaim to standardize, refine, and explain the regulations which had crystallized long before.

Teaching Judaism and Christianity

The above considerations must effect significant changes in the way the early histories of Judaism and Christianity are taught. The following basic observations concerning curricula and pedagogic questions are meant to relate to the different kinds of programmes in which we teach Judaism and Christianity at the turn of the era, and to show the importance, for both, of the results of Qumran research in evaluating the history of rabbinic Judaism.

The easiest place to begin is at the level of courses in which the Dead Sea scrolls are studied. If anything, this survey, which deals only with Jewish law but which can be paralleled for every area of study of the scrolls, shows that the Qumran materials are documents of Jews and Judaism. It is not intellectually legitimate to persist in teaching the scrolls as if the Qumran sect was simply a precursor of Christianity. This procedure results in a skewed perspective on the nature of Judaism in this period. Further, it effectively robs Judaism of its history. Of course, the large number of parallels between Qumran documents and early Christianity must be given adequate attention, but within the appropriate framework, and it must continually be emphasized that in the sect's eschatology, the future life was envisioned in the purity and perfection defined by Jewish law. Thus, legal texts must be accorded their deserved position in courses on the scrolls.

In teaching the early history of Christianity and the New Testament, the points of contact between Qumran and these traditions must be properly indicated, but without minimizing the Jewish character of the material. Specifically, Christianity has traditionally posited a discontinuity between the Judaism of the Hebrew Bible and that of the rabbis. It must be admitted that the history of Judaism can be traced from the Hebrew Scripture, to Second Temple literature, to rabbinic tradition. Christianity claimed to be the legitimate successor to prophetic tradition, presenting rabbinic Judaism as a development gone awry. Our presentation makes clear that, historically, there was no such discontinuity. We must now present Christianity and rabbinic Judaism as two different streams in the interpretation of the biblical traditions.

In courses on the history of rabbinic Judaism, or on talmudic texts, the tannaitic materials cannot be dealt with in a vacuum. It must be recognized and emphasized that many of the pertinent issues were previously argued in Second Temple materials. As a matter of fact, the talmudic texts often cannot be properly understood without knowledge of these earlier discussions. Further, we cannot continue to reconstruct the history of rabbinic Judaism as if the Qumran scrolls do not exist, and as if they do not necessitate a repainting of the picture of Second Temple Judaism.

Recent Qumran Discoveries and Halakhah
in the Hellenistic–Roman Period

Joseph M. Baumgarten

I

The study of the halakhah of the Qumran community is presently in a state of unprecedented ferment and expectation. The turning point in this development was, without doubt, the publication by Y. Yadin of the *Temple Scroll* (1977). This scroll, the largest of the Qumran texts, confirmed the antiquity of the halakhic corpus found in the *Zadokite Document*, which Solomon Schechter[1] and Louis Ginzberg[2] had already shown to have a close affinity with rabbinic halakhah. The *Temple Scroll* has considerably broadened the base of comparison between rabbinic halakhah and the exegesis of biblical law which prevailed in the Qumran community. Now further relevant material has come to the attention of scholars with the publication of discoveries from Cave 4. Among the fragments are texts which should be of intense interest to all scholars concerned with ancient halakhah. Suffice it to mention the initial description by Strugnell and Qimron of the text which they entitled *Miqṣat Ma'asei Torah* (4QMMT), an anthology of halakhic matters in which the Qumran sect differed from the contemporary traditions of the Pharisees.[3] Once a definitive edition becomes available, this text will open up new avenues of inquiry into pre-rabbinic halakhah.

A good model was provided by the late Professor Saul Lieberman,

1. S. Schechter, *Fragments of a Zadokite Work. Documents of Jewish Sectaries*, I (Cambridge: Cambridge University Press, 1910).

2. L. Ginzberg, *An Unknown Jewish Sect* (trans., rev. edn; New York: Jewish Theological Seminary, 1976), pp. 70-71.

3. E. Qimron and J. Strugnell, 'An Unpublished Halakhic Letter from Qumran', in *Biblical Archaeology Today* (ed. J. Amitai; Jerusalem: Israel Exploration Society, 1985), pp. 400-407.

who as early as 1952 noted the structural similarities between the Qumran *yahad* and the Pharisaic *haburah*. He also found possible echoes of Qumran practices in the Tosefta, where certain heterodox halakhic stringencies are labelled *derekh aheret*. Current developments in the study of the sect's halakhah appear to bear out a statement made in my extensive review of C. Rabin's Qumran studies published in 1957. I wrote then, with what now appears as the impetuosity of youth:

> In the end it may well be that the religious laws and practices in the Qumran documents will be more decisive in determining the position of the sect within the spectrum of pre-Christian Jewish movements than any of its theological and messianic speculations.[1]

The rest of this paper will be an attempt to show why this may after all have been a true prophecy, and to draw from it certain methodological lessons. I will confine my remarks to a discussion of already published materials, particularly to a few illustrations from sources which are not only significant in themselves, but may serve as testing grounds for the methodologies used in this area of research by modern historians of religion. In 1983, there appeared in Volume 7 of Discoveries in the Judaean Desert a small fragment edited by M. Baillet. It contains only nine words spread over four lines, which may be translated as follows:

> the waving of the Omer
> apart from the Sabbaths
> error of blindness
> not from the Law of Moses

The editor noted that this text must have something to do with the ancient controversy concerning the date of the Omer offering, but did not pursue the matter to gauge its full implications.

It is known that the rabbis interpreted the expression 'on the morrow of the Sabbath' which in Leviticus 23 marks the time of the Omer ritual, to refer to the day following the first day of the Passover festival. The same interpretation underlies the Septuagint translation. Thus, the barley required for the Omer meal offering was always to be harvested on the evening which followed the first day of the festival. But what was to be done if that evening happened to be the

---

1. 'Qumran Studies', *JBL* 72 (1958), pp. 249-57; reprinted in *Studies in Qumran Law* (Leiden: Brill, 1977), pp. 1-12.

eve of the Sabbath when all work is forbidden? Against a minority tannaitic opinion (*b. Menaḥot* 72b), the majority decision established that the Omer overrides the Sabbath. This is dramatically indicated in *m. Men.* 10.3:

> How did they use to do it (the Omer)? Officials of the court would go out on the eve of the holiday and bind it (the barley) into sheaves while attached to the ground so that it would be easy to harvest. All the villages nearby would gather there so that it might be harvested with much pomp. When it was dark, he would say to them: Has the sun set? They would say Yes...This scythe? They would say Yes...On the Sabbath he would say to them: On this Sabbath? They would say Yes: (On this Sabbath? They would say: Yes...) Three times for each thing, and they say to him: Yes, Yes, Yes. And why to such an extent? Because of the Boethusians who maintained that the harvesting of the Omer was not to be done on the night after the holiday.

The opposition of the Boethusians stemmed from the premise that the phrase 'on the morrow of the Sabbath' in Leviticus 23 was to be taken in its literal sense of the seventh day of the week, so that the Omer was always to be cut on Sunday. This was likewise the view of the Qumranites. They had adopted a solar calendar of 364 days per year, in which the first month began on a Wednesday, automatically precluding the possibility of any biblical holiday coinciding with the Sabbath.[1] In the *Zadokite Document* and the Cave 4 fragment cited above, this is reflected in the allusion to Lev. 23.38: 'These are the holidays of the Lord which you shall proclaim as holy...apart from your Sabbaths'. It now emerges from the new Cave 4 fragment that, in the eyes of the sectarian exegetes, the ruling of the Pharisaic sages that the harvesting of the Omer overrides the Sabbath was an 'error of blindness' and was 'not in accordance with the Law of Moses'. The Mishnah in *Menaḥot*, quoted above, shows that in reaction to this polemic, the Pharisees emphasized their position by directing that the Omer be cut on the Sabbath eve with a maximum of public participation and fanfare. Viewed in conjunction with the Qumran fragment, the account in the Mishnah provides us with a rare opportunity to observe an ancient halakhic controversy from both sides of the barrier

---

1. The issue is discussed in full in S. Talmon, 'The Calendar Reckoning of the Covenanters of the Judean Desert', *ScrHier* 4 (Jerusalem: Magnes Press, 1958), pp. 162-99.

which divided mainstream Judaism from dissident groups in the Second Temple period.

One cannot ignore the fact that some scholars had expressed reservations regarding the historical reliability of the Mishnah in *Menaḥot*. Yitzhak Baer, for example, doubted the accuracy of that Mishnah, based on the premise that the foundations of mishnaic law and the rituals of the Temple were already established as universal Jewish traditions before the Hasmonaean age, when we first learn about the emergence of the Sadducees and the related group of the Boethusians. He therefore suspected that the reference to the Boethusians in *m. Men.* 10.3 was a later interpolation.[1]

By contrast, a school of scholarship in the United States claims that the Mishnah is altogether unacceptable as a source for the historical realities of the Temple period, and rather is to be considered a literary product of the post-destruction academies of Yabneh and Usha. Therefore, one should not accept as reliable any tannaitic tradition or the attribution of a tradition to earlier teachers, unless it can be supported by external evidence or through an internal form-critical analysis. It is of interest to note that Jacob Neusner, in a work which attempts to offer a new approach to the historical analysis of rabbinic literature, does not refer to *m. Men.* 10.3 at all.[2] This, despite the fact that this source claims to relate actions of the sages of the Second Temple period that were intended to neutralize the Boethusian resistance to the Pharisaic tradition about the Omer. Since then a series of Neusner's studies of the mishnaic order of *Qodashim*, including the tractate *Menaḥot*, has appeared.[3] However, the reader is offered only a translation and a division of the text into literary units, without any evaluation of its historicity.

Let us consider another example. One excerpt from the afore-

---

1. Y. Baer, 'The Historical Foundations of the Halakhah', *Zion* 27 (1962), pp. 117-55. In the latter part of his career, Baer, a leading historian of the mediaeval period, applied his vast erudition in classical as well as Jewish sources to a fresh appraisal of the Second Temple period. The early Hellenistic age was, in his opinion, the formative period in the history of the halakhah and Jewish civilization.

2. See J. Neusner, *Rabbinic Traditions About the Pharisees* (Leiden: Brill, 1971).

3. See J. Neusner, *A History of the Mishnaic Law of Holy Things* (Leiden: Brill, 1978–80).

mentioned *Miqsat Ma'asei Torah* was cited by coincidence by Milik;[1] it reads as follows:

> And also concerning the streams (*mwṣqwt*) of liquid we say that they are not pure, for the wetness of the streams and the receptacle which receives them is one.

The word *mwsq*, in mishnaic Hebrew *missoq*, designates the stream of a liquid which is poured from one vessel to another. The question is whether the stream constitutes a connecting link that would transfer impurity from the (impure) receptacle to the source. The teachers of the sect asserted, and we note the polemical tone of 'we say', that the stream is indeed a connecting link which contaminates the vessel from which it originates. It is remarkable that this is precisely the subject of a controversy between the Pharisees and the Sadducees which is recorded in *m. Yad.* 4.7:

> The Sadducees say, 'We protest against you, O Pharisees, for you declare the *missoq* clean'. The Pharisees say, 'We protest against you, O Sadducees, for you declare clean a channel of water that flows from a burial ground'.

It is amusing to ponder in retrospect the ingenious efforts of Abraham Geiger a century ago to find some symbolic political meaning in this dialogue about the *missoq*.[2] The simple interpretation offered by the classical commentaries to the Mishnah, that this was a technical term from the elaborate semantic field of the laws of purity, failed to satisfy the proclivities of some modern historians who would not believe that such trivial questions were worthy to be disputed by Jewish groups in the Hellenistic period. Wellhausen, who did not understand the Mishnah, referred to it as *eine solche Lappalie*.[3]

Neusner made an important contribution when he directed attention to the centrality of purity in the religious life of the ancient world. Yet in his volume on the tractate *Yadayim*, he translates the Mishnah and describes its literary form, but does not evaluate its significance as a historical source for the Second Temple period. Yitzhak Baer was doubtless aware of the rabbis' pejorative characterization of certain

---

1. J.T. Milik, 'Le rouleau de cuivre provenant de la grotte 3Q (3Q15)', *DJD*, III (Oxford: Clarendon Press, 1962), p. 225.

2. A. Geiger, *Urschrift und Übersetuzungen der Bibel* (Breslau, 1857), II, chapter 1.

3. J. Wellhausen, *Die Pharisäer und die Sadducäer* (repr. Hannover, 1924), p. 64.

priestly groups in that period 'for whom the purity of utensils was of greater concern than bloodshed' (*b. Yom.* 23a). Yet he had difficulty in comprehending the Sadducaean complaints about the Pharisaic leniencies in terms of purity. Referring to the Mishnah in *Yadayim* he wrote, 'These things may be interpreted as pertaining to the Christians, who nullified the laws of purity altogether. One suspects that perhaps in the transmitted texts they wrote *ṣeduqim* in place of *minim* (Christians).'[1] This suggestion is as incredible as his notion that the Qumran *Manual of Discipline* stemmed from Christian sources.

It should nevertheless be noted that now there are reasons for reexamining the identity of the *ṣeduqim* mentioned in the Mishnah. It seems odd that the Sadducees, whom we are accustomed to portray as self-indulgent aristocrats, in this text are presented as being more meticulous about religious matters, and more stringent than the Pharisees concerning purity. It therefore seems possible that the Qumranites are another sort of *ṣidwqym*. They call themselves *bny ṣdwq*, or alternatively *bny ṣdq,* in my view probably because they were followers of the *mwrh hṣdq,* whose name, as some presume, may also have been *ṣdwq.* These Zadokites were decidedly stringent in halakhah, especially with regard to purity, as we know both from their scrolls and from Josephus's reports on the Essenes. The possibility that in rabbinic sources the name *ṣeduqim* served as an epithet not only for the aristocratic Sadducees, but also for the adherents of the Qumran sect, is indeed worthy of serious consideration.

We may further illustrate the controversy about purity laws by citing the peculiar procedure which the Pharisaic sages mandated in the ritual of the red cow, as described in *m. Par.* 3.7:

> They used to defile the priest who burned the cow, because of the Sadducees, that they may not say that it must be done by those who had waited for sunset.

That is to say, the Pharisees deliberately made the priest ritually unclean and then directed him to bathe before burning the cow, in order to demonstrate that one who had bathed but had not waited for sundown (called *tebul yom*) was still considered pure for performing rituals outside the Temple. I had occasion to suggest in a paper which

---

1. Y. Baer, 'Some Aspects of Judaism as Presented in the Synoptic Gospels', *Zion* 31 (1966), p. 127.

appeared in 1980[1] that the emphasis in the *Temple Scroll* on the requirement of waiting for sunset to achieve purity was directed against the Pharisaic treatment of the ritual of the red cow. It has since been reported by Strugnell and Qimron that the requirement that all who participate in the red cow ritual wait for sundown after purification is stated explicitly in *Miqṣat Ma'asei Torah*.[2] Also in this instance, the form-critical school characterized the account in *m. Parah* as an anachronistic myth created by the rabbis in the second century.[3] It can now be established that, on the contrary, the Mishnah reflects most reliably the essence of the sectarian controversy in the time of the Second Temple.

II

I have so far offered three illustrations of specific halakhot about which, as the Mishnah informs us, there were disputes with the Sadducees or the Boethusians. This fact is now confirmed in sources from the Hasmonaean period. My final example touches on a question of wider import—the unwritten transmission of the law. In *b. Kid.* 66a there is the well-known story about the alienation of Alexander Jannaeus from the Pharisees. A baraita records the following dialogue between Jannaeus and Elazar b. Po'irah, who represents the Sadducees:

Jannaeus:	What should I do?
Elazar:	Listen to my advice and stamp them out.
Jannaeus:	And what will become of the Torah?
Elazar:	Behold, it is written and placed in a corner.
	Whoever wishes to learn let him come and learn.

R. Naḥman b. Yitzhak comments thereupon: '[This shows that] he [Jannaeus] was already affected by heresy, for he should have responded, This is good and well for the Written Law, but what of the Oral Law?'

It goes without saying that this rabbinic aggadah need not be taken as a record of the *ipsissima verba* of the figures involved. As Urbach

---

1. J. Baumgarten, 'The Pharisaic–Sadducean Controversies about Purity and the Qumran Texts', *JJS* 31 (1980), pp. 157-70.

2. Strugnell and Qimron, 'Halakhic Letter', p. 403.

3. J. Neusner, *History of the Mishnaic Law of Purities, Part 22* (Leiden: Brill, 1977), pp. 224-50; cf. *Parah . Part 10* (Leiden: Brill, 1976), p. 223.

has argued,[1] we should understand the words attributed to Elazar as an expression of the Sadducaean position that only laws which are 'written and deposited', that is recorded in some official codex, are considered authoritative, and not those orally transmitted by the sages. This, in effect, is how R. Naḥman b. Yitzhak understood the above discussion, namely, as a repudiation of the method of transmission of the Oral Law. Yet, there are scholars who would dismiss as irrelevant this opinion of a talmudic teacher of the fourth generation.

Fortunately, in this case a parallel to the talmudic account is offered by Josephus. In *Ant.* 13.296 we find essentially the same story, although the names and some details vary. We are told that, reacting to an insult, John Hyrcanus 'abandoned the Pharisaic party and nullified the ordinances which they had established for the people and punished those who observed them'. Josephus notes parenthetically:

> Now I wish to state that the Pharisees had passed on to the people certain ordinances handed down by the fathers and not written in the Laws of Moses, for which reason they are rejected by the sect of the Sadducees, who hold that only those ordinances should be considered valid which were written down, and those which had been handed down by the fathers need not be observed (*Ant.* 13. 297).

Some scholars have tried to blunt the edge of this statement by construing it to say merely that the Sadducees accepted only the authority of the Pentateuch, while the Pharisees also accepted that of tradition. However, the plain sense of the text points to a contrast in the form of the laws, between those which were written (*ta gegrammena*) and those which came from ancestral tradition and were not written (*ouk anagegraptai*). The latter were rejected by the Sadducees because, not having been 'written and deposited', they were only part of that orally transmitted tradition known as *paradosis ton presbyteron*.

It is significant in this connection to note how the *Temple Scroll* paraphrases a pivotal verse in Deuteronomy which serves as the basis for the authority of future teachers to interpret the laws of the Torah. The biblical text reads:

> And you shall do in accordance with the thing which they shall tell you from that place which the Lord will choose, and you shall take heed to do according to everything which they teach you (Deut. 17.10).

In the *Temple Scroll* 56.3-4 we read:

> And you shall do in accordance with the Torah which they shall tell you
> and in accordance with the thing which they shall say to you from the
> book of the Torah and tell you in truth.

Instead of 'in accordance with the thing', the scroll emphasizes 'in accordance with the Torah'; and in place of 'which they shall tell you', it explicates 'which they shall say to you from the book of the Torah and tell you in truth'. That is to say, only that which is told to you on the basis of the book of the Law is acceptable as truth. As Yadin has already observed: 'There is virtually no doubt that these changes were designed to prohibit the fixing of any law according to oral tradition, i.e. any law not written and interpreted in the Pentateuch'.[1] Of course, in the eyes of the Qumranites, the *Temple Scroll*, and *Jubilees* as well, were considered to be Torah.

III

What are the methodological lessons to be learned from the current developments in the study of Qumran law? I have adduced four examples of rabbinic traditions about early halakhah which some scholars viewed with scepticism, and which are now seen to be authentic and historically reliable. The common denominator of our examples is the fact that they deal with matters that were disputed between the Pharisees and their ideological opponents. A priori, one would suppose that it is especially in such matters that we would confront the often discussed problematics of using rabbinic texts as historical sources—namely, their selectivity, tendentiousness, and the lack of concern on the part of the sages for questions which interest the modern historian. I do not propose to deny the existence of these problems. There can be little doubt that the rabbis were not given to writing history, even though Urbach has shown that they did not lack a sense of historical change.[2] Their central concern was the study and the fulfilment of the laws of the Torah as far as possible, in accordance with the tradition received from earlier generations. In the

---

1. Y. Yadin, *The Temple Scroll* (3 vols.; Jerusalem: Israel Exploration Society, 1977 [Hebrew]; ET, 1983).
2. E. Urbach, 'Halakhah and History', *Jews, Greeks, and Christians. Essays in Honor of W.D. Davies* (Leiden: Brill, 1976), pp. 112-28.

sphere of halakhah, the rabbis were trustworthy preservers of tradition. Indeed, in the light of the sources now available, one cannot but be impressed with the Mishnah as a repository of reliable information about ancient halakhah. There is no longer any reason to doubt that the mishnaic orders of *Qodashim* and *Toharot* reflect to a great extent the Pharisaic halakhah of the Temple period.

In order to recognize the significance of these observations, we may consider, by contrast, the view of a legal historian:

> Rabbinic sources do not usually purport to describe Second Commonwealth conditions. The discussion of those areas of the law which most contemporary opinion takes to have ceased to operate with the destruction of the state—parts of the ritual law which depended upon the existence of the temple, and parts of the criminal law—may be academic... All too often in the past any common denominators found in either Philo or Josephus or Qumran and some rabbinic source, often anonymously transmitted, have been taken to represent 'early halakhah'... Such argumentation only begins to approach credibility if it is assumed either that there was a single Second Commonwealth tradition of halakhah, or that the particular Second Commonwealth source stems from the same tradition as the forerunners of the rabbis. Neither assumption is justified.[1]

The purpose of this essay is not to establish that there was only one Second Commonwealth tradition of halakhah, but rather that the conflicting traditions show an awareness of each other's existence. That is to say, we can be sure that, in the areas of religious law which came under review, the normative halakhah of the Mishnah was essentially the same as that of the Pharisees which the Qumran teachers criticized. This means that the present perspective is markedly different from that of Abraham Geiger, who theorized that the early halakhah was displaced by the later halakhah of the Talmud. What emerges now, I believe, is the existence in the time of the Temple of a pattern of diverse halakhic traditions, including that of the Pharisees which ultimately became normative in talmudic law, and alongside it the heterodox exegesis displayed in the scrolls which occasionally survives in certain Targumim and peripheral rabbinic sources.[2]

Thus far we have been preoccupied with examples of halakhah. I

---

1. B.S. Jackson, *Essays in Jewish and Comparative Legal History* (Leiden: Brill, 1975), p. 5.

2. Cf. J. Baumgarten, 'Qumran and the Halakhah in the Aramaic Targumim', in *Proceedings of the Ninth World Congress of Jewish Studies* (Jerusalem: Magnes, 1987).

should like to conclude with an illustration which belongs to the sphere of theology. We are accustomed to associate the concept of the community as a 'temple' with Christian thought, as exemplified in Ephesians 2. However, in the *pesher* on 2 Samuel 7, commonly called 4Q Florilegium, the deuteronomic prohibition of certain illegitimate classes from entering the community is interpreted as an exclusion from the temple. The temple is there referred to as *mqdš 'dm*. I have argued[1] that this expression should be understood as a reference to a temple consisting of men, rather than a temple among men, as some Israeli scholars would have it. It is true that the *Temple Scroll* contains rules about the exclusion of converts from certain precincts of the Jerusalem sanctuary. Yet I believe we now have additional proof that an idea existed at Qumran of another sanctuary, not limited to the Temple precincts but rather consisting of holy men. In the Cave 4 texts entitled *Songs of a Sage* (4Q511 fr. 35), whose primary purpose was the exorcism of evil spirits, we find the following passage:

> Among the seven-fold purified, God will sanctify unto himself a sanctuary of eternity and purity among those who are cleansed, and they shall be priests, his righteous people, his host, and ministering (with) the angels of his glory.[2]

One may detect here both an echo of the biblical concept of a kingdom of priests (Exod. 19.6), and a precursor of the idea of the community as temple, demonstrating once again the remarkable continuity of religious concepts beyond the boundaries of time and confessional adherence.

IV

What bearing does all this have on the consideration of the sources for the academic teaching of Jewish civilization in the Hellenistic–Roman period? Clearly what we have indicated would require us to include tannaitic literature among these sources. In saying this, I am hardly proposing anything very revolutionary. It merely confirms the sound judgment of Emil Schürer who included a sampling of mishnaic halakhah in his *Geschichte des jüdischen Volkes im Zeitalter Jesu Christi*.[3] Schürer's limitations in handling halakhic texts, and his own

---

1. *Studies in Qumran Law*, pp. 82-83.
2. *DJD*, VII (ed. M. Baillet; Oxford: Clarendon Press, 1982), p. 237.
3. *Geschichte des jüdischen Volkes im Zeitalter Jesu Christi* (Leipzig: J.C.

rather skewed theological evaluation of such material, need not concern us here. Suffice it to say that he realized that *das Leben unter dem Gesetz*, as he called it, was an important aspect of the history of the Hellenistic–Roman 'inter-testamental' period, and that there was no source other than rabbinic literature from which to learn anything systematic about it. In contemporary scholarship, a growing number of non-Jewish historians have come to the same realization, though there is still a certain understandable diversity in their appreciation of this literature—reflecting, to a degree, differing areas of interest. The existence of specialists in the apocryphal and pseudepigraphical writings, alongside scholars who feel more at home in the dialectics of Jewish law, need not cause any difficulties as long as both parties realize that such specialization was not characteristic of the ancient world. The visionaries of Qumran were as much concerned with the minutiae of the laws of purity as they were with eschatology. A somewhat similar statement pertains to the later devotees of Jewish mysticism and their orientation toward the halakhah.

A more serious obstacle to the proper utilization of rabbinic halakhah for Second Temple history lies in the assumption that texts edited in a later period are of little value for illuminating phenomena of an earlier age. The burden of our examples has been to show that this is not necessarily the case. The same point was made by Ephraim Urbach in the introduction to his work on the halakhah:

> When one speaks of a literature which had for a long period been transmitted orally, the time in which the source was edited or composed cannot serve as an absolute proof for the time of the subjects included in it. It is possible that a work edited in a later period may contain authentic ancient material, while a work edited earlier may contain primarily material from that approximate time.[1]

Of course, this does not mean that we should not make every effort to determine the provenance of particular norms and ideas. But we should bear in mind that in religious history one rarely finds phenomena which totally lack precedents.

Hinrichs, 1898), II, pp. 464-95.

1. Urbach, *The Halakhah*, p. 4.

DEVIATIONS FROM SCRIPTURE IN THE PURITY LAWS
OF THE *TEMPLE SCROLL*

Jacob Milgrom

The deviations from Scripture in the postulates of Qumran's purity laws, rather than their biblical correspondences, hold the key to the Covenanters' distinctive ideology. The deviations were so numerous as to necessitate a sixth revealed book of the Torah, the *Temple Scroll* (11QT). This paper will focus on one purificatory requirement in 11QT in which Qumran specificity comes to light: the ritual ablution. It deviates from Scripture in four ways:

1. Corpse-contaminated persons must launder and bathe on the first day of their (week-long) purificatory period (49.16-17; 50.10-14; cf. 1QM 14.2-3). Those with seminal emissions must also launder and bathe on the first day of their (three-day) purificatory period before they may be admitted into the Temple-city (45.7-8). In neither case are such rites required by Scripture. Why?

2. The fundamental purity postulate of 11QT, as demonstrated by Yadin,[1] is that the Temple-city is equivalent in holiness to the Israelites' encampment on the eve of the Sinai theophany. At Sinai, Israel purified itself through laundering and ablutions for two days, and God revealed himself on the third day (Exod. 19.10-15). However, 11QT prescribes not two but three full days of purification (cf. 1QSa 1.25-26), with laundering and ablutions (for seminal emission) on the first and third day (45.7-10), before entry into the Temple-city is permitted. Why?

3. 11QT requires laundering whenever there are ablutions, even

1. Y. Yadin, *The Temple Scroll* (3 vols.; Jerusalem: Israel Exploration Society, 1977–83), I, pp. 287-89.

when it is not prescribed in Scripture. Here, to be sure, 11QT could take ablutions for granted, basing itself on the biblical practice. For example, in Leviticus 11 which deals with the impurity of carcasses, the clauses *yitma' 'ad-ha'areb* 'he will be impure till the evening' (24, 27, 31, 39) and *yekabbes begadayw* 'he shall launder his clothes' (11.25, 28, 40) clearly imply ablutions (cf. *Sifra* Shemini par. 4.7). But 11QT goes one step further: it requires laundering in addition to ablutions wherever Scripture prescribes (or assumes) only ablutions. For example, those who touch carcasses have to launder as well as bathe (51.1-2), though there is no warrant for this requirement in Scripture. Why?

4.   Moreover, 11QT mandates both laundering and ablutions on the third day of purification from corpse-contamination (49.18-19; 50.14), while there is no biblical basis for either prescription. Why?

In explanation of the first deviation, it should first be noted that biblical law requires one other severe impurity carrier, the leper, to launder and bathe on the first day of his week-long purificatory period; the ablution entitles him to re-enter the camp (Lev. 14.8). On the basis of the leper's example, I have previously proposed a tentative solution to this question.[1] Each ablution removes another layer (or degree) of impurity. The purpose of the first-day ablution of the corpse-contaminated person is to allow him to remain in his city without incurring banishment or quarantine. It is possible that 11QT ordained this same first-day procedure for other bearers of severe impurity. The beginning of the gonorrhaeic's purificatory process is described in Scripture as follows: *weki-yithar hazzab mizzobo*. Rendered literally this reads: 'when the gonorrhaeic becomes pure of his discharge' (Lev. 15.13). It seems obvious that in this text, *yithar* actually means '(when the gonorrhaeic) is healed'. However, the author of 11QT may well have reasoned: since the verb *tahar*, throughout the P source, refers to purification and never to healing,[2] *yithar* in this verse, and *tahara* in v. 28 must mean 'he/she purifies him/herself', that is, the gonorrhaeic bathes and launders before

---

1.   Cf. Milgrom, 'Studies in the Temple Scroll', *JBL* 97 (1978), pp. 512-18.

2.   Ostensibly, *taharato*, 'his healing' (Lev. 13.35; 14.2) is an exception. However, this word is a noun, not a verb.

commencing the purificatory period, namely, on the first day.[1] Further support for this interpretation could be adduced from the case of the parturient. Her purificatory period, called *yeme tohora* (Lev. 12.4, 6), expressly pertains to the thirty-three or sixty-six days which follow an initial impurity of one or two weeks terminated by ablutions.[2] Thus 11QT could have deduced from the case of the parturient that the purificatory period for all bearers of impurity must commence with ablutions.

The second deviation concerns the anomalous three-day purification for seminal emission, which calls for ablutions on the first and third day prior to entry into the Temple-city. Since this requirement is based on Israel's purification procedures at Sinai, it is imperative to examine the biblical text to see if there is any basis for 11QT's interpretation. First, one is struck by the unusual wording of the command given by Moses to the people: *heyu nekonim lišelošet yamim* (Exod. 19.15), which literally translates 'Be ready for three days'. (It should have been read *layyom haššeliši* 'for the third day', as in v. 11). This meaning is, paradoxically, buttressed by the view of Rabbi Jose that, since God commanded Moses, 'sanctify [i.e. purify] them today and tomorrow', Moses could not possibly have begun doing so that self-same day. He needed two complete days and, hence, the first ablution took place on the following day (*ARN* A2; *b. Shab.* 87a; *Yeb.* 62a; cf. *PRE* 41). Thus R. Jose agrees with 11QT that Israel spent three days preparing for the Revelation, and differs with it only in the timing of the two ablutions, holding that they occurred on the second

---

1. My interpretation has recently been confirmed by 4QOrd[c] in *DJD*, VII (ed. M. Baillet; Oxford: Clarendon Press, 1982), pp. 295-98, which (as noted by J. Baumgarten in *JSS* 31 [1980], p. 160) prescribes that a man suffering from a discharge (i.e. the *zab*) should bathe and launder on the first day of his seven-day purificatory period, so that he may eat pure food. The Karaites come to the same conclusion on the analogy of the parturient; cf. Keter Torah on Lev. 15.13 and the next note. Yadin argues similarly on the basis of Ezek. 44.26, pertaining to the purification of the corpse-contaminated priest (*Temple Scroll*, I, p. 333).

2. The ablution requirement for the parturient, or for the menstruant for that matter, is not explicit in Scripture (Lev. 15.19). However, since all statements regarding the duration of impurity automatically imply that it must terminate with ablutions, the statement that the severe impurity period of the parturient lasts seven or fourteen days, and seven days for the menstruant, must take ablutions for granted. Besides, if a minor one-day impurity such as seminal discharge requires ablutions (Lev. 15.16), all the more so the major genital discharges.

and third day, whereas 11QT opts for the first and third. The position taken in the scroll is easily defensible. The Bible expressly prescribes ablutions for seminal emissions on the first day (Lev. 15.16-18). Hence, 11QT engaged in an analogic comparison, or what I prefer to call the 'homogenization' (see below) of two different biblical texts and prescribes that entry into the Temple-city requires three days of purification consisting of two ablutions, just as Israel did at Mt Sinai— except that the first ablution occurs on the first day.

Moreover, it is my impression that 11QT was not just indulging in exegesis. More likely, it was following an ancient tradition. Philo informs us that after sex '(the husband and wife) are not allowed to leave the bed, to touch anything until they have had their ablution' (*Leg. All.* 3.63, 205). His view, that before the ablution they contaminate objects and persons, may fly in the face of rabbinic halakhah, but makes perfect sense in view of the impurity-removing function of the ablution. The impure male who wishes to enter the Temple-city must make two transitions—from impure (*ṭame'*) to common (*ḥol*), and from common to holy (*qadoš*). Or, to put it differently, he must eliminate two degrees of impurity—progressing to the common and to the sacred. Thus two ablutions are required, and precisely at the two points of transition: on the first day, when he washes off his initial impurity and is free to associate with the common, and on the third day, when he washes off his residual impurity and is qualified to be in the presence of the holy.[1] The graded effect of the ablutions can be represented diagrammatically as follows:

Purification for Seminal Emission

Stage	Effect upon the common	Effect upon the sacred
Pre-ablution	direct	airborne
First-day ablution	none	direct
Third-day ablution and sunset	none	none

11QT, in agreement with Philo, would maintain that prior to his initial ablution the impure male contaminates persons and objects by

---

1.   11QT assumes that the sunset proviso is part of the same purification unit as the previous ablution, and thereby it negates the rabbinic status of the *tebul yom*, as demonstrated by Yadin, *Temple Scroll*, I, p. 332.

direct contact, but that after having bathed he may contact them freely. A further postulate of the Priestly impurity system in Scripture is that the sacred is more vulnerable to contamination by one degree.[1] Thus, before the first ablution, the impurity is powerful enough to contaminate the sanctuary from afar.[2] Hence, he must leave the Temple-city and is not free to enter the sanctuary or partake of sacred food until he has bathed a second time. To be sure, the Priestly source, in conformance with its goal to demythologize impurity, has reduced this three-stage purification by eliminating one ablution.[3] Nonetheless, 11QT and Philo (in part) preserve the older view.

The third deviation is twofold in nature: laundering and bathing are mandated for the carcass-contaminated person, whereas only bathing is prescribed by Scripture; and both laundering and bathing are mandated for the corpse-contaminated person on the third day, whereas neither is prescribed by Scripture. This deviation is resolved by 11QT's innovative exegetical principle: the homogenization of Scripture.

Yadin has already pointed to what he calls 'harmonization' as one of the main organizing features of the Scroll. However, most of the examples he cites should really be described as a unification process: the fusion of the various laws pertaining to a single subject into one law—vows, 53.9–54.5 (Num. 30.3-16); judicial decisions, 51.11-18 (Exod. 23.6; Deut. 1.16-17; 16.18-19); mourning rites, 48.7-10 (Lev. 19.28; Deut. 14.1-2);[4] and contamination of foodstuffs and vessels, 49.7-10 (Lev. 11.33-34; Num. 19.15).[5] These unified blocks combine

---

1. Cf. J. Milgrom, 'The Priestly Impurity System', in *Proceedings of the Ninth World Congress of Jewish Studies, August 1985* (Jerusalem: Magnes Press, 1986), pp. 121-27.

2. Cf. J. Milgrom, 'Israel's Sanctuary: The Priestly "Picture of Dorian Gray"', *RB* 83 (1976), pp. 390-99.

3. Cf. J. Milgrom, 'The Graduated Purification Offering', *JAOS* 103 (1983), pp. 249-54, and 'The Paradox of the Red Cow (Num xix)', *VT* 31 (1981), pp. 62-72.

4. The prohibition against self-mutilation had already been enjoined upon priest and Israelite alike in the Priestly writings of the Torah (Lev. 19.28; 21.5) and, hence, cannot be the innovation of 11QT (*contra* Yadin, *Temple Scroll*, I, p. 324).

5. See his comments in *Temple Scroll*, I, pp. 74-77. For other examples, see items 1, 4, 7, 11-14, 19-21, 33, 35, 36, 38, 39, 47, 71 in the section 'The Themes of the Scroll', in Yadin, *Temple Scroll*, I, pp. 45-70.

laws that are either identical or supplementary, and they generally do not contradict each other. However, there are a few combinations, three according to my count, where the individual laws do conflict, necessitating true harmonization. These are: covering the blood, 52.11-12 (Lev. 17.13; Deut. 12.23-24); war spoils, 58.13-14 (Num. 31.27-28; 1 Sam. 30.24-25; cf. I, 360-62); and the 'ravaged virgin', 66.8-11 (Exod. 22.15-16; Deut. 22.28-29; cf. I, 368-71).

There is yet another exegetical principle, not dealt with by Yadin, that goes beyond harmonization; it may be called 'homogenization'. By this I mean that a law which applies to specific objects, animals, or persons is extended to other members of the same species. I shall cite one example of each: (1) Objects: everything within the house where death has occurred is impure (49.13-16, versus *m. Kel.* 10.1; *Sifre* Num. 126); (2) Animals: the prohibition of Lev. 22.28 falls on the sire as well as the dam of the slaughtered animal (52.6, versus the majority view in *Ḥul.* 78b); and (3) Persons: blemishes which disqualify priests from officiating in the Temple (Lev. 21.17-23) disqualify all Israelites from entering the Temple-city (45.12-14).

The *Temple Scroll*'s ruling on ablutions also falls into this homogenizing category. It requires laundering in addition to ablutions wherever Scripture only prescribes (or assumes) ablutions. For example, one who touches a carcass has to launder as well as bathe (51.1-2), though there is no warrant for it in Scripture. Of course, Scripture has to provide some warrant for this exegetical manoeuvre; and it does. The non-specific phrase *yitma 'ad-ha'areb,* 'he will be impure until evening', lends itself to the maximal ruling that laundering as well as bathing is required. The homogenization is more telling in the matter of corpse-contamination. The Scroll mandates both laundering and ablutions on the third day of purification from corpse-contamination (49.18-19; 50.14) but, again, without any explicit biblical basis.

The underlying exegetical process, I submit, is as follows: since the seventh day of purification from corpse-contamination explicitly prescribes aspersion, laundering and bathing (Num. 19.19), the Scroll deduces that the aspersion expressly required on the third day (Num. 19.12, 19) must also include laundering and bathing. The homogenization occurring here is further enhanced by the other innovation, that laundering and bathing are also required for the first day. After all, how could they be omitted for the third day on which aspersion is mandated, but prescribed for the first day when there is no aspersion?

Indeed, this major purificatory innovation is in itself a product of homogenizing exegesis. The case of the leper was the model. Scripture requires the leper to launder and bathe on the first day of his week-long purificatory period (Lev. 14.8). The ablution entitles him to reenter the camp. Similarly, by requiring the corpse-contaminated person to launder and bathe on the first day of his week-long purification, he need not be banished from his community (see Num. 5.2-4). The first-day ablution, I submit, is also required of the parturient, gonorrhaeic, and of all other major impurity-bearers even though there is no explicit statement to this effect in the Temple Scroll—again by the principle of homogenization.

The power of this hermeneutic can be gauged by the fact that it has no clear biblical foundation and that it also violates the Priestly system of impurities.[1]

The homogenizing tendency of 11QT can also help resolve an exegetical crux in a new Qumran document (4Q 394–399). According to E. Qimron and J. Strugnell,[2] among the many halakhic innovations in this text is the requirement that the leper must wait until sunset on the eighth day of his purificatory period before he may partake of sacred food. However, Scripture prescribes only sacrifices for this eighth day (Lev. 14.10-20, 23-31). How then, and why, did 11QT come up with its ruling? First, it should be noted that the rabbis also mandate additional purificatory measures for the eighth day: 'He whose atonement is yet incomplete (on the eighth day before bringing the sacrifices) needs to immerse himself (after the sacrifices) for sacred things' (*m. Ḥag.* 3.3). Thus, the rabbis added a proviso to the Torah that this last vestige of impurity preventing contact with the sacred cannot be lifted by sacrifices alone, but only by a subsequent ablution.

I am convinced that Qumran also prescribes this eighth day of ablution, since Scripture demands or assumes that sunsets be preceded by ablutions. However, Qumran goes beyond the rabbis in prescribing

---

1.   The three ablutions prescribed by 11QT for corpse-contamination cannot possibly be harmonized with the Priestly system requiring one ablution, unless the former has presumed that the person in contact with the corpse or under the same roof with it also contaminates by overhang (see the chart in Milgrom, 'The Priestly Impurity System').

2.   'An Unpublished Halakhic Letter from Qumran', in *Biblical Archaeology Today* (ed. J. Amitai; Jerusalem: Israel Exploration Society, 1985), pp. 400-407.

that the purification is not completed by the ablution, but by the subsequent evening. I submit that Qumran achieves this ruling by exegetical homogenization. In Scripture all minor impurities terminate in the evening following the ablution (Lev. 11.24, 25, 27, 28, 31, 32, 39, 40; 14.46; 15.5-8, 10, 11, 16, 19, 21-23, 27; 17.15; 22.26; Num. 19.7-8, 10, 21, 22). Major impurities, i.e., severe genital discharges (Lev. 12; 15), leprosy (Lev. 13–14), the corpse-contaminated Nazirite (Num. 6.9-12) and priest (according to Ezek. 44.26-27), terminate with sacrifices. Qumran appears to have reasoned as follows: if contact with sancta, the goal of the final stage of the purificatory process, requires prior ablutions and sunset for minor impurities, all the more so should ablutions and sunset be required as the final stage for major impurities.[1] Qumran might also have found scriptural support for this homogenizing exegesis in the wording of the purificatory rite for priests: a major impurity bearer 'shall not eat the sacred food until he is pure', '*ad 'ašer yithar* (Lev. 22.4), and a minor impurity bearer 'shall not eat the sacred gifts unless he has washed his body in water. As soon as the sun sets he shall be pure (*wetaher*) and afterwards he may eat of the sacred gifts' (Lev. 22.6-7). The indeterminate *yithar* for major impurities—so Qumran may have argued—is explicated by the *wetaher* specified for minor impurities, i.e. ablutions and sunset.[2]

Concerning the vexing question of whether 11QT is truly Qumranic, the impurity rules affirm that it is. The graded impurity, as reflected in the ablution scheme, conforms with the explicit gradations set out in 1QS 6.16-21.[3] That there was to be no sex in the Temple-city is echoed in CD 12.1-2, and that women and physically

---

1.   Strikingly, some tannaitic sources also opt for sunset as well as ablutions for the eighth day (e.g. *t. Šeq.* 3.3, 20; *b. Zeb.* 99a [bar]). These sources are collected and discussed in the Tosafot to *b. Ḥag.* 21a. Thus, despite the prevailing view that sacred food was permitted after the sacrifices for the eighth day, there were voices among the rabbis that insisted on a subsequent ablution, and others who even added the requirement of a subsequent sunset. Qumran clearly sided with the latter.

2.   As noted by J. Strugnell ('Halakhic Letter', p. 404) the commentator Yom Tov Lipman Heller reasons on *m. Par.* 3.7 as follows: '"As soon as the sun sets he shall be pure" (Lev. 22.7)' implies that the Sadducees would have required the termination of all impurity by sunset. This would be a remarkable anticipation of Qumranic exegesis, as now revealed in 4Q 394–399.

3.   Cf. J. Licht, *The Rule Scroll* (Jerusalem: Bialik, 1965), pp. 294-303 [Hebrew].

impaired men were excluded from it is duplicated in the prescriptions concerning the holy war camp (1QM 7.3-5). The more severe impurity of liquids (11QT 49.11-14) is confirmed by CD 12.15-18 and 1QS 6.16-21 (cf. Josephus, *War* 2.137-38). And the three-day purification for entrance into the Temple-city is also required for admission to the sacred assembly, 1QSa 1.25-26. Thus, the rules of the *Temple Scroll* are compatible with Qumran law and undergird it. Judging solely by its impurity rules, it is an organic part of the Qumran literature.

Potentially of even greater significance is the *Sitz im Leben* of the homogenization hermeneutic. The need for harmonization is self-understood; a society that lives by Scripture cannot tolerate conflicting rules. However, the extension of specific rules to others of the same species is not a scriptural necessity. There are no inconsistencies to iron out. What, then, is the *raison d'être* for this principle?

It seems to me that the legal precipitates of homogenization stem from earlier traditions. Qumran did not invent its laws of the three-day purification, the ablutions on the first day, the exclusion of women and impaired men, the impurity of everything in the house of the dead, the sunset requirement for the eighth day, etc. It is more likely that the Covenanters derived these laws from other sources, and subsequently anchored them in Scripture, through the technique of homogenization. If this is so, the homogenization changed exegesis into eisegesis and text into pretext.

I should like to suggest that the homogenized laws, being products of history—unlike the harmonized laws, the products of speculation—can be subjected to fruitful historical investigation.

QUMRAN IN RELATION TO THE APOCRYPHA, RABBINIC JUDAISM, AND NASCENT CHRISTIANITY: IMPACTS ON UNIVERSITY TEACHING OF JEWISH CIVILIZATION IN THE HELLENISTIC–ROMAN PERIOD

James H. Charlesworth

The discovery of the Qumran scrolls is one of the most significant of the sensational discoveries made in the Near East over the last forty years, and probably the most spectacular recovery of ancient manuscripts in the history of biblical research. These documents, popularly called the 'Dead Sea scrolls', rouse so much interest that a normal audience triples in size with the mere inclusion of that name in the title of a lecture. Students in the United States may be attracted to courses with 'Bible' or 'Jesus' in the title; but add the words 'Dead Sea scrolls' and the registration frequently quadruples.

The impact of the Qumran scrolls on university curricula has not been so dramatic. Very few colleges and universities offer courses on the Dead Sea scrolls. Very few of the universities which offer distinguished doctoral degrees in biblical or Jewish studies include regular course offerings on Qumran Hebrew, Qumran history, or Qumran theology.[1] Only a small number of undergraduate schools and seminaries offer a general course dealing with the Qumran scrolls.

Why is there such diversity between popular interest in the Qumran scrolls and curricular offerings? I know of no convincing answer to this question, but several can be suggested:

1. Such courses are almost always listed under 'religion', a subject which is frequently controlled by authorities in the Jewish community or in the Christian church. Each wants

---

1.   To the best of my knowledge, only Claremont, Duke, Princeton, New York University and Harvard; Göttingen and Tübingen; and the Hebrew University of Jerusalem offer specific courses on Qumran.

courses to teach what has long been recognized as important and essential for faithful adherence to cherished traditions. Each has been persuaded that the Qumran scrolls do not meet these needs.

2. Control of the unpublished Qumran material has been monopolized for four decades by a small group of scholars who, being specialists, can display evidence that may disprove potential doctoral theses. The fear of being judged uninformed, or even being exposed as the proponent of an impossible solution to a recognized problem, warns the student to shy away from forbidden areas. A PhD is a research degree; when data for research are denied to all but a very select group of students, it will obviously be considered wise to work in some other area. The PhD dissertation is also a 'rite of passage'; a flawed piece of research blocks appointments and careers.

There is another dimension to the problem of teaching the Qumran scrolls which needs exposing. A first-rate introduction to the scrolls is still lacking. The 'classic' introductions were published in the 1950s. Among these, the best were surely the authoritative books by F.M. Cross, and J.T. Milik. Cross's *The Ancient Library of Qumran and Modern Biblical Studies* appeared in 1958 and was revised in 1961.[1] John Strugnell's English translation of Milik's French book[2] appeared in 1959[3] and has long been out of print. Even more unfortunately, some of the sensational documents mentioned in these books have not yet been published. It is certainly not easy to teach a course without being able to suggest reliable books for the student to read. Teachers are left with the introduction and translation of selected Qumran texts, by G. Vermes.[4] Such books may suffice for beginning undergraduate

---

1. Cross's book was reprinted by Baker Book House in 1980 and is now out of print.

2. J.T. Milik, *Dix ans de découvertes dans le Désert de Juda* (Paris: Cerf, 1957).

3. J. Strugnell, *Ten Years of Discovery in the Wilderness of Judaea* (London: SCM Press, 1959).

4. G. Vermes, *The Dead Sea Scrolls: Qumran in Perspective* (London: SCM Press, 1982), and *The Dead Sea Scrolls in English* (London: Pelican, 1962); also *Discovery in the Judean Desert. The Dead Sea Scrolls and their Meaning* (New

classes; but they are not designed for advanced students.

Within a decade we shall fortunately have more of the as yet unpublished materials with which to work. John Strugnell is making available most of the data through lectures, articles, the work of reliable students,[1] and as the editor of the DJD series. He and Elisha Qimron have published an announcement about a letter designated 4QMMT which they claim dates from circa 150 BCE, and may have been sent by the Righteous Teacher to his opponent, the high priest in Jerusalem.[2] Cross also promises to publish, in the near future, the documents under his control; and Milik continues to work on his material, especially the fragments related to the *Testaments of the Twelve Patriarchs*.

The Princeton Dead Sea Scroll Project will republish through Princeton University Press all the documents already published. Over 170 documents will be published in three volumes. Volume I will contain the photographs, some new or unpublished. Volume II will have on the left page the Hebrew, Aramaic, or Greek, produced with the Ibycus Computer, and on the facing page a reliable but rather literal translation into English. Volume III will contain a concordance to the Hebrew, Aramaic, Greek and English. Subsequent volumes will include documents published after the commencement of the project. An international team of contributors has been assembled under my editorship.

The purpose of this paper is to review rapidly three phases in the modern study of Judaism prior to the destruction of Jerusalem in 70 CE, and to stress the present needs for incorporating the Qumran phenomena into the teaching of ancient Jewish culture.

Phase I

Phase I began with the scientific research in the wake of the European Enlightenment and closed with the discovery of the first of the Qumran scrolls. We may discern five characteristics of this phase:

1. The major source for the study of Jewish religious life prior to

York/Paris: Declée, 1956).

1. Noteworthy is Carol Newsom's published thesis, *Songs of the Sabbath Sacrifice: A Critical Edition* (Missoula, MT: Scholars Press, 1985).

2. 'An Unpublished Halakhic Letter from Qumran', in *Biblical Archaeology Today* (ed. J. Amitai; Jerusalem: Israel Exploration Society, 1985), pp. 400-407.

70 CE was the Mishnah. This collection of Jewish writings was acclaimed as the definitive, unedited evidence of Second Temple religious thought. This conception permeates H. Danby's authoritative Introduction to *The Mishnah* (1933)[1] which presents much valuable information. But the author does not sufficiently stress that the Mishnah is a post-70 CE selected and edited deposit of oral tradition. His opening statement will illustrate the point:

> The Mishnah may be defined as a deposit of four centuries of Jewish religious and cultural activity in Palestine, beginning at some uncertain date (possibly during the earlier half of the second century BC) and ending with the close of the second century AD (p. xiii).

Danby surely knew that the 'deposit' was shaped by post-70 social and religious phenomena, but he did not adequately grasp the extent to which the Mishnah was, at least in part, a second-century CE compilation.

Other scholars wrote as if the Mishnah were an unedited 'deposit' of reliable historical information from pre-70 Palestinian religious life and thought. This assessment seems valid for most scholars working before 1950. It is also true that a large group of Christian authors pursued their studies and published the results in ignorance of the Mishnah, despite the sound advice of experts like E. Schürer and H. Danby. For many New Testament scholars, the paradigmatic source of Early Judaism (which they called 'Intertestamental Judaism'—an unfortunate term still widely used for pre-70 Judaism), was the New Testament, although they did bring the Apocrypha to bear on the issue.

2. Josephus was celebrated as the reliable historian of 'Intertestamental Judaism'. The veneration of Josephus is evident both by the repeated appearance of W. Whiston's translation of Josephus in private libraries, and by the subtitle of that work, *The Life and Works of Flavius Josephus: The Learned and Authentic Jewish Historian and Celebrated Warrior*. Generations of students have read Josephus's account as if he supplied us with an 'authentic' description of early Palestinian Judaism.

3. Many experts assumed that Philo of Alexandria represented faithfully the thought of Egyptian Jews. They pointed out that the so-called

---

1. *The Mishnah. Translated from the Hebrew with Introduction and Brief Explanatory Notes* (London: Oxford University Press, 1933).

'Hellenistic' Judaism was actually distinctly different from Palestinian Judaism. Many specialists even assumed that there were two Bible canons. Hellenistic Jews had an expanded canon which is represented by the Septuagint. Palestinian Jews read only the twenty-four books of the Hebrew Bible whose text was identical, even in Samuel and Jeremiah, with the received Hebrew text (MT).

4. Palestinian Judaism was perceived as being cut off from the rest of the world; it was geographically, culturally and religiously isolated. Virtually no Greek influence had 'contaminated' the Jewish religion. Many experts misunderstood *m. Ab.* 1.1 which states, 'the men of the Great Synagogue' said that one should 'make a fence around the Law'.

5. Finally, it was also assumed that Christianity did not develop in Palestine. Under the influence of Paul, it was shaped by Greek norms and ideas. It was rightly held that Judaism had not been influenced by the oriental mystery religions. Despite the brilliant work by R.H. Charles, E. Kautzsch and others, Christianity was judged by numerous experts to have been shaped by the mystery religions, whose influence was especially noticeable in the origin and development of the two major sacraments, namely, the Eucharist and Baptism. Judaism and Christianity, it was claimed or assumed, had different origins.

Today scholars concur that the most prominent religious thought in pre-70 Palestinian Judaism was apocalyptic and eschatological. A distinguished specialist of apocalypticism before the Second World War and even before the First World War was R.H. Charles, the editor of the first English edition of the Old Testament Pseudepigrapha. He was a Victorian, however, who often emended the apocalypses and even developed a subjective hypothesis regarding the redactional nature of the Apocalypse of John.

Charles did not appreciate the lack of logic which is often evident in the Jewish and Christian apocalypses; he did not grasp that the essence of apocalypticism required redundancies and inconsistencies. The distinguished scholar T.W. Manson offered the following evaluation of Charles's appreciation of apocalyptic thought:

> Yet there was a sense in which the language of Apocalyptic remained a foreign language to him. He could never be completely at home in the world of the Apocalyptists. And this made it impossible for him to achieve

that perfect understanding which demands sympathy as well as knowledge.[1]

Charles, like all of us, was shaped by the tenor of his times. Victorian Christians looked forward to the triumph of the Kingdom of God in the present ever-improving world. There was no need for apocalyptic eschatology; God's own kingdom was slowly becoming manifest in European and American societies. In this intellectual atmosphere a full recognition and appreciation of pre-70 Jewish apocalypticism was practically impossible.

Having said that much, I would wish to add that Charles, unlike many of his contemporaries, had a high regard for the apocalyptist. He contended that some of the authors of the *Apocalypse of Enoch* 'belonged to the true succession of the prophets...' The 'general trend' of the *Books of Enoch*, he judged, was 'onward and upward'.[2] When he describes the transhistorical eschatological thrust of *1 Enoch* 91–104, he does not use disparaging words, as might be expected of a man of his time. He describes the abandonment of hope for the present earth and the projection of Utopia to another world and age as one of 'endless development in every direction' (p. cviii).

Of course, Charles is devoted to disclosing the roots of Christianity. Adjacent to the above quotation he says: '...the way was thus made possible for the rise of Christianity'. In perceiving the *Jewish* origins of Christianity, generally speaking, he differed from many of his contemporaries.

To sum up: in phase one, Jewish and Christian scholars were largely ignorant of Jewish and Christian origins. Now, however, the vast increase in documentary and archaeological evidence allows us to perceive the complex, variegated, and cosmopolitan nature of Palestinian Judaism.

Phase II

With the discovery and publication of the Qumran scrolls in the late forties, early fifties, and mid-sixties, a major shift occurred. The prevalent picture of pre-70 Judaism was examined and found

1. *The Dictionary of National Biography 1931–1940* (ed. L.G. Wickham; Oxford, 1949), p. 170.

2. *The Book of Enoch or 1 Enoch* (Oxford: Clarendon Press, 1912), p. x.

misrepresentative. The Qumran Scrolls—which included not only the unique writings of the Qumran group but also, *inter alia*, some of the previously maligned Old Testament Pseudepigrapha—displayed aspects of Palestinian Judaism that had not been perceived earlier.

Scholars turned again to the presumably historical sections of the Old Testament Apocrypha, especially 1 Maccabees, and read the history of the second and first centuries BCE in a different light. In the classroom many teachers had their students read 1 Maccabees 14, pointing to the apparent acknowledgment that Simon Maccabaeus and his sons were not legitimate high priests, and to the prohibition for priests to nullify or oppose any of Simon's decisions or to gather in groups (1 Macc. 14.41, 44). Any infraction of these laws resulted in severe punishment (1 Macc. 14.45). Numerous teachers rightly explained that this historical break with past customs and traditions aptly described why at least one group of priests was forced to leave the Temple and the official cult and flee into the wilderness. The Qumran scrolls often describe in a similar way the origins of the Covenanters' community, especially in the *Rule of the Community*, the *Hodayot*, the *Damascus Document*, and the *Habakkuk Pesher*. They were a priestly group that once had been powerful in the Temple cult, but became disenfranchised.

Five major shifts began to be discerned in scholarly publications.

1. It was at first slowly, and then more widely, acknowledged that Palestinian Judaism had not been monolithic. No one theology reigned as normative throughout Palestine. The Old Testament Pseudepigrapha were not insignificant writings of scattered groups on the fringes of an orthodoxy centred in Jerusalem. The rabbinic writings were imperfectly transmitted records of pre-70 Palestinian religious life.

2. Palestinian Judaism was not representatively divided into four sects, as Josephus reports. Scholars began to study anew the dates when the Pharisees, Sadducees, Essenes—probably the three major groups—and especially the Zealots originated. Gradually they tended to affirm that the Zealots did not consolidate as a religious 'sect' until the first great revolt against Rome in 66 CE, although scattered groups of revolutionaries and extremists existed before that time. Early Palestinian Judaism was characterized by more than a dozen groups and subgroups. Perhaps the term 'sect', which had been refined in

sociology, was not a term that adequately represented the character of Early Judaism and its many divisions.

The historical writings of Josephus were now read in an appreciably different light. On the one hand he misrepresents Palestinian Judaism by describing it in terms of four sects. On the other hand he seems to portray with accuracy the origin of the Zealots at the beginning of the first great revolt. Unfortunately in universities, colleges, seminaries—both Christian and Jewish—churches and synagogues, the old unexamined clichés continue to exert their influence. Even today, many research students come to graduate school with the unexamined false presupposition that pre-70 Palestinian Judaism was 'normative' and at the same time composed of four 'sects'.

3. The best scholars, especially W.D. Davies, D. Flusser and S. Talmon, began to emphasize that pre-70 Judaism must not be bifurcated into Hellenistic Judaism and Palestinian Judaism. The beginning of Mishnah *Abot* is not to be read uncritically; there was no 'wall' built around Judaism. As many scholars have attempted to demonstrate, especially Martin Hengel of Tübingen, Greek influences penetrated deep into almost every sector of early Judaism. But one must also pay attention to indigenous forces that shaped Judaism. Historically, this is the Hellenistic age. Hence, the term 'early Judaism' is synonymous, to a degree, with Hellenistic Judaism, in distinction to earlier exilic and post-exilic Judaism, and to later rabbinic Judaism.

Rapid means of communication, the defeat of Mediterranean pirates, the flow of commercial goods from east to west, from north to south, and indeed in all directions, created what is recognized by classical scholars like F.W. Walbank as the first world culture, or the 'Hellenistic world'. He rightly states that to a certain extent we can talk about 'the unity and homogeneity of Hellenistic culture'.[1] The origins of this unification can be traced to Alexander the Great, and even to the developments that anteceded him, as we know from the pre-Alexandrian Samaritan Papyri, which were sealed with impressions that depict scenes from the Greek classics.

Another aspect of the Hellenistic world has not been adequately recognized. Despite rapid advances in the transmission of data information, indigenous centripetal forces were effective in the Hellenistic

---

1. F.W. Walbank, *Hellenistic World* (Cambridge, MA: Harvard University Press, 1981), p. 65.

period. In ancient Iran, Zoroastrianism and Zurvanism remained strong centralizing forces in Persian and Parthian cultures.

Most especially in Palestine an indigenous culture continued to be a unifying force. We know this aspect of early Judaism thanks to traditions preserved in the Pseudepigrapha (especially *Jubilees*), the Qumran scrolls, the Mishnah, and predominantly from the descriptions of the Maccabaean rebellion in the Apocrypha and from Josephus's report on the origins of the first revolt. Virtually all our literary sources point to the normative influence and centralizing power of the writings canonized as sacred Scripture by both Jews and Christians. Unfortunately most of these insights are shared by scholars in closed meetings. They are seldom found in popular textbooks, or in the curricula of Christian seminaries or rabbinic academies.

4. Jerusalem was not cut off, nor was it geographically isolated in an inaccessible mountainous region. The walls of this vibrant centre, which was more than a religious symbol, did not dissuade foreigners from entering. Quite the contrary, the city attracted Persians, Greeks, Egyptians, Syrians, Parthians and Romans. Especially after Pompey's integration of Jerusalem into the Roman Empire in 63 BCE and Herod's massive constructions beginning around 20 BCE, Jerusalem increasingly moved to the centre-stage of world attention.

Progress in the classroom comes slowly. It is an unfortunate fact that R. Bultmann's *Primitive Christianity in its Contemporary Setting* had, and may still have, a wide reading. Bultmann was a great scholar who developed the methodological approach to New Testament literature which is pivotal to modern scholarship. But he incorrectly claimed that pre-70 Palestinian Judaism, which he called 'Israel', had 'cut herself off from the outside world and lived in extraordinary isolation'.[1]

5. The posited 'vast difference' between Judaism and Christianity is no longer stressed. Prior to the discovery of the Qumran scrolls, Christianity was often studied in terms of non-Jewish phenomena, including the Hellenistic mystery religions. The origin of the Gospel of John, for example, was sought in Greek philosophical systems. The words, 'In the beginning was the word', which open that Gospel, were characteristically examined in terms of Stoicism, Heraclitus, and

---

1. R. Bultmann, *Primitive Christianity in its Contemporary Setting* (New York: World Publishing Co., 1956), p. 60.

Plato. With the discovery of the Qumran scrolls, the Gospel of John was seen in a new light. Many of the so-called Johannine symbols, terms, phrases, perspectives and exhortations were found to be deeply embedded in the theology of pre-70 Palestinian Judaism. What was once hailed as the Gospel of the Greeks is now widely recognized to be one of the most Jewish of the Gospels.

Judaism and Christianity are no longer portrayed in antithetical terms. To be sure, one reason for the misrepresentation of Christian origins was the latent anti-Semitism, actually anti-Judaism, running through Western society, especially in the decades before 1947 when the first Qumran scrolls were discovered. Another reason for the change is the recognition of the great breadth, depth and creativity of early Judaism. Among other factors, it was the Qumran scrolls that convinced scholars of the vast complexities of early Jewish thought.

It has become increasingly difficult to decide in many an instance whether an expression, a thought, and even a document, is of Jewish or Christian origin. *Joseph and Aseneth*, and the *Prayer of Manasseh*, for example, are no longer considered 'Christian' because of their elevated thoughts or piety. They are clearly Jewish works. Today it is not easy to discern if some documents are originally Jewish or Christian. The best example, of course, is the *Testaments of the Twelve Patriarchs*.

Sadly only a portion of this revolutionary advance in research is shaping our curricula. Many Christian theologians continue to focus on the uniqueness of Christianity, emphasize the post-150 CE Greek and Roman influence on early Christian thought, and stress in dogmatic terms the divinity of Jesus. Likewise, some Jewish theologians tend to present modern Judaism as if it were virtually identical with pre-70 Palestinian Judaism, and consider Christianity not in terms of what it was prior to 135 CE but as it has evolved after almost 2,000 years.

The key question then becomes to what extent the historical study of origins can correct both distortions. From my own experiences, I see the welcome dawning of a new consciousness which, hopefully, will not lead to a minimizing of significant differences. The best publications in the field show an awareness of the fact that we must acknowledge the existence of a plurality of Judaisms, not one, and that both nascent Christianity and rabbinic Judaism developed at the same time and in the same place, out of a complex early Jewish culture. In different ways, both inherited much from early Judaism (250 BCE–200 CE) and from the antecedent forms of Israel's religion, notably post-exilic Judaism, exilic Judaism, and the biblical religion of the First Commonwealth. As Alan F. Segal shows, rabbinic Judaism and early Christianity shared the same mother—early Judaism.[1]

The second phase in the study of Jewish and Christian origins, in terms of the academic teaching of Jewish civilization, reveals a lack of integration of the new discoveries and insights into the curriculum. We see a continuation of the old way of teaching. While some courses add a new section, and occasionally new courses are introduced, these are but minor additions to old ways and approaches. Fortunately, advances are more noticeable in the scholarly periodicals and monographs.

Phase III

No clear chronological break separates phase two from phase three, which began about a decade ago in some of the most advanced institutions of higher learning. Curricula were revised and tended to incorporate the new perspectives. This incorporation is precisely what is now required; all relevant courses must be reshaped by the new understanding of early Judaism which is shared by the leading Jewish and Christian scholars.

In the Jewish centres of learning, the New Testament documents should be studied in terms of what they can teach us about the emergence of rabbinic Judaism; they also should be examined historically with a view to their pneumatic interpretation of Torah. The Palestinian Jesus Movement shared such biblical exegesis with many other Jewish groups, especially the Qumran Covenanters who developed the *pesher* method of exegesis and hermeneutics. Jews and Christians should struggle with this question: how can the New Testament writings be studied within the history of Judaism?

Christian scholars must advance beyond viewing pre-70 Judaism as mere background material that must be pursued before beginning what is considered to be the really essential task, namely reading and attempting to understand the message contained in the documents of

---

1.   A.F. Segal, *Rebecca's Children* (Cambridge, MA: Harvard University Press, 1986).

the New Testament. Scholars must acknowledge that what had been categorized as *background* is now clearly part of the *foreground*. This means that early Judaism is not a mere presupposition for the study of the theologies in the New Testament; it is part of these theologies. Such key terms as Son of Man, Messiah, Son of God, living water, eschaton and apocalypse are as much part of the essence of early Jewish theology as of early Christian theology. The movement of thought from metaphor, through personification, to hypostatization, advanced far in early Judaism and left an indelible impression on early Christian thought, especially with the concepts of Word, Wisdom and Voice.

I am encouraged by the observation that this enlightened view is finding its way into books that are now used in the classroom. C.J. Roetzel stresses that the Hellenistic–Roman world 'was far more than background, it was also the homeground and foreground of the early church'.[1] M.J. Borg rightly rejects the tendency to treat the background of early Christianity as mere '"backdrop", a setting which at best might illuminate some references made by the actors who appear on the stage of the New Testament'. Borg wisely states that the 'background has become foreground, though the change has not produced a simple reduction to social causation...'.[2]

Teachers need to be apprised of these developments. Courses must be rethought and restructured in light of the new insights. The entire curriculum needs to be revamped. There is no alternative. Misrepresentations of origins cannot be tolerated; they should be replaced by the challenges arising out of new discoveries and a new understanding. The excitement of unparalleled breakthrough in perception will attract the best students.

We must also acknowledge another aspect of what we have learned. A startling new source of information, the Qumran scrolls, showed us how ignorant we were of Jewish and Christian origins. We must be ever circumspect regarding the little we really do know of pre-70 Jewish life and thought. We must humbly acknowledge how lucky we

---

1. C.J. Roetzel, *The World That Shaped the New Testament* (Knoxville, TN: John Knox Press, 1985), p. vii.
2. M.J. Borg, *Conflict, Holiness and Politics in the Teachings of Jesus* (New York / Toronto: Edwin Mellen Press, 1984), p. 18.

have been during our own lifetimes to be handed such precious literary and archaeological reminders of our origins.

Conclusion

Jewish and Christian scholars must admit the difficulties that confound honest dialogue with each other and the search for a better understanding of Jewish and Christian origins. We clearly have commitments to our own traditions. For each of us, as for our home universities or other institutions of higher learning, the reward of our labour inheres in an evaluation of how our work furthers scholarship, but also in how it helps our own religious communities. The question of canon and authority may always relegate the study of Qumran phenomena into the status of second-class citizenship in our curriculum.

We scholars together must seek ways to move beyond the isolation that tends to characterize the study of the Apocrypha, Pseudepigrapha and Qumran scrolls. The new insights and paradigms for understanding pre-70 Palestinian Jewish phenomena must affect the teaching of every course on Judaism and Christianity, at least in some respect. Courses in anthropology, sociology and the economics of the Hellenistic world will be significantly enriched by the Qumran realia and data still undigested and to a certain extent unpublished.[1]

Qumran represents more than a collection of precious ancient scrolls. It reveals a community, with realia unearthed, rules translated, dreams perceived and lives lived out in the common struggle for meaning in a hostile world. Entering into the Qumran community, sauntering among the ruins, reflecting in the caves, and pensively attending to the Qumran world of thought, changes our perceptions, and then our conclusions and methods. The windows of the classroom need to be thrown open to the fresh breezes.

---

1.   The publication of Elisha Qimron's *The Hebrew of the Dead Sea Scrolls* (Missoula, MT: Scholars Press, 1986), and Claus Beyer's *Die aramäischen Texte vom Toten Meer* (Göttingen: Vandenhoeck & Ruprecht, 1984) certainly assist those of us who teach doctoral seminars in Qumran philology.

THE QUMRAN FRAGMENTS OF *1 ENOCH* AND OTHER APOCRYPHAL WORKS: IMPLICATIONS FOR THE UNDERSTANDING OF EARLY JUDAISM AND CHRISTIAN ORIGINS

George W.E. Nickelsburg

The manuscript collections from the Qumran caves contain, in addition to copies of biblical texts and of sectarian documents hitherto unknown to us, Aramaic and Hebrew fragments of non-canonical texts that were previously known only in translations once or twice removed from their Semitic originals. The main texts in question include parts of the *Books of Enoch*, the *Book of Jubilees*, material related to the *Testaments of the Twelve Patriarchs*, and the Book of Tobit.[1] In lieu of a better term I shall refer to these as apocryphal writings. Several significant issues have arisen as a result of the discovery of these fragments, with consequences for the interpretations of early Judaism and of the beginnings of Christianity in its Jewish matrix.

The Texts

The Qumran Enoch Fragments

Chief among these texts are writings that represent a literary corpus ascribed to the ancient patriarch Enoch who, it is alleged, ascended to heaven and travelled to the outer reaches of the cosmos, where the secrets of God, the demonic world, and the universe were revealed to him.[2]

---

1. In addition, one fragment each of Sirach and the Epistle of Jeremiah have been identified (*DJD*, III [Oxford: Clarendon Press, 1962], pp. 75-77, 143).

2. See J.T. Milik, *The Books of Enoch: Aramaic Fragments of Qumran Cave 4* (Oxford: Clarendon Press, 1976). For a bibliographic summary, see G.W.E.

1. *Fragments from the early strata of* 1 Enoch—*the reconstruction of early apocalypticism.* Although the Qumran MSS of the *Books of Enoch* are to be dated to the last two centuries BCE,[1] critical analysis of their contents indicates that the earliest strata of the corpus derive from the late Persian and early Hellenistic periods, that is from about 400–165 BCE.[2] This early dating for the *Book of the Heavenly Luminaries* (chs. 72–82) and the *Book of the Watchers* (chs. 1–36), reveals these works to be substantially older than the final redaction of the Book of Daniel and, therefore, of considerable consequence for the reconstruction of the history of early Jewish apocalypticism.

Several decades ago, it was customary to refer to the Book of Daniel as the earliest apocalypse, and to cite it and the New Testament Book of Revelation as model apocalypses.[3] With Daniel taken to be the earliest exemplar, scholars emphasized the historical concerns of the apocalypticists. Central was the receiving and interpreting of visions and dreams that predicted the future and, especially, the broad sweep of history under God's control.

Close inspection of what we now know to be the earliest Enochic writings indicates that early Jewish apocalypticism was a broader and more variegated phenomenon that creatively combined aspects of both prophetic and sapiential streams of Israelite thought and drew freely, though selectively, on material of non-Israelite provenance.

Enoch's commissioning in the heavenly courtroom resembles the call of Ezekiel (cf. *1 Enoch* 14–16 with Ezek. 1–2), although in this case the seer is taken to heaven.[4] The introduction to the corpus

---

Nickelsworth, 'The Books of Enoch in Recent Discussion', *Religious Studies Review* 7 (1981), pp. 210-17.

1. Milik, *Books of Enoch*, pp. 5-6.

2. For chs. 72–82, see Milik, *Books of Enoch*, pp. 7-8; for chs. 1–36, see G.W.E. Nickelsburg, 'Apocalyptic and Myth in 1 Enoch 6–11', *JBL* 96 (1977), pp. 389-91.

3. See, e.g., H.H. Rowley, *The Relevance of Apocalyptic* (London: Lutterworth Press, 2nd edn, 1972); and D.S. Russell, *The Method and Message of Jewish Apocalyptic* (Philadelphia: Westminster Press, 1964). For a critical analysis of the discussion, see J.J. Collins, 'Apocalyptic Literature', in *Early Judaism and its Modern Interpreters* (ed. R.A. Kraft and G.W.E. Nickelsburg; Philadelphia/Atlanta: Fortress Press/Scholars Press, 1986), pp. 345-70.

4. G.W.E. Nickelsburg, 'Enoch, Levi, and Peter: Recipients of Revelation in Upper Galilee', *JBL* 100 (1981), pp. 576-82.

(chs. 1–5) is written in the style of a late prophetic oracle. The *Woes and Exhortations* of the last chapters are reminiscent of biblical prophecy.[1] But woven into this material are idioms and literary forms at home in Jewish wisdom literature, and 'wisdom' is a term not infrequently used to describe the content of this section (92.1; 93.8, 10; 94.5; 104.12; 105.1; see also 5.8).

Consonant with this is a concern with the heights and depths and hidden recesses of the created world.[2] Although the seer speaks of future events, the certainty of the advent of these events is often documented by reference to the outer reaches of the cosmos, where the places and apparatus of eschatological reward and punishment exist as part of God's creation.[3] Human inconstancy is contrasted with the predictable cycles of nature (see especially chs. 1–5 and 101).[4] Thus, in a way that is reminiscent of the emphases and concerns of wisdom literature, the apocalypticist appeals not to the events of history, but to the realities of creation.

The peculiar nature of this appeal differs, however, from much traditional wisdom speculation. In contrast to Job 28, which denies that humanity has access to wisdom and to the created marvels of the celestial and cosmic realms, Enoch claims to have visited the storehouses of the winds and the sources of the Deep, and to have counted the stars (see especially 93.11-14). Two things go hand-in-hand. These texts are marked by a dualism between the known, inhabited world and the hidden cosmos, and between experienced history and the hidden future. In tension with this is the seer's claim that what is hidden has been revealed to him. Wisdom is *revealed* wisdom. This element of revelation leads one to consider *1 Enoch* in the context of the Book of Daniel. The comparison underscores the breadth of the

---

1. G.W.E. Nickelsburg, 'The Apocalyptic Message of 1 Enoch 92–105', *CBQ* 39 (1977), pp. 309-28.

2. M.E. Stone, 'Lists of Revealed Things in the Apocalyptic Literature', in *Magnalia Dei: The Mighty Acts Of God. Essays on the Bible and Archaeology in Memory of G. Ernest Wright* (ed. F.M. Cross, W.E. Lemke and P.D. Miller; New York: Doubleday, 1976), pp. 414-52.

3. See especially chs. 17–19; 21–36, discussed briefly in G.W.E. Nickelsburg, *Jewish Literature between the Bible and the Mishnah* (Philadelphia: Fortress Press, 1981), pp. 54-55.

4. E. Rau, *Kosmologie, Eschatologie und die Lehrautorität Henochs* (Dissertation, Hamburg, 1974), pp. 31-124.

early Enochic material and its interest in the many aspects of the creation that are the guarantors of divine order and that promise the inevitable enactment of divine justice. Of these matters the later Book of Daniel scarcely offers a hint.

Another feature of the Enochic writings is their pervading concern with the demonic origins of evil. Creatively drawing on the resources of ancient Near Eastern and Greek myth, the authors transform biblical traditions in order to explain the nature, presence and ultimate eradication of evil.[1] Although God is not responsible for evil, humanity is in a substantial way its victim. Evil results from a realm of malevolent spirits who have rebelled against God and bred evil into the world. As was often the case in classical Israelite religious thought, the idiom and imagery of this speculation are drawn from non-Israelite sources.

The historical settings of the Enochic writings antedate the foundation of the Qumran community by up to two-and-a-half centuries. The texts, which emanate from unnamed circles that in some cases could be called 'sectarian', were composed by sages or seers, who made prophet-like claims in language that was often akin to what we have tended to associate with 'wisdom' literature. These texts clearly derive from a complex and transitional period in Israelite religious and cultural history, a period whose form was scarcely imagined by pre-Qumranic scholars.[2]

2. *The absence of the Parables*. Among the puzzles presented by the Qumran manuscript discoveries is the complete absence of the section of *1 Enoch* known as the *Parables* or *Similitudes* (chs. 37–71). Although every other major section of the corpus is represented among the Cave 4 fragments, it appears that none of the MSS included the section that especially interests New Testament scholars because of the dominating presence therein of a heavenly saviour figure known variously as 'the Chosen One', 'the Righteous One', and 'the son of man'.

---

1.   See P.D. Hanson, 'Rebellion in Heaven, Azazel, and Euhemeristic Heroes in 1 Enoch 6–11', *JBL* 96 (1977), pp. 195-233; and Nickelsburg, 'Apocalyptic and Myth', pp. 395-404.

2.   For a comparison of *1 Enoch* and the Qumran texts and their possible relationships, see G.W.E. Nickelsburg, '1 Enoch and Qumran Origins: The State of the Question and Some Prospects for Answers', in *SBL 1986 Seminar Papers* (Number 25; ed. K.H. Richards; Atlanta, GA: Scholars Press, 1986), pp. 341-60.

The absence of the *Parables* in the Qumran Enochic writings has led their editor, J.T. Milik, to conclude that this section is very late—indeed, that it was written in the Byzantine period—and that it is a Christian composition based on the New Testament.[1] Although this particular formulation of the hypothesis has not found wide acceptance, many scholars agree that the absence of the *Parables* from the Qumran finds indicates that the section is indeed late and, specifically, that it is too late to have any bearing on the interpretation of the New Testament.[2]

The argument from silence has serious shortcomings. The earlier strata of *1 Enoch* are pre-Qumranic, and there is no a priori reason to suppose that the Enoch tradition was transmitted only through Qumran. The *Parables*, which are a unique reshaping of the Enochic tradition, could have been composed and transmitted in circles that had a common ancestor with Qumran.[3] In those circles, God's eschatological judgment was believed to have been delegated to a transcendental figure that filled the descriptions of the Davidic messiah, Second Isaiah's exalted Servant, and Daniel's 'one like a son of man'.[4]

The Gospels make frequent reference to 'the son of man', and with a few minor exceptions, the son of man is identified as Jesus. Analysis of the material indicates that these Christian references to the son of man cannot be explained simply on the basis of Daniel 7. Indeed, it is possible to detect elements in the Gospels that are best explained as reflections of the same blend of traditions to be found in the Enochic *Parables*.[5] Notwithstanding the silence of Qumran, the *Parables* remain a body of Jewish evidence that helps us to understand early

1. Milik, *Books of Enoch*, pp. 89-98.
2. On this and related matters, see D.W. Suter, 'Weighed in the Balance: The Similitudes of Enoch in Recent Discussion', *Religious Studies Review* 7 (1981), pp. 217-21.
3. Nickelsburg, *Jewish Literature*, pp. 214-33.
4. G.W.E. Nickelsburg, 'Salvation without and with a Messiah: Developing Beliefs in Writings Ascribed to Enoch', in *Judaisms and their Messiahs at the Turn of the Christian Era* (ed. J. Neusner, W.S. Green and E. Frerichs; Cambridge: Cambridge University Press, 1987), pp. 49-63.
5. The evidence and argument to support my contention that the Gospels know and use a Jewish tradition very close to if not identical with the Parables is laid out in my article 'Son of Man', in *The Anchor Bible Dictionary* (ed. D.N. Freedman; Garden City: Doubleday, forthcoming).

Christian speculation about Jesus of Nazareth, the risen and exalted Christ.

Thus, the evidence from Qumran underscores the point that has already been made. Around the turn of the era, as in the Hellenistic period, Jewish religious thought is characterized by a remarkable diversity. The traditions of early Enochic apocalypticism mingle with an element from later Danielic tradition, and as these elements blend they are transformed. The Danielic son of man is construed not as the heavenly patron of Israel's dominion after the judgment, but as the agent of that judgment. Whereas the early Enochic authors expected that God would function as judge, the author(s) of the *Parables* await a divinely appointed and anointed agent of judgment. However, the 'anointed one' of biblical tradition is envisioned not as a scion of David, but as a glorious heavenly saviour figure, who is identified as Isaiah's Servant and Daniel's cloud-borne 'son of man'.

This strain of transcendental messianism, in turn, informs important aspects of the Gospels' claims about Jesus and is one of the formative elements in primitive Christian belief. At the same time, it must be emphasized that many Jews, the Qumranites evidently among them, did not subscribe to this particular form of messianism. For these people, Christian claims about the messianic status of the risen and exalted Jesus would hardly be acceptable. Indeed, we can go a step further; for the author of the *Parables*, the heavenly Chosen One never had an earthly existence. It was only by a complex twist of the tradition that the crucified Jesus was identified as the exalted son of man.[1] Thus, many Jews who subscribed to the *Parables'* messianism may not have accepted the claim that Jesus was that messiah.

The Book of Jubilees

Like the Enoch material, the *Book of Jubilees* is known in its entirety only in an Ethiopic rendition of a Greek translation of a Semitic original—in this case a Hebrew original. Hebrew fragments of perhaps a dozen MSS found at Qumran attest to the remarkable accuracy of the secondary rendition.[2]

The Ethiopic version indicates that *Jubilees* is a running paraphrase

1. Nickelsburg, 'Son of Man'.
2. J.C. VanderKam, *Textual and Historical Studies in the Book of Jubilees* (HSM, 14; Missoula, MT: Scholars Press, 1977), pp. 1-205.

of Genesis and the first part of Exodus, with many alterations, additions and deletions.[1] The most obvious and remarkable characteristic of the book is its calendrical framework. The events in Genesis and Exodus are placed within a chronology that presumes and uses a 364-day solar calendar, and the author polemicizes against the use of other calendars, which are defined as 'gentile' (6.35).

Related to this calendrical framework are the copious references to the Enochic literature. At appropriate places in the Genesis story, the author expands his source in the Torah by citing or quoting traditions that we know from *1 Enoch* (*Jub.* 4.17-26). Enoch is identified as the one who revealed the structures of the universe that attest the created basis of the solar calendar (*Jub.* 4.17, an allusion to *1 Enoch* 72–82 or its sources). The story of the sons of God and the daughters of men is elaborated in a form closely allied to *1 Enoch* 6–11 (*Jub.* 5), and the origins of the demonic world, presumed throughout the work, are traced to a variant of the Enochic story (*Jub.* 7.21-28; 10.1-12).

In addition to the Enochic material, *Jubilees* contains a plethora of earlier traditions about other patriarchs, notably Abraham and Levi.[2] Whatever the status and authority of Genesis may have been for the composers of these traditions, it is clear that the Genesis material was already the subject of a lively, imaginative and elaborative tradition in the third century BCE. Haggadic narrative had made its appearance.

Haggadah was complemented by halakhah, and the patriarchal stories are frequently interpolated with references to the heroes keeping laws written on heavenly tablets. These laws include not only the Enochic calendaric Torah, but many other laws as well.[3] The extent to which the Torah of *Jubilees* agrees with, differs from, or polemicizes against the specific legal interpretations of the Qumranites and the Pharisees is still a matter of discussion.[4] However this question is finally resolved, it is important to note the author's claim—paralleled

---

1. G.W.E. Nickelsburg, 'The Bible Rewritten and Expanded', in *Jewish Writings of the Second Temple Period* (CRINT 2.2; ed. M.E. Stone; Assen/Philadelphia: Van Gorcum/Fortress Press, 1984), pp. 97-104.

2. Nickelsburg, 'Bible Rewritten', pp. 98-99.

3. Nickelsburg, 'Bible Rewritten', pp. 97-98.

4. C. Albeck, *Das Buch der Jubiläen und die Halacha* (Berlin: Schocken, 1930); L.H. Schiffman, *The Halakha at Qumran* (SJLA, 16; Leiden: Brill, 1975), pp. 10-11; S. Safrai, 'Halakha', in *The Literature of the Sages* (CRINT, 3.3, part 1; ed. S. Safrai; Assen/Philadelphia: Van Gorcum/Fortress Press, 1987), pp. 140-43.

in parts of *1 Enoch*—that the law here promulgated is revealed and necessary for salvation.[1]

The *Book of Jubilees* presents many historical puzzles that remain to be sorted out. Its solar calendar and citations of parts of *1 Enoch* indicate important historical connections with that work and with some of the communities in which it originated and was transmitted. The calendar and the book's presence at Qumran and its citation in the *Damascus Document* point to another connection.[2] *Jubilees* presents an additional testimony to the complex Judaism that is ancestral to Qumran. The peculiar calendar leads some to call the work sectarian, yet the text is remarkable for its lack of sectarian vocabulary. The significant division of which *Jubilees* speaks is not between different groups of Israelites, but between Israel and the nations.[3]

The Testamentary Literature

The *Testaments of the Twelve Patriarchs* are, in their present form, a Greek composition of Christian provenance. Whether there ever existed a Jewish collection of twelve such testaments is a hotly debated question that can probably not be resolved on the basis of the presently available evidence.[4] Here, too, the Qumran texts tease us with evidence that raises new questions.

Among the fragments of Caves 1 and 4 are some Levi materials related to the Greek *Testament of Levi* and *Testament of Naphtali*. The nature of the relationship must await full publication of the texts.[5] However, a few details are clear. One published Aramaic fragment of a Levi text attests a version of the material which is considerably

---

1. G.W.E. Nickelsburg 'The Epistle of Enoch and the Qumran Literature', *JSS* 33 (1982), pp. 334-43.

2. VanderKam, *Studies*, pp. 268-83.

3. See R.H. Charles, *The Book of Jubilees or the Little Genesis* (Oxford: Clarendon Press, 1902), pp. lv-lvi.

4. For a critical analysis of the discussion, see J.J. Collins, 'The Testamentary Literature in Recent Scholarship', in *Early Judaism*, pp. 268-76; for the most recent major discussion, see M. de Jonge, 'The Testaments of the Twelve Patriarchs: Central Problems and Essential Viewpoints', in *Aufstieg und Niedergang der römischen Welt*, Part 2, Vol. 20.1 (ed. W. Haase; Berlin: de Gruyter, 1987), pp. 359-420.

5. For a discussion of the Semitic testamentary material and its implications, see M. de Jonge, 'Testaments', pp. 370-84.

longer than its counterpart in the Greek *Testament of Levi* (although, curiously, its contents were known to the scribe of one Greek MS, who interpolated the section into his text).[1] This indicates that at least in part the *Testaments* in their present form are a reduction of fuller Jewish traditions.

The discovery in Cave 4 of testaments ascribed to Qahat and Amram, the son and grandson of Levi, was totally unexpected.[2] In counterposition to testaments of the twelve sons of Jacob were a series of three testaments that traced the priestly line. To complicate matters further, Levi's account of his being appointed as priestly patriarch (*T. Levi* 2–5) is located at the same place as Enoch's ascent to heaven in *1 Enoch* (12–16); a close comparison of the two accounts indicates that they describe the events in a similar manner.[3] This suggests a historical connection between the circles that produced the Levi material and those that generated the Enoch material. That both texts have been found in the Qumran collections supports this assumption and suggests, in turn, that these circles were ancestral to the Qumran community.

The Book of Tobit

Cave 4 has yielded fragments of four Aramaic MSS and one Hebrew MS of the Book of Tobit.[4] The find helps to clarify the textual history of the book. The longer text form, represented by the Codex Sinaiticus and the Old Latin version, is clearly original, and not the shorter form that was customarily used as the base for English translations.[5]

The number of copies of the text is noteworthy. The only writing of the Hebrew Bible not found at Qumran is Esther.[6] However, Cave 4 contained five copies of another literary work that treats in an overtly

---

1. On this fragment, see de Jonge, 'Testaments', pp. 370-71.
2. For these texts, see J.T. Milik, '4Q Visions de 'Amram et une citation d'Origène', *RB* 79 (1972), pp. 77-97.
3. Nickelsburg, 'Enoch, Levi, and Peter', pp. 588-90.
4. J.T. Milik, 'La Patria de Tobie', *RB* 73 (1966), p. 522.
5. Students should be referred for the text to the Jerusalem Bible, the New American Bible, the New English Bible and, when it is published, the revised form of the Revised Standard Version.
6. F.M. Cross, *The Ancient Library of Qumran and Biblical Studies* (rev. edn, Garden City: Doubleday, 1961), p. 40.

religious way some of the central problems of Jewish life in the eastern Diaspora, namely Tobit. This book was not accepted into the Hebrew canon, but the evidence of Greek biblical MSS indicates that it was highly revered in Alexandria. Apart from a fragment of the letter of Jeremiah and a few fragments of Sirach, it is the only text from the more comprehensive Greek collection that is represented at Qumran. While we must be cautious in our conclusions about the biblical canon at Qumran, the number of MSS indicates substantial interest in Tobit.

It is not possible to discuss here in detail the content of Tobit, although it is relevant to our topic. I have suggested relationships between *Enoch, Jubilees* and the Levi material on the one hand, and the religious thought and historical matrices of the Qumran community on the other hand. Such relationships are far from clear in Tobit, but a number of interesting parallels between that work and parts of *1 Enoch* may not be irrelevant to the presence of the Book of Tobit at Qumran.[1]

Finally, the existence of the Hebrew text of Tobit raises an interesting question: why, in a time and place that attest the development of Aramaic targums of biblical books, do we find a Hebrew translation of a work originally composed in Aramaic?

General Implications for the Teaching of Jewish Civilization

Judaism in the Hellenistic–Roman Period

This brief discussion of individual apocryphal texts found at Qumran suggests some broad historical considerations of significance for teachers of Jewish civilization. First, the discovery of these scrolls has affected our understanding of Judaism in the Hellenistic and early Roman period.

1. *The historical setting*. It is important to alert students to the fact that these writings were composed after most of the Hebrew Bible had been written, but before some of it came to be considered authoritative. For Jews and Christians, and also for many informed Westerners

---

1. G.W.E. Nickelsburg, 'Tobit and 1 Enoch: Distant Cousins with a Recognizable Resemblance', in *SBL 1988 Seminar Papers* (Number 27; ed. D.J. Lull; Atlanta: Scholars Press, 1988), pp. 54-68.

who do not identify existentially with either tradition, the canonical collection fixed near the beginning of the Common Era is accepted as given; one thinks of it as the Bible and not simply as a historical legacy from the past. This complicates the act of historical imagination that allows one to stand in a past time when that canon was not yet fixed.

This act of imagination is crucial, however. These texts reveal a period of considerable literary fertility, when authors are composing writings that do not yet have the status of being excluded from a fixed collection. Tobit, *Enoch*, and *Jubilees* are not yet judged by some authoritative body to be of less worth than Ecclesiastes or Esther. While some books already written will eventually become part of the canon, they do not yet enjoy canonical status, and new religious texts continue to be written. Indeed, it is likely that in some circles the Enochic literature, at the very least, has an authority not yet ascribed to some works that will later be included in the Hebrew canon.[1] For some, this quality—suggested by the Enochic authors' prophetic idiom—may blend indistinguishably into the authority of the books that will be formally defined as the latter prophets.

2. *Mindset and purpose.* I labour this point for several reasons. First, it is important that students tune in to the mindset of these authors and try to understand their purposes in writing their work. A proper historical assessment of these texts requires that one should block out the later canonical categories and attempt to appreciate these authors on their own terms and with respect to their own self-understanding. To the extent that one does this, one begins to appreciate the immense diversity of belief and religious expression in this period.

Secondly, emphatic analysis of the texts helps one to see the great diversity of these authors' attitudes toward literature that later came to be considered canonical and biblical. The authors of this period were not treating the works of the Hebrew Bible in the same way that the rabbis would. The Qumran *pesharim* show that in the late Hellenistic

---

1. For a recent discussion of the Jewish canon, see R. Beckwith, *The Old Testament Canon of the New Testament Church and its Background in Early Judaism* (London: SPCK, 1985). This treatment, however, dates the fixing of the canon too early, and does not account for the popularity of *1 Enoch* in sectors of both Judaism and early Christianity.

period people were composing formal commentaries on Scripture. But the apocryphal writings indicate that, at an earlier time, authors were developing elaborate extensions of the material contained in the Torah and the Prophets, and that these traditional developments had an importance, and perhaps an authority of their own, which may have been perceived as equal to that of the older texts. For the author of the *Parables of Enoch*, his elaborate eschatological scenario was the right way to read parts of Isaiah, the Psalms and Daniel.

3. *Interrelationships of communities*. In addition to the literary and theological issues, it is important to note the multiplicity and complexity of religious communities that most probably generated the literature in question. What do we really mean by the term Essene? What does the term 'Hasidim' connote? Whatever the precipitating cause or causes for the move to Qumran, the Enoch literature, *Jubilees*, and perhaps the Levi material, indicate that all was not well between all Jews and the Temple establishment. To some extent—in complex ways that we do not understand—the people at Qumran were heirs of a broader and multifaceted reform movement or series of reforms. Terms like Hasidim, proto-Essene, proto-Pharisaic and proto-Apocalyptic may create more confusion than is useful, and more certainty than is possible.[1]

Rabbinic Literature in this Earlier Context
Although this paper has focused on Jewish texts from the Hellenistic–Roman period, the renewed study of these writings in the light of the Qumran scrolls provides a fresh context in which to approach the rabbinic literature generated in subsequent centuries. Several considerations may be suggested here.

1. *What was law, for whom, and when*? Before the destruction of Jerusalem and in its immediate aftermath, there was considerable

---

1. On the problems relating to the identity of the 'Hasidim', see P.R. Davies, 'Hasidim in the Maccabean Period', *JJS* 28 (1977), pp. 127-40; and G.W.E. Nickelsburg, 'Social Aspects of Jewish Apocalypticism', in *Apocalypticism in the Mediterranean World and the Near East: Proceedings of the International Colloquium on Apocalypticism, Uppsala, August 12–17, 1979* (ed. D. Hellholm; Tübingen: Mohr, 1983), pp. 641-48.

diversity concerning the Torah. It comes to light in *Jubilees*, and there are some hints of it in *1 Enoch*. These texts ascribe unimpeachable authority to certain interpretations of the law, and indicate that their proper observance is a prerequisite for divine blessing and for deliverance in the face of the coming judgment. Nonetheless, the authors indicate that many do not agree with them on this matter. The nature of the disagreement and its implications differ from the halakhic debates recorded in the rabbinic texts. To the extent that legal debates revolved about the Temple and priesthood, the events of 70 CE doubtless rendered such debates irrelevant, except perhaps for speculations about the causes of the destruction of Jerusalem and the Temple.

2. *Early evidence for haggadah and haggadic traditions*. The authors and compilers of the rabbinic texts were aware of and made use of haggadic traditions that are attested in detail in much earlier texts, such as *Jubilees*, Pseudo-Philo, and the *Apocalypse of Abraham*. We do not know in what forms and through what channels they knew these traditions, but there are real continuities—as Ginzberg suggests at many points. Perhaps we are beginning to develop some tools that will help us better understand the social settings behind this literary evidence. We may then see more clearly not only the differences between rabbinic Judaism and its predecessors, but also some of the continuities.

3. *How do we explain the demise of apocalypticism?* It is perhaps time to reconsider and revise earlier theories about the demise of so-called apocalypticism. For some, the logical chain has been simple. Apocalyptic thought promoted rebellion. Rebellion led to destruction. Apocalypses were proscribed to prevent further rebellion and disaster. Once it becomes evident that apocalypticism was a variegated phenomenon, which may or may not have countenanced revolt and whose common theme is a claim of revelation, the issue looks different. Were apocalypses proscribed, or excluded, or ignored, in part because their content was perceived to be irrelevant and because their particular theories of inspiration or claim to authority were deemed unacceptable? A reductionist explanation of the demise of apocalypticism seems to be problematic.

Interpreting the Rise of Christianity

Interpretations of the rise of Christianity have been inextricably linked to corresponding interpretations of first-century Judaism. Indeed, Christian apologetic has generated particular compatible models of early Judaism. The new inductive study of Jewish texts triggered by the discovery of the Qumran scrolls requires us to re-think some of the accepted wisdom about the rise and early development of Christianity.

1. *Jesus among Jewish teacher/revealer figures.* A careful analysis of the Enoch materials belies older ideas about the so-called demise of prophecy. The Qumran literature in general adds many nuances to the question. There were people in first-century Palestine who talked and acted as if they were prophets or successors to the prophets, and we will have much to learn about who they were, what they called themselves, who followed them, and why. This situation suggests a caveat for simple assertions about the claims and style of Jesus of Nazareth and about contemporary perceptions of him. Many New Testament exegetes and historians of early Christianity still talk as if the old generalizations are still valid. This is not helpful if we are interested in understanding the rise of Christianity and its interactions with the contemporary Judaism.

2. *Early christology in the context of Jewish eschatological speculation.* A new perception of the variety which marked early Jewish religious thought and expression helps to highlight the broad range in Jewish eschatological speculation. This, in turn, can sharpen our perception of the different nuances in early Christian speculation about Jesus of Nazareth. Both of these factors may help us better understand why and in what ways Christianity was attractive to some Jews, and why and how it was unacceptable or irrelevant to others.

3. *Daniel and Enoch in early Christianity.* In the New Testament, the Danielic and Enochic traditions are treated paradoxically. Daniel—especially Daniel 7—is often cited, quoted and closely paraphrased. Enochic traditions are also known and used with some frequency in the New Testament,[1] but with the exception of the Epistle of Jude,

---

1. For the use of the *Book of the Watchers* in the New Testament, see

they are never formally cited or quoted. In the case of the 'son of man' material, the shadow of *Enoch* is everywhere, although the work is never mentioned. *Enoch* is the hermeneutical key for the interpretation of Daniel 7, but Daniel is the text that is quoted and appealed to. This situation probably reflects a transition period in Judaism and Christianity; the authority of Daniel is increasing, while the prestige of Enoch is diminishing. The shift is slower in Christianity. Prominent second- and third-century writers, like 'Barnabas', Irenaeus, Tertullian and Origen still appeal to Enochic authority. But in the end, the *Books of Enoch* are excluded from the canons of both traditions. There is one exception within Christianity. The collection known as *1 Enoch* is part of the Bible of the Ethiopian church, and through this version alone we are able to gauge how the Enochic form of the 'son of man' traditions influenced early Christology.

Conclusion

The chance finds at Qumran have enabled us to recognize the significance of ancient Jewish texts that have long been known to us. In this sense the Qumran scrolls are a boon for students of both early Judaism and primitive Christianity; but at the same time they sound a warning that interpretations based on them also have their limitations and should be undertaken with circumspection.

R. Rubinkiewicz, *Die Eschatologie von Henoch 9–11 und das Neue Testament* (Österreichische biblische Studien, 6; trans. H. Ulrich; Klosterneuberg: Österreichisches katholisches Bibelwerk, 1984).

THE 'TEACHER OF RIGHTEOUSNESS' AND JESUS:
TWO TYPES OF RELIGIOUS LEADERSHIP
IN JUDAISM AT THE TURN OF THE ERA

Hartmut Stegemann

Introduction

In the phenomenology of religions it is easy to denote some person as a 'religious leader', to describe the kind of his 'religious leadership', and to demarcate some of its elements. But it is very difficult to compare two religious leaders with one another, as no standard pattern of religious leadership exists. What could be a common denominator of such different figures as Moses, the Buddha, Gautama, Jesus, Mani, or Muhammad? Each was the founder of a religion. They all had followers who revered them—but in quite different ways. The significance of their leadership in the groups in which they were active differed in many respects; and even the constitutive elements of their leadership were established in quite different ways. This is the case also with the priestly Qumranic Teacher of Righteousness and the Jesus from Galilee who had no distinct religious-social status by his birth or education. Thus it seems almost impossible to compare them with one another.

On the other hand, we can point to some essential features that relate the Teacher of Righteousness and Jesus to one another. Both of them lived within the Judaism of the Second Temple period, when there was no clearly defined and established Jewish 'orthodoxy', and when Judaism was marked by a variety of different religious groups or movements. Both the Teacher and Jesus functioned in Palestine, close to Jerusalem and its Temple. Indeed, the departure of the Teacher of Righteousness from Jerusalem led to the establishment of a separate community, while the circumstances of Jesus' last arrival in Jerusalem were basic to the creation of the Christian church. Both religious leaders had a particular relationship to Jerusalem and to its religious institutions, establishing their specific leadership in altercations with other religious groups and institutions, such as the Temple priesthood. But at the same time both stood in a positive relationship to traditional Jewish authorities of the past—the Torah and the Prophets. And, finally, both regarded themselves as 'teachers'—even if of quite different kinds of teaching; and both had 'followers'— though they were organized in quite different ways. Let us, therefore, try to compare these two religious leaders with one another, despite the inherent difficulties. I will start by referring to several literary sources, which when read in a critical manner can help in revealing the historical facts.

I will begin with the assumption that the 'Teacher of Righteousness' was the author of most of the hymns collected in the *Hodayot*, columns II–VIII.[1] Probably, he was also the author of a 'halakhic letter' addressed to the high priest at the Jerusalem Temple around the mid-second century BCE. Some of the contents of this still unpublished letter have been described by E. Qimron and J. Strugnell.[2] Other characteristics and deeds of this 'Teacher of Righteousness' were extolled by members of his community after his death. We find them recorded in the 'Admonitions' of the so-called *Damascus Documents* (CD I–VIII/XIX–XX) and in two Qumranic *pesharim*, 1Q *Pesher Habakkuk* and 4Q *Pesher Psalms[a]*.[3] Those literary sources provide us with reliable information about the 'Teacher of Righteousness' though there are some differences between his self-evaluation which is

---

1. See G. Jeremias, *Der Lehrer der Gerechtigkeit* (Göttingen: Vandenhoeck & Ruprecht, 1963), pp. 168-77; J. Becker, *Das Heil Gottes* (Göttingen: Vandenhoeck & Ruprecht, 1964), pp. 50-56; H.-W. Kuhn, *Enderwartung und gegenwärtiges Heil* (Göttingen: Vandenhoeck & Ruprecht, 1966), pp. 21-24.

2. The sigla of the six MSS of this 'letter' are 4QMMT[a-f]. See E. Qimron and J. Strugnell, 'An Unpublished Halakhic Letter from Qumran', in *Biblical Archaeology Today* (ed. J. Amitai; Jerusalem: Israel Exploration Society, 1985), pp. 400-407; E. Qimron and J. Strugnell, 'An Unpublished Halakhic Letter from Qumran' (text of this article differs from the previous one, with a photograph of one fragment), *The Israel Museum Journal* 4 (1985), pp. 9-12. This 'letter' may be mentioned in 4QpPs[a] IV.8-9.

3. For a discussion of these documents see Jeremias, *Der Lehrer*, pp. 140-66; H. Stegemann, *Die Entstehung der Qumrangemeinde* (Bonn: Rheinische Friedrich-Wilhelms-Universität, 1971), pp. 34-38, 39-87, 88-115, 128-85.

mirrored in the *Hodayot*, and the appreciation of his function and significance expressed in texts written by others (see below).

The access to the historical 'Teacher of Righteousness' is much easier than the approach to the historical Jesus who has left for us no written documents from his hand, so that we must have recourse solely to third-, fourth-, or fifth-hand information about him. These data and traditions come from many different informants who were more interested in telling of Jesus' significance for themselves and for the salvation of all humanity, rather than in reporting for later historians or scholars the events of his life, his acts and teachings. These are generally recognized difficulties. There are no two contemporary scholars whose descriptions of the historical Jesus dovetail completely, in spite of their using the same literary sources—the four Gospels of the New Testament, and a few hints from the Pauline letters and other sources—and applying the same methods of literary and historical analysis.[1] Therefore, my statements regarding the historical Jesus as a religious leader will be much more open to queries than those concerning the Teacher of Righteousness.

In this essay I shall concentrate on four aspects of religious leadership. First, the specific authority of the 'religious leader'—its foundations, problems of the office, competence, etc. Second, the relations between the 'leader' and his 'followers'—the organization of these followers, the kind of devotion to the leader, etc. Third, the uniqueness of the leader—his relation to other, opposing figures, leadership succession in the group, political implications of religious leadership, etc. In each of these sections the Teacher of Righteousness will be discussed first, followed by consideration of Jesus. These figures will not be explicitly compared with one another, either historically or phenomenologically, but only by implication.

In the fourth section I will briefly consider more general issues, such as types of leadership in Judaism and in Christianity, the circumstances which demand or produce 'leadership', and specific religious notions which render some kind of leadership necessary.

---

1.   See, *inter alia*, H. Conzelmann, 'Jesus Christus', in *Die Religion in Geschichte und Gegenwart*, III (Tübingen: Mohr [Paul Siebeck], 1959), pp. 619-53; H. Merklein, *Jesu Botschaft von der Gottesherrschaft* (Stuttgart: Katholisches Bibelwerk, 1983; 3rd edn, 1989); E.P. Sanders, *Jesus and Judaism* (London: SCM Press, 1985).

I propose to draw only on the most significant or remarkable aspects. I also shall reduce to a bare minimum methodological remarks, and references to the work of other scholars. Rather than produce a definitive review of the entire body of relevant material, I hope to stimulate discussion on this subject.

In concluding these introductory remarks, let me refer to the comparison of the Teacher of Righteousness and Jesus presented by A. Dupont-Sommer, and others, after the publication of the first texts from the Qumran caves in the early 1950s. At that time, many parallels between both figures were affirmed, almost all of them quite unjustifiable and without foundation. These early speculations are convincingly refuted by G. Jeremias in his study of the Teacher of Righteousness, *Der Lehrer der Gerechtigkeit*.[1]

1. *The Authority of the Religious Leader*

The Teacher of Righteousness

The literary sources of the Qumran community leave no doubt that the Teacher of Righteousness was a priest. In 4QpPs[a] 3.15, the *gever* of Ps. 37.23 is identified with *hkwhn mwrh hsdq*, 'the priest, the Teacher of Righteousness'.[2] Elsewhere in the *pesharim* he is called only *hkhn* the priest (1QpHab 2.8; 4QpPs[a] 2.19). His titles *mwrh sdq* (CD 1.11), *mwrh hsdq* (1QpHab 1.13; 2.2; 5.10; etc.), *mwrh hyhd* (CD 20.1), or *dwrš htwrh* (CD 7.18), also classify him, within the framework of the specifically Qumranic texts, as a priest. For in this community, *drš htwrh* 'to inquire of the Law', and *yrh* 'to teach', were restricted to the priests who alone were invested with this authority, along with such traditionally priestly privileges as pronouncing cultic blessings and offering sacrifices on the altar. The *Hodayot* do not use the term *hkwhn;* but in the hymns composed by the Teacher himself (1QH 2–8), the priestly self-image of their author is evident.

Born to an Aaronite family and educated to function as a priest, the Teacher of Righteousness was from his earliest years a member of a leading family. He was also destined to become a mediator between the God of Israel and his people, which was the cultic role of priests

---

1. Jeremias, *Der Lehrer*, pp. 319-53; cf. pp. 268-307.
2. Jeremias, *Der Lehrer*, pp. 147-48.

during the Second Temple period. Thus, from his birth, the Teacher of Righteousness was some kind of a potential Jewish religious leader, independent of the concrete functions he assumed during his lifetime and of his particular priestly career at the Temple in Jerusalem.

Furthermore, the definite article in his designations, *hkwhn*, the priest *kat' exochen; mwrh hṣdq*, the (only) right teacher; *mwrh hyḥyd*, the (unique) teacher; or *dwrš htwrh*, the (most authoritative) interpreter of the Law, characterize him clearly as the high priest of his time. According to the tradition, this meant that he considered himself the only true high priest in Judaism, from the day of his anointment until his death.[1] Historically, he was—in my opinion—the predecessor of the first Hasmonaean high priest, Jonathan, who violently removed him from office about 152 BCE. The teacher may have officiated at the Temple during the *intersacerdotium,* which was erroneously assumed by Josephus because of the lack of evidence for this period in his literary sources.[2] Even if this high priest was only in office for seven years at the most,[3] in his own view he continued to be the high priest of all the people of Israel to the end of his life.

The *Eigenverständnis,* or the self-image, of the Teacher of Righteousness as being the true high priest of his time is indirectly evidenced by the later Qumran literary sources in which he is given the titles *dwrš htwrh, mwrh hṣdq, hkwhn,* etc. In my opinion, this is also directly evidenced by the *Hodayot* which he composed.[4] G. Jeremias considered the Teacher to be endowed by God with some special mission, like a prophet, enabling him to be a powerful teacher of his people or his community. But the specific power of the Teacher was basically not rooted in some kind of instruction, or in his

1.   J. Jeremias, *Jerusalem zur Zeit Jesu* (Göttingen: Vandenhoeck & Ruprecht, 3rd edn, 1962), p. 179. Cf. the fate of the high priest Onias III, who was removed from his office in 175 BCE, but regarded himself as the true high priest in spite of his deposition by his brother. He was murdered three years afterwards.

2.   See Stegemann, *Die Entstehung*, pp. 212-20.

3.   This is the duration of the *intersacerdotium* according to Josephus, *Ant.* 20.10.3 (237), while in *Ant.* 13.2.3 (46), he reduced this period of time to four years.

4.   My theories are independently upheld by P. Schulz, *Der Autoritätsanspruch des Lehrers der Gerechtigkeit* (Meisenheim am Glan: Anton Hain, 1974). G. Jeremias (*Der Lehrer*) did not realize this aspect of a high priestly author of those *Hodayot.*

appointment as a prophet. It was inherent in his office as high priest, in the sense of a 'character indelebilis' enduring despite his deposition by his enemies, foremost by the parvenu Jonathan backed by the Pharisees who regarded Jonathan and his followers as high priests although they were descendants of a non-Zadokite family.

The *Hodayot* give expression to the self-image of their high priestly author, for example, by phrases such as *rz hbth by*, 'the secret that thou hast concealed within me' (5.25) or *twrtkh hbth by*, 'the Torah which thou hast concealed within me' (5.11), which designate the Teacher as the only and central authority in Israel for the correct interpretation of the Mosaic Law. Only by being the high priest could he identify the *bryt 'l*, the everlasting covenant which God had given to Israel through Moses, with *bryty* 'my covenant', which others *b'y bryty*, could also enter (5.23)—a formulation quite foreign to all biblical literature. The Teacher of Righteousness speaks here clearly as *the* central representative of the holy covenant which had departed its traditional place at the Temple in Jerusalem together with him: *bmgwr* 'at a place of exile', *lmšpt ysdtny* 'hast thou (God) established me as [the determinative institution of] justice', *wmzh bryt ldwršyh* 'and from that [time] onwards [or: 'and because of this event'] the covenant exists for those who search for it' (1QH 5.8-9f.). This statement implies that only they who enter of their own free decision into the community led by this high priest are still within God's covenant with Israel, the 'true Israel'. Although only a part and a remnant of Judaism, this community is regarded as its central and only legitimate representative.

Thus, the authority of the Teacher of Righteousness as a religious leader rested, on the one hand, on the traditional authority of a high priest. On the other hand, with his deposition from the Temple in Jerusalem, he also achieved the rank of a leader of a religious community. The then already existing 'community of pious ones' (*synagoge, Asidaioi, 'adat [ha]hasidim*) of pre-Maccabean times, founded about 172 BCE and called in the 'Admonitions' of the *Damascus Documents hbryt hḥdš b'rṣ dmšq*, 'the New Covenant [established] in the Land of Damascus' (CD 6.19; 7.21/19.33-34f.; cf. 20.12), gave him refuge. The Teacher then caused a split in this group when he demanded to be permanently acknowledged as the only true high priest in Israel. Many of the members of that community acceded to his demand; they became the so-called Qumran community, or 'the Teacher's community', historically identified with the *Essaioi* or *Essenoi* mentioned by Philo of Alexandria, Josephus, and Pliny the Elder. Their settlement at Ḥirbet Qumran was the residence of one small group, serving as a study centre of the broader movement. The other wing of the '*adat (ha)hasidim* became the so-called Pharisees, 'schismatics', who rejected the demand of the Teacher and continued to participate in the sacrificial service at the Temple of Jerusalem. In their opinion, the sacrificial offerings demanded by the Torah took precedence over the question of the legitimacy of the currently officiating high priest. This was the historical breaking-point between the (Qumran) Essenes and the Pharisees; the decision of the first group caused the high priestly Teacher to become the founder and religious leader of an autonomous community.

The Qumran *pesharim* referred to this event in several ways. On the one hand, this break is mentioned in 1QpHab 5.9-12, where the '*yš hkzb*—in my opinion *hmbkr 'šr lkwl hmhnwt,* i.e. the leading figure of the '*dt (h)hsydym* at that time—*m's 't htwrh bkwl 'dtm* 'neglected the [commandments of the] Torah in [an assembly of] their entire community', and did not accept the special demand of the Teacher to be acknowledged as the only true high priest. On the other hand, this '*yš hkzb,* 'the Liar', and his followers were labelled by the adherents of the Teacher *byt 'bšlwm,* 'house of rebellion' (because they acted like David's rebellious son, Absalom) (1QpHab 5.9), or *byt plg* 'house of schism' (4QpNah 4.1; CD 20.2), some of the earliest designations of the Pharisees.[1]

In this way, the so-called Teacher of Righteousness became the founder of a new community, which is described by 4QpPs[a] 3.15-17: 'The priest, the Teacher of [Righteousness] whom God called to arise, and whom he appointed to build up for him a community [...] and guided him to his truth'. According to this text, God himself granted the Teacher special authority, making him the founder of this community, and 'guided him to his truth' in the sense that all further decisions of that Teacher proved to be right. This account was obviously formulated by members of the Teacher's community at a later date; but it agrees with the references to those events in *Hodayot* composed by the Teacher himself—including the statements that God had installed him in his office, and that God saved him and guided him

---

1.   See Stegemann, *Die Enstehung*, pp. 48-52, 92-93, 179-83.

through all the difficulties and the rebellions against him or against his special demands.

The Teacher organized his new community in a rigidly hierarchical manner, with the priests at the top (the Zadokite priests being an elite group above all others), the Levites after them, and the common people of Israel in the third rank. In this community, the Teacher was regarded as the eminent interpreter of the Torah for all his adherents, that is to say, he was the leading authority in all questions of halakhah, and no one in the community could act against his will. For the members of this group, their Teacher was the main representative of God's will on earth. This view accords with the self-image of the Teacher in the *Hodayot*; he states that God himself guided him in all that happened to him, that he determined all his deeds and decisions, and that God's will alone was behind all the decrees which the Teacher established for his followers.

An additional aspect of the special authority accorded to the Teacher should be considered here. 1QpHab states that God gave into his (the Teacher's) heart the 'insight to explain everything the prophets had told' (2.8-10; cf. 7.3-5). This statement does not imply that the Teacher was regarded, or regarded himself, as a prophet. But by his priestly authority he discerned that what the biblical prophets had written related to the future, and that his own days were the time of fulfilment of the prophets' words. His own days were *'ḥryt hymym*—'the last days' before the final salvation of Israel.

The Teacher's understanding was clearly recognized in the hermeneutical approach of his *Hodayot*. Many sayings of the biblical prophets, and of the Psalter attributed to (the prophet) David, are indirectly quoted to explain the fates of the authors of those hymns as predicted by God, and to conform to the situation at 'the end-of-days'. In the Qumran *pesharim,* and in other midrashim written by members of the Teacher's community after his death, the perspective is broader. The sayings of the biblical prophets are related not only to the lifetime of the Teacher, but also to the longer timespan of the existence of his community up to the final extermination of all their enemies. In later Qumran writings, like 1QpHab, the Teacher was only presented as the authoritative source of this kind of knowledge or hermeneutics, not as the last eschatological figure before the time of fulfilment.

Jesus

It is extremely difficult to describe the authority of Jesus as a religious leader in Second Temple Judaism. Jesus was not a priest, nor an educated religious leader, and there is no record which would be construed as his 'call to office' in the tradition of the New Testament. Some scholars consider the events at his baptism, as reported by Mk 1.9-11 (cf. Mt. 3.13-17; Lk. 3.21-22), as such a call to office. But in every case, this is not a report from Jesus himself, but a rather late statement formulated in a Christian community. The historian cannot detect the source of Jesus' authority. We only know that he began as a follower of John the Baptist. He later became independent of his early 'master', but did not transmit to us any information about why this happened, or where his new orientations came from. The field remains open for academic speculation.

It is my view that one day Jesus experienced 'events' which he could not explain in any way other than to conclude that God had started to act on earth again, that is, that the eschatological end-of-days had already set in. His basic experience may have been the 'withdrawal of demons' from ill people, and their suddenly being restored to health without the application of any magical healing practices. No one except God could have done that. Jesus saw himself implanted in this process: 'If I by the "finger of God" [i.e. by God's own power] cast out the demons, the kingdom of God is already established amidst you' (Lk. 11.20; cf. Mt. 12.28). This is the background of the many New Testament narratives and other traditions depicting Jesus as a 'healer'. He found himself involved in those events, but without fulfilling any specific role or even displaying leadership attributes. Indeed, he sent his followers to distant places, to have the same experience of driving out of the world the evil tangible in the demons (see, e.g., Mk 6.7; Mt. 10.5-8). Some of those healed in contact with Jesus, and others who were impressed by such deeds, may have considered him to be a powerful religious leader. But the narratives which stress this aspect of his life are all *Gemeindebildungen,* community traditions, and there is not one saying of the 'historical Jesus' which attributes such a leading role to him.

The meals which Jesus shares with his disciples and many other people testify to another aspect of his religious experience. The participants in those meals were often 'impure' people (see, e.g., Mk 2.15-17; Lk. 19.1-10), and even if the numbers were large, the food became so plentiful that only 'the heaven' (i.e. God himself) could be seen as the true host. In this case too, all the narratives that report such meals are *Gemeindebildungen,* with Jesus figuring as the host (see, e.g., Mk 6.30-44; 8.1-10; Jn 6.1-13; cf. also Mt. 11.18-19/Lk. 7.33-34). However, this specific role accorded to him is clearly secondary, styled by tradition; Jesus himself saw God as the true host of such meals, acting again as the creator of the world and feeding his people abundantly in a 'heavenly' manner (Mt. 6.25-34/Lk. 12.22-31; cf. also Mt. 6.11/Lk. 11.3). Jesus was clearly included in such meals, but only as a participant, not as a host or leader.

The teachings of Jesus convey the same impression; he comments on the events in his time, and explains that God himself has started the breakthrough of his kingdom on earth. By his impressive parables and many sayings, Jesus argues against those who doubted his understanding and his interpretation of current events as 'traces' of the again-acting God of Israel. Consequently, Jesus was regarded not only as a 'healer' and as an 'eater and drinker', but also as a religious 'teacher'.

Later, his adherents, or the Christian communities, considered him to be a mediator of the kingdom of God, a royal messiah, 'the son of God', and so on. To Jesus himself such views were quite strange; he was witness to and involved in God's actions, but he did not feel that he had the leading role or function in this cosmic drama.

How can one describe the authority of Jesus within the framework of such indirect religious leadership? He was not like John the Baptist, who was born into a priestly family and, therefore, could become a mediator, who is 'more than a prophet' (Mt. 11.9/Lk. 7.26); by baptizing penitent people he could save them from their approaching punishment in the final judgment. Jesus did not consider himself to be such a priestly mediator. All his authority came from God, and from his followers. He did not think of himself as possessing a specific authority, neither initiated by a religious 'call' nor inaugurated by a 'messianic' office. He became a 'leader' only by extra-personal authority drawn from God, from the people, and from the belief of the Christian communities in his resurrection.

3. *The Relation between the Leader and his Followers*

The Teacher of Righteousness

The officiating high priest at the Temple in Jerusalem was the head of all cultic affairs, of the priestly personnel in the Temple administration, and also of the political and juridical affairs of the Jewish people—at least in Jerusalem and in Judea. He was at the same time their high priest and their governor, *mwšl*. He had to care for them 'like a father for his children'. But the Jewish people of this time were not his 'followers' in the narrow specific sense of this term.

We have no direct information related to this part of the life or career of the Teacher of Righteousness. But, on the basis of similar circumstances, we may assume that, being a high priest, he had in the various areas of his responsibilities several trusted individuals who enjoyed his special confidence. This circle may have included Zadokite and other priests, Levites and laymen as well. When he was violently removed from his office at the Temple, most of those close confidants also had to leave. This is only a supposition, but it is an obvious and reasonable one. These associates then became his 'followers' and partners in his fate. Most of them probably followed him into his exile, or refuge, and joined one of the local groups, called 'camps' of the 'community of pious ones', where the Teacher started the second phase of his career as a religious leader.

From the *Hodayot* we learn that at this critical juncture, the Teacher had a distinct group of individuals associated with him, whom he called *nṣmdy swdy* or *'nšy 'ṣty* (1QH 5.24). These close adherents of the Teacher were not identical with the other members of his community, whom he denotes in the previous line as *r'y*, 'my fellows', and as *b'y bryty*, 'they who entered my covenant' (1QH 5.23). As a leader of his community he had, therefore, a close inner circle of men of special confidence, perhaps his 'followers' from the Temple who may have been his counsellors in problematic affairs, as well as a wider circle of 'followers', i.e. all the other men who were simple members of his group (*yḥd* or *'dh*).

The information that can be culled from the *Hodayot* or from 1Q *Serekh ha-Yaḥad*, 'the Rule of the Community', points to well-organized relations between the Teacher as the leader of his group and members in their different ranks. The organizational system was hierarchical, with strict obedience expected from the lower to the upper ranks. As long as the Teacher lived, all final decisions were his. He was their unique religious leader. This role did not derive from his personal authority or the persuasive power of his teaching. His leadership derived exclusively from his permanent function as a high priest of 'all of Israel', even if that recognition was now limited to the members of his community. Every Jew could enter this community and thus become a follower of the Teacher. No longer did birth from Jewish parents determine who was a 'true' Jew—but rather, adherence to the demands of this Teacher. For the first time in Jewish history, the religious society was not only constituted by genealogical descent, but also by 'following' a specific religious 'leader'.

Jesus

According to the Gospels of Mark and Matthew, Jesus 'called' to his disciples in a godlike fashion, bidding them: 'Follow me!' And they followed him without being motivated by a miracle to do so, or by any kind of persuasive preaching (see, e.g., Mk 1.16-20; 2.14; Mt. 4.18-22; 9.9). The psychologist Luke noticed this curious manner of enlisting followers, and he replaced it with a more plausible version: Simon Peter and the two sons of Zebedee are now driven to become followers of Jesus by an impressive miracle (Lk. 5.1-11).

All traditions of this kind are secondary and cannot be traced back to the historical Jesus and to the ways in which he gained followers and 'disciples'. His call of 'the Twelve' (Mk 3.13-19/Mt. 10.1-4; cf. 1 Cor. 15.5) was similarly modified by Luke to the call of the 'twelve apostles' (Lk. 6.12-18; cf. Acts 1.13). These twelve were clearly considered the representatives of the twelve tribes of Israel in the 'new age'. I do not believe, however, that Jesus restricted God's renewed acting in history only to Israel (in contrast to the world-wide perspective of John the Baptist; see Mt. 3.7/Lk. 3.8). Therefore, the tradition of his call of 'the Twelve' may also be regarded as having been conceived by the early Jewish-Christian community after his death.[1]

---

1. P. Vielhauer, 'Gottesreich und Menschensohn in der Verkündigung Jesu', in *Festschrift für G. Dehn* (Neukirchen–Vluyn: Neukirchener Verlag, 1957), pp. 62-64; reprinted in *Aufsätze zum Neuen Testament*, I (München: Kaiser, 1965), pp. 68-71. He adduces convincing arguments against the notion that 'the Twelve' were established by the historical Jesus.

What remains, then, if all these traditions are regarded as not true in the historical sense?

The Gospel of John reports that the first followers of Jesus were former 'disciples' of John the Baptist, who sent them to Jesus (Jn 1.35ff.). The idea that John the Baptist 'sent' them to Jesus may be a secondary tradition; but it may be true that some of his first adherents had formerly joined John the Baptist, but 'followed' Jesus after the death of their master, or after Jesus started his own 'preaching'. Others of his followers may have been people whom he 'healed' from their demons (see, e.g., Mk 5.18-20; Lk. 8.23), or people impressed by his deeds or by his preaching (Lk. 19.1-10).

How did Jesus himself react to people 'following' him? According to some New Testament traditions, most of which are gathered in Matthew 10, Jesus sent them away to other places to tell their experiences of the new 'kingdom of God' on earth, to preach that kingdom and to drive out demons. Contrary to the descriptions in the Gospels, Jesus did not want to have a circle of close adherents accompanying him, either as 'followers', or as 'disciples'. But he could not stop the devotion of those adherents. Some, like Simon Peter, the sons of Zebedee, and even several women who honoured him as their 'teacher' or 'healer' (see, e.g., Lk. 8.1-3), continued to accompany him. But Jesus never initiated a close circle of followers, nor anything resembling a 'community', or a 'church'. During his lifetime there were only some devoted disciples who regarded him as their 'master'; the organizational framework of his followers actually only developed after his death. Jesus preferred to divert his followers' faith to the God acting in the world, not to his own person. He became a religious 'leader' of sorts against his will, very much in contrast to the Teacher of Righteousness of the Qumran community.

Despite his personal inclinations, the followers of Jesus perceived his deeds and teachings as testifying to his personal qualifications as their 'master' and 'prophet'. In their belief, Jesus was authorized by God to establish the final truth. In this indirect way, Jesus became a 'religious leader', without ever having claimed this function or having assumed such a role.

4. *The Uniqueness of the Leader*

The Teacher of Righteousness

As already stated, the Teacher of Righteousness claimed to be in his lifetime the unique religious leader of 'all of Israel'. Being the only true high priest, he could not view himself in any other way. As long as the Teacher lived he was regarded as the unique religious leader of Israel and the central authority in the interpretation of the Torah of Moses—at least in his own evaluation and in the opinion of his community. He believed that the opposing high priest who then officiated at the Temple should resign from office and follow the halakhah according to the interpretation of the Torah which he, the Teacher of Righteousness, offered. This claim is clearly demonstrated by his so-called 'halakhic letter'.[1] It was impossible to have two high priests in Judaism at the same time. According to the personal claim of the Teacher of Righteousness, he had been and remained the unique leader of 'all of Israel', even if, due to circumstances, his authority was acknowledged temporarily only by one segment of a split community. The opposing leader of the other part of that community, later known as the 'Pharisees', was condemned as 'the liar who flouted the Law' (1QpHab 5.11-12).

After the death of the Teacher of Righteousness—probably close to the end of the second century BCE—no successor was acknowledged as the true high priest and the unique leader of the community. His community continued to exist as the Essene group within Judaism, at least until the first Jewish revolt against the Romans (66–73 CE). This group was now guided by a council of twelve (lay-)men and three priests (1QS 8.1), some rights being reserved solely for the priests, headed by the leading family, the sons of Zadok (see, e.g., 1QS 5.2-9). Instead of electing a successor, the members of the community hoped that in the future a priestly 'messiah of Aaron' (1QS 9.11; CD 19.10-11; 20.1) would emerge who would again be the true religious leader of 'all of Israel'. He should be assisted by a 'royal messiah' descended from King David. The deceased Teacher of Righteousness was now called 'the unique teacher' as in the 'Admonitions' of the *Damascus Documents* composed about 100 BCE (CD 20.1). Whatever this unique

---

1. See the description of 4QMMT[a-f] (above p. 195 n. 2).

Teacher had decided or taught became, after his death, a guiding principle for his community. Only the future 'period of final consummation', with the emergence of new authorities, could change this situation (see, e.g., 1QS 9.10-11).

In the Teacher's self-image, his 'uniqueness' pertained to every aspect of the office of the high priest in his time. He was the true *archiereus* in charge of priestly affairs, he was the only *hegoumenos* serving as a political leader and as the head of administration, and he was the unique *prophetes* who defined every kind of basic religious orientation, even if his execution of power in this threefold office was restricted to his community alone. The members of his group confirmed the manifold authority of their unique Teacher after his death, for the duration of the community's existence up to the 'latter' or 'last days'.

Jesus

Jesus did not achieve his uniqueness as a religious leader in opposition to some other Jewish leader. He became independent from John the Baptist, but never his opponent (see, e.g., Mt. 11.7-11/Lk. 7.24-28). If indeed he was in conflict with the high priest of his time (see Mk 14.60-64; Jn 18.19-21), this was a last episode shortly before his death, and had no importance for his self-image during his lifetime.

As I have said, Jesus believed that during his lifetime God had begun to establish his everlasting reign on earth. Jesus did not believe in the coming of a 'messiah', or conceive of himself as such. Neither Jesus nor anyone else could assume an 'official' role where the almighty God himself was acting. The high priest in Jerusalem and his function on the Day of Atonement were no longer necessary if a sinless 'people of God' started to spread throughout the world. The religious leaders of the Sadducees, the Pharisees, the Zealots, the Essenes, and all other Jewish groups or organizations were rendered totally unnecessary wherever God himself had taken over.

In accord with this concept, Jesus did not claim uniqueness, nor was such uniqueness attributed to him. Uniqueness was attributed exclusively to God and to the events of his final coming, the inauguration of which Jesus experienced in his lifetime, an event never before experienced nor ever to be experienced in the future.

But, quite independent of his self-understanding, some of the 'followers' of Jesus started even during his lifetime to regard him as their unique 'master' or 'religious teacher'. After his death, they continued to believe in his function as their religious leader. Progressively they included Jesus within the uniqueness of God's acting-in-history, and in this way Jesus finally was cast in the role of the unique saviour of all humanity. This aspect of Christian belief cannot be traced back to the historical Jesus who attributed all uniqueness of leadership to God alone.

5. *Types of Religious Leadership*

Two very different types of religious leadership are evident in the above descriptions of the Teacher of Righteousness and of Jesus. The Teacher of Righteousness was indeed the unique religious leader of 'all of Israel' during his lifetime, even if political circumstances restricted his influence to a particular community during the last decades of his life. In contradistinction, Jesus attributed uniqueness to God alone. He did not consider himself to be a religious 'leader', or the royal 'messiah'. He was merely a witness of God's eschatological deeds, in which he was involved. He conveyed his observations to others, commented on them, and argued against opponents who did not believe his view of the now-acting God. Jesus did not interpret the Torah or the Prophets better than others, nor did he perform miracles to convince others of his religious power. But whatever he did or said, his followers felt themselves 'guided' by his views—or by his deeds. In this indirect way, Jesus became a religious leader of his time, an everlasting 'master' for his followers, and finally the founder of a new community, the Christian church. Thus after his death he gained a status which is, in some respect, similar to that which the Teacher of Righteousness enjoyed within his community.

One may question whether these two individuals who were active about the turn of the era exemplified 'types' of religious leaders within the framework of Second Temple Judaism. Although each arose as a result of circumstances that were perhaps 'typical' for that time, each was a unique figure, and the types of religious leadership they exemplified were not similar—indeed they were atypical for Judaism. Never again did Judaism—or Christianity—produce a religious leader like the Teacher of Righteousness or like Jesus.

What were the more representative types of religious leadership in Judaism and in Christianity in the centuries at the turn of the era? In

Judaism, the typical religious leader eventually became the sage, or the rabbi. At first, he was a *dwrš htwrh*, an interpreter of the Torah, and later also a *doresh dibre ḥakhamim*, an interpreter of the sayings of the sages. There was no need for this interpreter to be of priestly stock; laymen could exercise the same kind of authority. The rabbis were for the most part heads of schools in Mesopotamia or in Palestine.

This type of religious leader may have originated in the 'community of pious ones' of pre-Maccabaean times about the middle of the second century BCE; perhaps, the *mbqr* of a single *mḥnh*, i.e. the religious leader of a local group of pious men, or some learned individual, *mskyl*, was the archetypal figure. The Pharisees favoured this type of religious leadership, and under their influence the rabbi became the decisive leader figure in Judaism after the destruction of the Second Temple. By the end of the first century CE, the priests had lost most of their traditional importance, and the era of the sages or rabbis was inaugurated.

Early Christianity was marked by a rather diffuse plurality of religious leadership in its beginnings. Some types emerged from Judaism, others from Hellenistic patterns. At first, 'the Twelve' existed in Jerusalem as representatives of the eschatological Israel; however their true function is as yet unknown. Afterwards, three *styloi* (pillars) were the leaders of the Christian community in Jerusalem (Gal. 2.9), while other groups were headed by an *apostolos* who had founded them, for example, as Paul had founded local communities. Other Christian communities were guided by a collective group of *presbyteroi* (elders), while *prophetai* and *didaskaloi* held different offices under them. Only after a century of pluralistic Christianity did a special type of *episkopos* (bishop) begin to attain religious leadership, at first as head of a local community and later as a representative of a broader segment of the church. This specific Christian type of religious leader put its stamp on the church during the centuries when the sages were active in rabbinic Judaism. The roots of the office of the bishop are still debated; perhaps it first developed from the Hellenistic associations and only later received its religious connotation. But whatever its origins, the Christian bishop and the Jewish rabbi exemplified quite different types of religious leadership and cannot legitimately be compared.

I conclude that one can enumerate some types of religious leadership in Judaism and in Christianity in the centuries around the turn of the era, but that it is impossible to compare them. They were formed by interests and duties too different for comparison. The Teacher of Righteousness and Jesus were both Jews, but they became religious leaders under rather different historical circumstances, and represented quite different aspects and tendencies of Second Temple Judaism. They are similar, perhaps, in that their adherents' fervour made them unique leaders for all time, to the end-of-days. Concomitantly their followers held that all other branches of Judaism were in error, for the righteousness of a religious leader is exclusive and *ipso facto* turns all others into false pretenders and liars. This is the basic problem of every kind of 'religious leadership'.

BETWEEN THE BIBLE AND THE MISHNAH:
QUMRAN FROM WITHIN

Shemaryahu Talmon

Four Decades of Research:
Achievements and Unsolved Problems

Some forty years have passed since the accidental discovery of a cluster of ancient scrolls in a cave near a site in the Judaean Desert known by the Arabic name Qumran.[1] In the ensuing systematic exploration of that wilderness area, scholars produced a hoard of partial scrolls and fragments from eleven of the many more caves which were methodically investigated. The finds opened an entirely new field of intensive research. Notwithstanding the energy and expertise brought to bear on the elucidation of the intricate problems which these documents pose for us, all the acumen and wisdom mustered by a legion of scholars cannot dispel the doubts which beset the solutions that have been offered to the questions which abound in the Qumran documents. Unlike the Covenanters of Qumran who gave twenty years as the length of the period of their own initial bewilderment (CD 1.9-10), we have in fact been 'like the blind groping their way' in respect to most of the issues which have come under review, for the stereo-

1. An account of the circumstances surrounding the discovery of the scrolls is offered in several comprehensive surveys. See *inter alia*: F.M. Cross, *The Ancient Library of Qumran and Biblical Studies* (New York: Doubleday, 1961, 1980); J.T. Milik, *Ten Years of Discovery in the Wilderness of Judea* (trans. J. Strugnell Naperville, IL: Allenson, 1959); G. Vermes, *The Dead Sea Scrolls: Qumran in Perspective* (London: SCM Press, 1982). While these surveys are twenty years apart, they address themselves in essence to the same basic issues and problems. See further, J.A. Sanders, 'The Dead Sea Scrolls: A Quarter Century of Study', *BA* 36 (1973), pp. 110-48; M.A. Knibb, *The Qumran Community* (Cambridge Commentaries on Writings of the Jewish and Christian World 200 BC to AD 200, 2; Cambridge: Cambridge University Press, 1987).

typical span of forty years which biblical tradition accords to the aberrant wilderness generation and henceforth to every generation.[1]

Judging by the past achievements, which have resulted in only partial success, one wonders whether at the end of the next decade (which will mark the jubilee of Qumran research) we shall be better informed on these perplexing issues. It remains to be seen whether we shall then have reached the terra firma of an adequate and full understanding of what these scrolls were meant to tell their ancient readers, exactly who these readers were, and why and by whom the manuscripts were deposited in the caves and thus preserved for posterity.

In view of the unsolved problems, current Qumran research patently stands in need of a periodic assessment of the state of the art,[2] even though a considerable part of the documents salvaged from the caves still has not been made available for study. The publication of additional materials is bound to enlarge the compass of the evidence on which theories can be founded. Some of the extensive manuscripts and fragments which still remain unpublished may eventually shed new light on several unresolved pivotal questions, and others may even hold surprises. But the experience of recent decades prompts the assumption that we should not expect a fundamental reformulation of any of the mainline theories propagated in the past. The considerable volume of materials, published over the last two or three decades, albeit fragmentary, has not appreciably corroborated or countervailed proposals put forward in the first ten or fifteen years on the basis of the documents available then. It suffices to make reference only to the

---

1. For this motif see S. Talmon, 'midbar, arābāh', *ThWAT* 4 (1983), col. 660-95, and 'The "Desert Motif" in the Bible and in Qumran Literature', in *Biblical Motifs. Origins and Transformations*, III (ed. A. Altman; Studies and Texts of the Philip L. Lown Institute of Advanced Judaic Studies; Cambridge, MA: Harvard University Press, 1966), pp. 31-63.

2. Such an assessment was indeed proffered in several conferences convened to celebrate four decades of Qumran discoveries. The proceedings of these meetings should provide a detailed picture of the state of the art. For the present, see the partial overview given by M. Wise, 'The Dead Sea Scrolls, Part 1: Archaeology and Biblical Manuscripts', *BA* 49 (1986), pp. 140-56, and 'The Dead Sea Scrolls. Part 2: Non-biblical Manuscripts', *BA* 49 (1986), pp. 228-43. Some of the papers presented at a conference held at the Warburg Institute in London were published in *JJS* 39 (1988), pp. 5-79. See also G. Vermes, *The Dead Sea Scrolls Forty Years On. The Fourteenth Sacks Lecture* (Oxford: Centre for Postgraduate Hebrew Studies, 1987).

most important of these more recently published manuscripts and fragments: the several volumes in the DJD series,[1] extra-series publications such as the *Targum of Job*,[2] the Palaeo-Hebrew Exodus[3] and Leviticus Scrolls,[4] and the *Temple Scroll*.[5] They did not provide any pertinent new information which would lead to a fully satisfactory solution of old questions, but rather added new queries to the extant roster.

Some offbeat hypotheses which were formulated in the early stage of Qumran studies have indeed been abandoned. They are now passed over in silence or are cursorily referred to in retrospective surveys of Qumran research. We need but mention the most conspicuous of these phased-out theories: the attempted invalidation of the scrolls by debunking them as spurious modern fabrications;[6] their presentation as mediaeval documents of Karaite origin;[7] the various proposals to affiliate their authors with sundry factions that flourished in the early Christian era—the Ebionites,[8] or in the outgoing Second Temple

1.   J.A. Sanders, *The Psalms Scroll of Qumran Cave 11 (11QPs^a)* (DJD, 4; Oxford: Clarendon Press, 1965); J.M. Allegro, *Qumran Cave 4*, I (*4Q158–4Q186*) (DJD, 5; Oxford: Clarendon Press, 1968); R. de Vaux and J.T. Milik, *Qumrân Grotte 4*, II. *Archéologie; Tefillin, mezuzot et targums (4Q128–4Q157)* (DJD, 6; Oxford: Clarendon Press, 1977); M. Baillet, *Qumran Grotte 4*, III (*4Q482–4Q520*) (DJD, 7; Oxford: Clarendon Press, 1982).

2.   A.S. van der Woude and J.P.M. van der Ploeg, *Le Targum de Job de la Grotte XI de Qumran* (Leiden: Brill, 1971); R. Weiss, *The Aramaic Targum of Job* (Tel Aviv: Tel Aviv University, 1979 [Hebrew]).

3.   J.E. Sanderson, *An Exodus Scroll from Qumran. 4QpaleoExod^m and the Samaritan Tradition* (HSS, 30; Atlanta, GA: Scholars Press, 1983).

4.   D.N. Freedman and K.A. Mathews, *The Paleo-Hebrew Leviticus Scroll (11QpaleoLev)* (Winona Lake, IN: American Schools of Oriental Research, 1985).

5.   Y. Yadin, *Megilath haMiqdash. The Temple Scroll* (Jerusalem: Israel Exploration Society and Hebrew University, 1977 [Hebrew]; ET, 1983).

6.   S. Zeitlin voiced this opinion in a series of essays published in *JQR*. See especially *The Dead Sea Scrolls and Modern Scholarship* (JQRMS, 3; Philadelphia: Jewish Quarterly Review, 1956).

7.   Foremost, Zeitlin, *The Dead Sea Scrolls*; N. Wieder, *The Judean Scrolls and Karaism* (Oxford: Clarendon Press, 1962); N. Golb, 'Literary and Doctrinal Aspects of the Damascus Covenant in Relation to Those of the Karaites', *JQR* 47 (1957), pp. 354-74.

8.   This identification had already been proposed by Kaufmann-Kohler on the basis of the Zadokite Fragments from the Cairo Genizah, but was developed by J. Teicher on the strength of the Qumran discoveries in a series of essays published in

period—the Samaritans[1] or the Zealots.[2] These and similar theories have altogether lost credibility. The ever-increasing cumulative evidence brought to light by scholarly investigation in a variety of disciplines—history, archaeology and numismatics,[3] palaeography,[4] and science[5]—has proven them to be unfounded.[6] But on the whole,

---

JJS 2–5 (1950–54). See especially 'The Dead Sea Scrolls: Documents of the Jewish–Christian Sect of Ebionites', *JJS* 2 (1951), pp. 67-99; 'The Damascus Fragments and the Origin of the Jewish-Christian Sect', *JJS* 2 (1951), pp. 115-43; 'Jesus in the Habakkuk Scroll', *JJS* 3 (1952), pp. 53-56; 'The Teachings of the Pre-Pauline Church in the Dead Sea Scrolls', Part I, *JJS* 3 (1952), pp. 111-18, Part II, *JJS* 3 (1952), pp. 139-50; Part III, *JJS* 4 (1953), pp. 1-13; Part IV, *JJS* 4 (1953), pp. 49-58; Part V, *JJS* 4 (1953), pp. 93-103; Part VI, *JJS* 4 (1953), pp. 139-53; 'Jesus' Sayings in the Dead Sea Scrolls', *JJS* 5 (1954), p. 38.

1. See J. Bowman, *The Samaritan Problem: Studies in the Relationships of Samaritanism, Judaism and Early Christianity* (Pittsburgh: Pickwick Press, 1975).

2. C. Roth, *The Historical Background of the Dead Sea Scrolls* (Oxford: Basil Blackwell, 1958).

3. See R. de Vaux, *Archaeology and the Dead Sea Scrolls. The Schweich Lectures of the British Academy, 1959* (Oxford: Oxford University Press, 1973); R. de Vaux and J.T. Milik, *Qumrân Grotte 4, I. 1. Archéologie* (DJD, 6; Oxford: Clarendon Press, 1977), pp. 3-28.

4. See *inter alia*: S.A. Birnbaum, *The Hebrew Script. Part One. The Texts* (Leiden: Brill, 1971), and *The Hebrew Script. Part Two: The Plates* (London: Paleographia, 1957); N. Avigad, *The Paleography of the Dea Sea Scrolls and Related Documents* (ed. C. Rabin and Y. Yadin; *ScrHier*, 4; Jerusalem: Magnes Press, 1958), pp. 56-87; M. Martin, *The Scribal Character of the Dead Sea Scrolls* (Louvain: Publications Universitaires, 1958); F.M. Cross, 'The Development of the Jewish Scripts', in *The Bible and the Ancient Near East: Essays In Honor of W.F. Albright* (ed. G.E. Wright; New York: Doubleday, 1961), pp. 133-202; J.P. Siegel, 'The Scribes of Qumran. Studies in the Early History of Jewish Scribal Customs, with Special Reference to the Qumran Biblical Scrolls and to the Tannaitic Traditions of Massekhet Soferim' (PhD dissertation, Brandeis University, 1972).

5. See, e.g., O.R. Sellers, 'Radiocarbon Dating of Cloth from the 'Ain Feshkha Cave', *BASOR* 123 (1951), pp. 24-26.

6. The discovery at Masada of fragments of the *Širat 'Olat Haššabat,* the Ben Sira Scroll, and some additional fragments which are Qumran-related, provides the definite *ante quem* date of 73 CE for the Covenanters' community and their literature. See Y. Yadin, *The Ben Sira Scroll from Masada* (Jerusalem: Israel Exploration Society and Shrine of the Book, 1965), and 'Qumran and Masada', *BIES* 30 (1966), pp. 117-27, esp. 123-27 [Hebrew]. Further, C. Newsom and Y. Yadin, 'The Masada Fragment of the Qumran Songs of the Sabbath Sacrifice', *IEJ* 34 (1984), pp. 77-88; C. Newsom, *Songs of the Sabbath*

scholars remain entrenched in positions which they had originally taken up, steadfastly defending hypotheses worked out on the strength of the evidence available then, and passing them on to new generations of their disciples. We seem to have reached an impasse.

It is appropriate at this juncture that we are reminded of the enthusiastic reactions when news of the initial discovery of the Qumran scrolls came to the attention of scholars. Expectations soared. The manuscripts appeared to hold out great promise for opening up new possibilities of scholarly inquiry into the late Second Temple period before the emergence of Christianity. In the early 1950s, H.H. Rowley assured students of the Hebrew Bible troubled by a nagging doubt whether significant contributions could yet be made in that intensively ploughed-over field of research, that the new documents would provide at least two generations of scholars with interesting, problematic, and yet revealing materials into which they could sink their teeth.[1]

The veritable 'megillo(th)mania' which spread in the 1950s and 1960s seemed to prove that prognosis correct. The new art of 'scrolling' attracted many scholars who had previously been engaged in other areas of Ancient Near Eastern Studies.[2] The new pursuits caused an avalanche of scroll publications in the one and a half decades after the discovery of the Qumran caves. In the first volume of the comprehensive Qumran bibliography published in 1957, Christoph Burchard could already list approximately 1,500 entries.[3]

Sacrifice: A Critical Edition (HSS, 27; Atlanta, GA: Scholars Press, 1985); J. Strugnell, 'The Angelic Liturgy at Qumran: 4Q Serek Širot 'Olat Haššabat' (Oxford Congress Volume; VTSup, 7; Leiden: Brill, 1960), pp. 318-45.

1.   This may be an 'oral tradition'. I cannot trace this remark to a written source. A similar appreciation was expressed by A. Dupont-Sommer: 'It is clear the Qumran studies, affecting as they do all sorts of spheres—palaeographic, linguistic, literary, historical, theological—will continue to develop, and will require the cooperation of very many scholars for a long time to come, whether with regard to the biblical manuscripts or the non-biblical writings' (*The Essene Writings from Qumran* [trans. G. Vermes; Oxford: Blackwell, 1961]).

2.   In 1959 Mitchell Dahood voiced the complaint that the Qumran finds turned students away from the pursuit of Ugaritic studies, due to widespread feeling that 'the Ras Shamra tablets have contributed as much to biblical studies as they ever will' (M. Dahood, 'The Value of Ugaritic for Textual Criticism', *Bib* 40 [1959], pp. 160ff.).

3.   C. Burchard, *Bibliographie zu den Handschriften vom Toten Meer*

In the second volume, which brought the survey up to 1962, the number of entries grew to some 4,500.[1] No comprehensive inventory is available for the quarter-century after 1962.[2] While it cannot be established for certain whether the appearance of publications continued at the same pace, we may presume that it did not slow down perceptibly.

A possible explanation of this rapid development lies in the fact that, since the inception of critical Judaic research, scholars have never before had access to pristine copies of Hebrew writings which date from the otherwise undocumented latter half of the Second Temple period. All previously available information relative to those times gleaned from Hellenistic, Jewish, or Christian sources is retrospective. It derives from reports in which that period is viewed from the vantage point of later generations that were removed from it by several centuries. In contradistinction, the writings which emanate from the Qumran caves were evidently produced by Jewish authors who lived in the last centuries before and the first century after the turn of the era. These documents thus contain contemporaneous, firsthand evidence which relates directly to this crucial period. One could expect with much justification that they would enlighten us on that 'dark age' in the history of Judaism.

These great hopes did not materialize. The most painstaking analysis of the Qumran documents has not shed new light on historical events which affected Judaism as a whole in those times, nor on significant developments which then occurred in Jewish concepts and beliefs. Moreover there remains much uncertainty even in regard to

---

(Berlin: Töpelmann, 1957).

1.   C. Burchard, *Bibliographie zu den Handschriften vom Toten Meer*, II (Berlin: Töpelmann, 1965).

2.   See, *inter alia*: W. Lasor, *Bibliography of the Dead Sea Scrolls 1948–1957* (Pasadena, CA: Fuller Theological Seminary, 1958); M. Yizhar, *Bibliography of Hebrew Publications on the Dead Sea Scrolls 1948–1964* (Cambridge, MA: Harvard University Press, 1967); B. Jongeling, *A Classified Bibliography of the Finds in the Desert of Judah 1958–1969* (Leiden: Brill, 1971); J. Fitzmyer, *The Dead Sea Scrolls: Major Publications and Tools for Study* (Missoula, MT: Scholars Press, 1977); C. Koester, 'A Qumran Bibliography 1974–1984', *BTB* 15 (1985), pp. 110-20; E. Schürer, *The History of the Jewish People in the Age of Jesus Christ* III/1 (ed. G. Vermes, F. Millar, M. Goodman; Edinburgh: T. & T. Clark, 1986), pp. 380-469; further: the current bibliographical information given in *RevQ* and *Bib*.

matters which pertain specifically, in fact exclusively, to the Qumran Covenanters themselves: *inter alia*, the genesis, history, and societal structure of their community, their particular theology and ritual code.

In the present framework a full review of all the relevant issues cannot be offered. It must suffice to list only some important questions which remain under scrutiny and are debated with the same or similar pro and con arguments that were adduced when Qumran research was in its infancy.

We have as yet no universally accepted identification of the Covenanters' community. We cannot establish for certain the identity of the authors who presumably produced the substantial number of documents which exhibit a specifically Qumranite stance. Nor do we know any better the provenance of writings in the collection which were probably not produced locally by members of the New Covenant but had been brought to Qumran by new recruits who joined the *Yaḥad*.[1]

The proposed identification of the Covenanters with the Essenes is certainly more persuasive than all other suggestions and has accordingly attracted wide scholarly acclaim. But at the same time, it met from the outset with some opposition which may now draw strength from new sources.[2] The first halakhic document which issued from

---

1.   There are as yet no generally agreed-upon criteria for differentiating imported from locally produced manuscripts. There is much to be said for E. Tov's proposal to use objective linguistic and scribal criteria, such as defective vs. (excessive) plene spelling as a means for telling one group from the other. See E. Tov, 'The Orthography and Language of the Hebrew Scrolls found at Qumran and the Origin of These Scrolls', *Textus 13* (1986), pp. 31-57, and 'Hebrew Biblical Manuscripts from the Judean Desert: Their Contribution to Textual Criticism', *JSS* 38 (1988), pp. 5-37. The hypothesis that all scrolls were brought to Qumran from (the Temple archives in) Jerusalem is not convincing, since it disregards the obvious connection of the manuscripts with the Qumran caves and the nearby settlement. See, *inter alia*, K.H. Rengstorf, *Ḥirbet Qumran und die Bibliothek vom Toten Meer* (Studia Delitzschiana, 5; Stuttgart: Kohlhammer, 1960); E.Y. Kutscher, *The Language and Linguistic Background of the Isaiah Scroll (1QIsaᵃ)* (Leiden: Brill, 1974), pp. 89-95; N. Golb, 'The Problem of Origin and Identification of the Dead Sea Scrolls', *PAPS* 124 (1980), pp. 1-24.

2.   There is no need to give a list of the proponents of the Essene theory. The reader is referred to the surveys and bibliographies mentioned above, especially Jongeling's classified bibliography. The identification of the Covenanters with the

the fourth Qumran Cave, *mqṣt m'sy/dbry htwrh* (4QMMT), so far only known in general outline, presumably reflects legal and ritual peculiarities which rabbinic tradition associates with the Sadducees.[1] For this reason and because of some other particular traits which mark Qumran theology and religious practice (which had indeed been known for a long time but were not given the attention they deserve), the prevalent identification of the Qumran community with the Essenes must again be brought under review.

No manifest progress can be registered in the endeavour to establish conclusively the identity of the central protagonists in the contention between the Covenanters and their adversaries. The designations 'Teacher of Righteousness' and 'Evil Priest', by which they are known in the Qumran literature, have an enigmatic ring to them in the ears of the modern reader and cannot be related unequivocally to historical figures of whom the classical sources speak. The epithets *dwrš htwrh* and *mtyf hkzb* may equally pertain to these opposing leaders. Alternatively they may designate some other *dramatis personae* who at a later stage played an important role in the controversy between the *Yaḥad* and the main community.[2]

Essenes was rejected by several scholars. See, e.g., C. Roth, 'Why the Qumran Sect Cannot Have Been Essenes', *RevQ* 1 (1958–59), pp. 417-22, and 'Were the Qumran Sectaries Essenes? A Re-examination of Some Evidences', *JTS* ns 10 (1959), pp. 87-93. I have recurrently questioned the proposed identification. See 'The New Covenanters of Qumran', *Scientific American* 225.5 (1971), pp. 72-81; 'Qumran und das Alte Testament', *Frankfurter Universitätsreden* 42 (1971), pp. 71-83; 'The Calendar of the Covenanters of the Judean Desert', *ScrHier* 4 (1988), pp. 162-99; 'Waiting for the Messiah: the Conceptual Universe of the Qumran Covenanter', in *Judaism and their Messiahs at the Turn of the Christian Era* (ed. J. Neusner, W.S. Green and E.S. Frerichs; New York: Cambridge University Press, 1987), pp. 111-37 = *WQW*, pp. 147-85, 273-300.

1.   See the preliminary report by E. Qimron and J. Strugnell, 'An Unpublished Halakhic Letter from Qumran', in *Biblical Archaeology Today* (Jerusalem: Israel Exploration Society, Israel Academy of Arts and Sciences, and American Schools of Oriental Research, 1985), pp. 400-407.

2.   The question whether the titles *mwrh hṣdq* and *dwrš htwrh* designate the same or different personalities does not need to occupy us here. The same pertains to the titles *kwhn hrš'* and *mtyf hkzb*. The reader is referred to the publications listed by Jongeling,   to   which   should   be   added,   *inter   alia*, B. Thiering, *Redating the Teacher of Righteousness* (Sydney: Theological Explorations, 1979); J. Carmignac, 'Qui était le Docteur de Justice?', *RevQ* 38

The arguments adduced in favour of the thesis that the Covenanters entertained a vision of 'Twin Messiahs' who were expected to arise in an undetermined future have not materially changed since this issue came to the attention of scholars in the wake of the discovery of the *Zadokite Fragments* (CD) in the Cairo Genizah. The same holds true for the counter-arguments which the defenders of the 'One Messiah' thesis brought to bear upon the matter.[1]

Similarly, novel theories concerning the history of the text of the Hebrew Bible and its historical development, promulgated on the strength of the two Isaiah scrolls which issued from Cave 1 (1QIsa[a] and 1QIsa[b]), and some additional biblical manuscripts published in the first decade of Qumran research, are in the main still discussed on the same premises that initially formed the basis of the debate.[2]

Again, no discernible progress was made in gauging the process of the gradual emergence of the 'Hebrew Bible Canon' and its final closure. The questions pertaining to this matter remain unanswered. They result, *inter alia*, from the absence in the Qumran manuscript finds of even one fragment of the book of Esther or of one evident quotation from that book in the Covenanters' particular literature. The publication over the last quarter of a century of a large number of additional, partial copies and fragments of biblical books and of typical Qumranite works did not contribute new data which would induce scholars to change their earlier pronouncements on the issue of canon-formation.[3]

(1980), pp. 235-46; H. Burmann, 'Wer war der Lehrer der Gerechtigkeit?', *RevQ* 40 (1981), pp. 553-78; B.Z. Wacholder, *The Dawn of Qumran. The Sectarian Torah and the Teacher of Righteousness* (Cincinnati: Hebrew Union College, 1983).

1.   See Wacholder, *The Dawn*; Talmon, 'Waiting for the Messiah'.

2.   See the collection of pertinent studies in F.M. Cross and S. Talmon (eds.), *Qumran and the History of the Biblical Text* (Cambridge, MA: Harvard University Press, 1975) [hereinafter *QHBT*]; G. Vermes, *The Dead Sea Scrolls*; E. Tov, 'Hebrew Biblical Manuscripts', pp. 5-37, and 'A Modern Textual Outlook Based on the Qumran Scrolls', *HUCA* 53 (1982), pp. 11-27; E. Ulrich, 'Horizons of Old Testament Textual Research at the Thirtieth Anniversary of Qumran Cave 4', *CBQ* 46 (1984), pp. 613-36.

3.   See S. Talmon, 'Heiliges Schrifttum und kanonische Bücher aus jüdischer Sicht: Überlegungen zur Ausbildung der Grösse "Die Schrift" im Judentum', *Mitte der Schrift? Ein jüdisch-christliches Gespräch. Texte des Berner Symposions vom 6–12. Januar 1985* (Judaica et Christiana, 11; ed. M. Klopfenstein, U. Luz, S. Talmon, E. Tov; Berne: Peter Lang, 1987), pp. 45-79.

There is no need to proliferate examples to buttress the conclusion that the materials published since the mid-sixties have not introduced new arguments into the debates over questions raised in the past, nor have they perceptibly affected the insights gained in the preceding period.[1]

The Uniqueness of Qumran and its Documents

Before proceeding it should again be emphasized that the Qumran documents must be judged an unprecedented phenomenon in the study of ancient Jewish history and civilization. Viewed comprehensively, they provide the means for reconstituting to an impressive extent an exceedingly detailed and intricate self-portrait of a closely knit socio-religious entity in Second Temple Judaism such as cannot be gained from any other ancient sources. The emerging picture has, moreover, the quite special distinction of being contemporaneous with the events which it depicts. This literature provides information on a non-conformist movement which flourished in the Judaism of that period, and must be accorded more, and certainly not less, credibility than the retrospective reports found in Hellenistic, rabbinic, and Christian sources on other groups of dissenters. True, the Qumran evidence needs to be viewed with circumspection. It is most probably marred by distortions which can be expected to occur in such a literary self-portrait. But we should bear in mind that the classical sources are also tainted by their authors' prepossessed notions and are to a large measure founded on hearsay. Therefore they too must be taken *cum grano salis*.

Because of the characteristics of the Qumran literature, it is appropriate to study the scrolls first and foremost with the aim of extracting from them substantive and intimate information on the Covenanters' community and their *Eigenbegrifflichkeit*.[2] It is to be expected, however, that when all is said and done there will still remain unsolved and possibly unsolvable problems which result from the many veiled references and an often baffling terminology which abound in the Covenanters' writings. However, these enigmatic allusions should not

---

1.   See the surveys provided by Vermes, Sanders, Knibb and Wise (above).
2.   For this term and the underlying concept, see B. Landsberger, 'Die Eigenbegrifflichkeit der babylonischen Welt', *Islamica* 2 (1926), pp. 355-72.

be construed as evidencing the writers' calculated attempts at mystification. It stands to reason that in antiquity the seemingly elusive references were fully understood by the initiated. The Qumran authors did not compose their opuscules as missionary tracts intended for outsiders whom they wished to attract into their fold, as some scholars opine.[1] Their compositions addressed an informed audience and were expressly designed to transmit instructive and normative teachings which were to regulate the life of the individual member and the communal life of the *Yaḥad*.

These considerations prescribe the methodology which will govern the ensuing discussion: the *Yaḥad* literature will primarily be viewed and analysed as first-hand documents which give witness to the particular world of ideas and the history of an ancient, self-contained, *sui generis*, socioreligious entity. Once a comprehensive understanding of the Qumran commune has been achieved, as far as this is possible, the comparative approach can be attempted. A premature comparison and the hypothetical identification of the novel phenomenon with one or another schismatic group known from the classical sources, on the strength of discrete features which they appear to have in common, is bound to obfuscate the Covenanters' idiosyncratic religious and societal profile. In the comparison, attention should be given not solely to similarities which the *Yaḥad* shares with one or the other *Strömung* in Second Temple Judaism, but also to dissimilarities which set it apart from all other known contemporaneous socioreligious manifestations. Moreover, the emerging analogous and disparate features should not be assessed in isolation but rather should be accorded their specific weight in the holistic makeup of each of the groups under consideration. Only thus can we hope to gauge the specific historical, social, and credal characteristics of the *Yaḥad* and define its place in late Second Temple Judaism. The Qumran commune will probably emerge from this analysis as a unique socioreligious configuration of Judaism in the transition period from the biblical to the rabbinic era.

In the ensuing deliberations I seek to highlight the distinctive posture of the *Yaḥad*. I purport to show that the Qumran Covenanters

---

1.   See especially J. Murphy-O'Connor, 'An Essene Missionary Document? CD. II,14–VI,l', *RB* 77 (1970), pp. 201-29; P.R. Davies, *The Damascus Covenant* (JSOTSup, 25; Sheffield: JSOT Press, 1983).

were poised between an ideational attachment to the world of the Hebrew Bible and the emerging world of the Mishnah. They hovered between the historical reality of the Hellenistic Roman era and a utopian identification with the historical past of biblical Israel. This setting in an existential twilight zone appears to cause a good many of the immense difficulties which confront the modern interpreter of the Covenanters' literature and their spiritual universe.

The Qumran View of the End of the Biblical Age

The above depiction of the historical setting and the ideational character of the *Yaḥad* connects the issue under review with a well-known problem to which some thought must now be given. There is no universally or even widely accepted criterion by which one can securely define the termination of the biblical age. The total lack of reliable historical data defies any attempt to delimit the ending of that period in precise chronological terms. Therefore, in endeavouring to draw the demarcation line between the biblical and the post-biblical era, scholars tend to have recourse to a variety of somewhat intangible indicators.

There is a prevalent disposition to distinguish between a 'Biblical Israel' and an 'Early Judaism', and to conceive of the one as being entirely different from the other. This radical disjunction is determined by subjective predilections rather than by conclusions which result from an objective scholarly analysis. It is predominantly based on theological notions or credal preconceptions and not on chronological facts and historical considerations.[1]

One registers attempts to define the ending of the biblical era by equating that critical caesura in the history of ancient Israel with the effective closing of the Hebrew canon of Scripture.[2] However that literary-cultural phenomenon also cannot be dated unequivocally.[3]

---

1. An illustration of this approach may be found, *inter alia*, in M. Noth, *The History of Israel* (New York: Harper, 1960), p. 454. See R. Rendtorff's criticism of this modus operandi: 'Das Ende der Geschichte Israels', in *Gesammelte Studien zum Alten Testament* (München: Chr. Kaiser Verlag, 1975), pp. 267-76; further, S. Hermann, *A History of Israel in Old Testament Times* (Philadelphia: Fortress Press, 1975).

2. See Talmon, 'Heiliges Schrifttum'.

3. The discussion of this matter is surveyed, *inter alia*, in S.A. Leiman, *The*

Scholarly opinion remains divided in respect to the chronological determination of almost every phase in the progressive accumulation of the collection of books contained in the Hebrew canon. No reliable criteria are at hand for convincingly and accurately dating the inclusion of the Book of Esther, assumedly the last book that was accepted into the corpus of Holy Scriptures.[1] Likewise there is no *communis opinio* relative to the date and the circumstances pertaining to the closure of the third major constituent part of the Hebrew Bible (the 'Writings'), which would have been coterminous with the culmination of the cumulative process and the fixation of the comprehensive canon.

It appears that, already in antiquity, concrete and precise data pertinent to the issue were no longer available. A rabbinic dictum which connects the closure of the corpus of biblical writings with the demise of the last prophets (Haggai, Zechariah, and Malachi), when 'divine inspiration departed from Israel' (*t. Soṭ.* [ed. Zuckermandel] 318.21-23; *b. Soṭ.* 48b; *t. Sanh.* 11a; *t. Yom.* 9b), is altogether indeterminate. The same pertains to a later saying which probably evolved out of the former, in which the cessation of prophetic inspiration is dated to the time of Alexander the Macedonian[2] (cf. Josephus, *Apion* 1.40-41). It is more than doubtful that these pronouncements reflect reliable information of which the sages could avail themselves, but of which we have no knowledge. They seem, rather, to reveal the ancient tradents' ignorance of the precise circumstances which surrounded the definitive delimitation of the canon of Holy Scriptures. They also point up the ancients' ignorance of the exact conditions under which the new and distinct literary genres which mark the commencement of the rabbinic age emerged.[3]

Canonization of Hebrew Scripture: The Talmudic and Midrashic Evidence (Transactions of the Connecticut Academy of Arts and Sciences; Hamden, CT: Archon Books, 1976); B.S. Childs, *Introduction to the Old Testament as Scripture* (Philadelphia: Fortress Press, 1979), pp. 27-67; J.A. Sanders, *From the Sacred Story to Sacred Text. Canon as Paradigm* (Philadelphia: Fortress Press, 1987).

1. See S. Zeitlin, 'An Historical Study of the Canonization of the Hebrew Scriptures', *PAAJR* 3 (1931–32); repr. in S.Z. Leiman (ed.), *The Canon and Masorah of the Hebrew Bible* (New York: Ktav, 1974), pp. 164-99.

2. See B. Rabner (ed.), *Seder Olam Rabba* (Vilna, Romm, 1897), repr. with an introduction by S.K. Mirsky (Jerusalem: Rabbi Kook Foundation, 1966).

3. See below, pp. 231-41.

We should turn our attention to a prominent and telling character-istic which the ancient rabbinic sayings (concerning the closure of the Hebrew canon and the termination of the biblical era) seem to share with modern scholars' opinions in these matters. The dichotomy between the world of 'Biblical Israel' and the world of 'Early Judaism' is thrown into sharp relief as a result of focusing solely on the one central configuration of Second Temple Judaism that came into full view in the tannaitic period, the first and second centuries CE. From then on, it constitutes the mainstream community, which G.F. Moore has designated 'normative Judaism'.[1] Persuasive validity attaches to the claim that the roots of that core community of the tan-naitic age can be traced to the preceding centuries, back to the return from the exile in the sixth and fifth centuries BCE.[2] But this very plausible assumption cannot be substantiated by tangible contempora-neous evidence.

In this context the significance of the Qumran scrolls becomes apparent: they reflect a socioreligious entity in Second Temple Judaism which did not link up with either the 'normative' community that crystallized in the tannaitic era or with nascent Christianity. The cluster of dissidents who established the 'New Covenant' and consoli-dated the *Yaḥad* in the Judaean Desert remained outside the compass of rabbinic Judaism and Christianity, each of which perceived (through its own interpretation) biblical Israel as the source from which its particular societal-credal universe sprang.[3]

This conceptual implantation in the biblical world was also shared by the *Yaḥad*. However, as will yet be specified, the Covenanters' ideational integration into the framework of biblical Israel rests upon a rather singular interpretative notion that differs fundamentally from the perception of the biblical legacy by both Judaism and Christianity. A close reading of the Qumran documents reveals some hitherto unknown aspects of the spiritual make-up of Jewry before the turn of the era. These particular facets evince a possible unique existential

---

1.   G.F. Moore, *Judaism in the First Century of the Christian Era: The Age of the Tannaim,* I (Oxford: Clarendon Press, 1927), p. 3.
2.   See S. Talmon, 'The Emergence of Jewish Sectarianism in the Early Second Temple Period', in *King, Cult and Calender* (Jerusalem: Magnes Press, 1986) [hereinafter *KCC*], pp. 176-201.
3.   Talmon, 'Jewish Sectarianism', *KCC*, pp. 186-201.

understanding of the meaning and import of the biblical heritage which that group fostered and which has left no lasting imprint on the later Jewish and Christian evaluation and formative exegesis of the Hebrew Bible. Notwithstanding the ephemeral nature of their community, the Covenanters' idiosyncratic attachment to the biblical world throws further light on the internal multiformity within Jewry at the height of the Second Temple period.[1]

At this juncture we need to remember that a substantial number of the Covenanters' writings stem from the second or possibly even from the third century BCE. This means that they were written when biblical literary creativity was still ongoing. Now it is a *communis opinio* that the book of Daniel, or at least its second part, was probably composed somewhat later in the Hellenistic period.[2] Many scholars concur that the book of Esther was also written at that time.[3] Some maintain that it was integrated into the Hebrew canon only in the second century CE.[4] (While various aspects of these conjectures remain under debate, the comparative lateness of those books is a matter of scholarly consensus.) Accordingly it may be considered certain that various Qumran works originated concurrently with the latest books contained in the Hebrew canon, and that the historical reality of the *Yaḥad* coincided with the last stage of the waning biblical age.

1.   Talmon, 'Jewish Sectarianism', *KCC*, pp. 176-97.

2.   See R.D. Wilson, 'The Book of Daniel and the Canon', *Princeton Theological Review* 13 (1915), pp. 352-408. A concise presentation of the arguments is given by Childs, *Introduction*, pp. 608-23; further, S. Talmon, 'Daniel', in *The Literary Guide to the Bible* (ed. R. Alter and F. Kermode; Cambridge, MA: Harvard University Press, 1987), pp. 343-56. The discovery at Qumran of fragments of several Daniel manuscripts has added a new dimension to the discussion. See E. Ulrich, 'Daniel Manuscripts from Qumran, Part I: A Preliminary Edition of 4QDan^a', *BASOR* 268 (1987), p. 17; 'It [4QDan^a] is closer to the time of the original composition than any other extant manuscript of a book of the Hebrew Bible. The early semicursive script of 4QDan^a is to be dated in the "late second century" BC "no more than about half a century younger than the autograph", c. 168–165, of that book' (quoted from Cross, *The Library*, p. 43).

3.   A summary of the arguments may be found, *inter alia*, in S. Talmon, 'Wisdom in the Book of Esther', *VT* 13 (1963), pp. 419-22; Childs, *Introduction*; H. Bardtke, 'Neuere Arbeiten zum Estherbuch. Eine kritische Würdigung', *Ex Oriente Lux* 19 (1965–66), pp. 519-49.

4.   See Zeitlin, *PAAJ* 3 (1931–32), pp. 12-14.

This partial chronological overlap with the end phase of the biblical era also applies to the mainstream Jewish community of the last two centuries BCE, the days of the *zugoth*, the pairs of contending sages, the founding fathers of rabbinic Judaism. However, the partial concurrence of their existential situation with the biblical world generated in the Qumran *Yaḥad* and in the community of the Sages intrinsically different responses. (Proto)-rabbinic Jewry viewed the biblical era as a closed chapter and their own times as being profoundly different from that preceding age. In contradistinction, the Covenanters perceived themselves as standing within the orbit of the biblical era, and their community as the rejuvenated embodiment of biblical Israel. They were the 'righteous remnant' whom God had spared when he delivered Judah and Jerusalem to the sword of the Babylonians; they were divinely appointed to reconstitute Israel of old in the present (CD 1.1-8), and to write the next chapter in the yet ongoing history of the biblical people.

The Yaḥad *and Rabbinic Judaism*

The fundamental divergence of the stance of the *Yaḥad* from that of rabbinic Judaism surfaces in various facets of the two communities' public life and spiritual universe. Some of these will now be brought under consideration.

Torah shebiktab *and* Torah shebe'al peh

From the early days of the mishnaic or protomishnaic period, the sages accorded a special status of sanctity to the biblical books. They were *in toto* designated *Torah shebiktab* and were considered to have been authored under divine inspiration. The corpus of 'Holy Writings' was distinguished from all other compositions then known. These also included the teachings of the sages, which were subsumed under the comprehensive appellation *Torah shebe'al peh*. The Hebrew expressions and their prevalent English translations, 'Written Law' and 'Oral Law', convey the notion that the distinction between the two corpora of traditions is rooted in a purely technical circumstance: one could and should be handed down in writing; the other should exclusively be transmitted orally (*j. Meg.* 4.1, 74d; cf. *b. Git.* 66b; *Tem.* 14).[1]

---

1. See S. Lieberman, *Hellenism in Jewish Palestine* (New York: Jewish

This understanding of the collocations is based on fully justified etymological considerations. The implied technical particularity of transmission may indeed initially have set apart one category of literary works from the other. But in a subsequent stage of development, the *Torah shebe'al peh* was also committed to writing. Therefore its presumed differentiation from the *Torah shebiktab* by the merely technical criterion of 'oral' versus 'written' fails to do justice to the intrinsic significance of these collocations. They should be understood, rather, as ciphers for 'biblical', viz. 'holy' books conceived under divine inspiration, and 'extra-biblical' books which are not thus distinguished, irrespective of their being transmitted orally or in manuscript form.

Rabbinic tradition considered the category of biblical books to be totally different in tenor from the works of the sages. They were distinguished from each other by the distinct 'language' in which they are severally clothed: 'the language of Torah (i.e. the books of the Bible) is one matter; the language of the (teachings of the) sages is another matter' (*b. 'Abod. Zar.* 58b; *Men.* 65a). In this context the term 'language' should not be taken to connote only the linguistic medium in which one or the other complex of writings was cast. Its meaning also extends to the terminology in which they were couched, to style and conceptual content.[1] In short, the above pronouncement declares the biblical literature in its totality to be essentially different from the rabbinic writings.[2]

The traditions which evince this distinction are mostly attributed to talmudic teachers of later generations, viz. to *amora'im*. It follows that in their present wording they stem from the third to the fifth century CE. But it may confidently be assumed that they reflect a situation

Theological Seminary, 1962), p. 87.

1.   For the style and formulation of mishnaic legal literature see J. Neusner, 'The Meaning of Oral Torah', in *Early Rabbinic Judaism* (Leiden: Brill, 1975), pp. 1-33; and 'Accomodating Mishnah to Scripture in Judaism: The Uneasy Union and its Offspring', *Michigan Quarterly Review* 22 (1983), pp. 465-79.

2.   See E. Rivkin, *A Hidden Revolution: The Pharisaic Search for the Kingdom Within* (Nashville: Abingdon Press, 1978), pp. 223-27. This distinction may explain the striking circumstance noted by W.D. Davies 'that the Oral Law of Judaism often bears little relation to the Written Torah'; see 'Reflections about the Use of the Old Testament in the New in its Historical Setting', *JQR* 74 (1983), p. 132.

which obtained from the days of the very first *tanna'im* or from even earlier times.

Various categories of literary compositions were excluded from the corpus of 'Holy Writings'. Some were of a patently secular nature, like the *Sifrei Hamiran*, possibly a mispronunciation of *homeros* (*m. Yad.* 4.6), which were current either in an original Greek version or else in Hebrew translation. Others, especially the Proverbs of Ben Sira, admittedly contained significant teachings. But they were nevertheless relegated to the extracanonical status of *hisonim*,[1] since they did not meet with the above-mentioned qualitative and temporal requirements (*m. Sanh.* 10.1), viz. they were not conceived under divine inspiration and were known to have been authored after *mikan wa'elek*. Standardized prayer texts and compilations of prayers[2] were similarly precluded from inclusion in the Book of Psalms and thereby from becoming an integral part of the biblical canon.

The canonical books *in toto* come under the headings *Migra, Kitbe Hagodesh, Torah*, and so on.[3] They are further defined by the phrase *metam'im et hayadayim*, which sets them apart from all other books. The exact signification of this designation too cannot be unequivocally established. Its meaning may, in fact, have already escaped the knowledge of the rabbinic tradents who offer seemingly far-fetched suggestions for its explanation.[4] The prevalent English rendition, '(books which) defile the hands', is etymologically correct. But it does not convey the intrinsic technical sense of the Hebrew term. There is no reference to an actual ritual 'defilement' incurred by the handling of these so-designated books. Nor is there any mention of an ensuing purification rite required after contact with the 'defiling' objects. These circumstances prompt the conclusion that the characterization

---

1. The Hebrew expression *hisonim* is echoed in the Aramaic term *baraita*, which defines an extra-compendium mishnah.

2. On the exclusion of prayers from the 'Holy Writings', see S. Talmon, 'The Emergence of Institutionalized Prayer in Israel in the Light of Qumran Literature', in *Qumran, sa piété, sa théologie et son milieu* (ed. M. Delcor; BETL, 46; Paris/Leuven: Duculot/ Leuven University Press, 1978), pp. 265-84 = *WQW*, pp. 200-43.

3. For the use of these terms in rabbinic literature, see Leiman, *Canonization*, pp. 56-72.

4. The putative rabbinic explanations of this term are surveyed in Leiman, *Canonization*, pp. 102-20.

of the biblical books as 'defiling the hands' does not show that they actually impart 'impurity'. Quite the contrary. The expression defines and highlights their unique sacred and authoritative status, in which no extra-canonical book has a part. This term too must be understood as a cipher which had a specific and restricted applicability. It pertains positively to acclaimed biblical books only. In the negative sense it applies exclusively to writings which appear to have stood a chance of infiltrating the canon and therefore needed expressly to be precluded from entering it. In neither of these connotations was the phrase ever used in reference to a work for which no one claimed a 'biblical' status, nor to rabbinic compositions of the *Torah shebe'al peh* category. While these works were held in highest esteem, they were extra-biblical by definition.

In sum, the above technical terms and others not mentioned, which in rabbinic literature pertain exclusively to canonical books and segregate them from all non-biblical writings, reveal the sages' perception of the Hebrew canon as a closed corpus to which nothing can be added and from which nothing can be subtracted.

The Qumran Covenanters' outlook was entirely different. There is no explicit or implicit statement in their literature which could give pause to think that they subscribed to a similarly clear-cut distinction between books which 'defile' and others which 'do not defile the hands'. Likewise, nothing indicates that they discriminated between books of the category *Torah shebiktab* and others which were subsumed under the category *Torah shebe'al peh* irrespective of whether these terms are understood as distinctive designations of canonical *vis-à-vis* extracanonical works as proposed above, or whether, in accord with the prevalent opinion, they distinguish between books which should be transmitted in writing and others which should be orally tradited. The total absence of relevant pronouncements suggests that the Covenanters did not subscribe to such a categorization of the literary works which they preserved.

This conclusion is borne out by the large number of distinctive *Yahad* opuscules which issued from the Qumran caves. These finds prove beyond doubt that the prolific *Yaḥad* scribes committed to writing a considerable amount of various, partly–legal, materials of a type which the sages would have deemed to belong to the category *Torah shebe'al peh*.

I mention here only some instructive examples. From Cave 1 came the *Serek Hayyaḥad* (1QS), a compilation of legislation peculiar to Qumran. Extrapolations of biblical laws and additional injunctions are also contained in the Zadokite Documents (CD 9.1-12.22). This work is known *in extenso* from mediaeval manuscripts which stem from the Cairo *Genizah*.[1] But its *Yaḥad* origin is proven beyond doubt by manuscript fragments of the work which were found at Qumran.[2] Further statutes surface in the War Scroll (1QM) and in the *Temple Scroll* (11QTemple). Special weight must be accorded in this context to the treatise *mgṣt m'sy/dbry htwrh* (4QMMT), only partially preserved and not yet published, which lists a series of halakhic rulings in which the Covenanters differed from their opponents.[3] The tractate is extant in fragments which hail from six different copies, evidence to the exceeding importance which the Covenanters attached to it.

These distinctive extrabiblical law compilations, which differ from each other in their stylistic formulations, were handed down at Qumran in manuscript form, viz. as *Torah shebiktab*. They were invested with a binding force that was evidently on a par with the normative nature of the legal decrees and dispensations which in the contemporaneous rabbinic community of that time were transmitted exclusively as *Torah shebe'al peh*. The transmission in writing of such extrabiblical legislation at Qumran sustains the conclusion that the Convenanters, unlike mainstream Judaism, did not distinguish between a 'Written Law' and an 'Oral Law'.

The Withdrawal of Divine Inspiration

It can equally be shown that the *Yaḥad* did not embrace the rabbinic distinction between the books contained in the biblical canon which were believed to have been authored under divine inspiration in the

1. S. Schechter, *Fragments of a Zadokite Work in Documents of Jewish Sectaries*, I (Cambridge: Cambridge University Press, 1910).

2. M. Baillet published the fragments from Cave 6 in *Les 'Petites Grottes' de Qumrân* (DJD, III; Oxford: Clarendon Press, 1962), pp. 128-31; J.T. Milik published a fragment from Cave 5 (*DJD*, III, p. 181), and another fragment from Cave 4, 'Fragment d'une source de psautier (4QPs 89) et fragments des Jubilés, du Document de Damas, d'un phylactère dans la grotte 4 de Qumran', *RB* 73 (1966), p. 105.

3. See the preliminary report by Qimron and Strugnell (above). For a discussion of the specific Qumran *halakhah* see, *inter alia*, L.H. Schiffman, *The Halakhah at Qumran* (Leiden: Brill, 1975); J. Baumgarten, *Studies in Qumran Law* (Studies in Judaism in Late Antiquity, 24; ed. J. Neusner; Leiden: Brill, 1977).

era that preceded the caesura termed *mika'n wa'elek*, and all other works known to have been composed after that indefinable date when divine inspiration (viz. the prophetic spirit) had withdrawn from Israel.

Nothing indicates that the Covenanters subscribed to the notion that prophecy was phased out after the demise of the last biblical prophets. Quite the contrary. The prophetic spirit was still seen to be implanted in some of their leaders, even though the inspiration of the Teacher of Righteousness[1] and possibly the author of the *Hodayot* (1QH) was expressed in forms which differed from the hypostatizations of prophecy in the biblical age.

The Covenanters preserved in writing commentaries on books of the biblical prophets, such as the *Pesher Habakkuk* (1QpHab) or *Nahum* (4QpNah); midrashic extrapolations of biblical books such as the *Genesis Apocryphon* (1QapGen);[2] translations of biblical books into Greek[3] or Aramaic;[4] sundry prayer collections;[5] and also several extracanonical works which in rabbinic parlance would come under

---

1.   See G. Jeremias, *Der Lehrer der Gerechtigkeit* (Göttingen: Vandenhoeck & Ruprecht, 1963).

2.   A.N. Avigad and Y. Yadin, *A Genesis Apocryphon* (Jerusalem: Magnes and Shrine of the Book, 1956).

3.   Only a few fragments of a Greek translation of the Bible were preserved at Qumran: pap7QLXXExod, 4QLXXLev[a], pap4QLXXLev[b], 4QLXXNum, 4QLXXDeut. See P.W. Skehan, *The Qumran Manuscripts and Textual Criticism* (VTSup, 4; Leiden: Brill, 1957), pp. 155-59; and '4QLXXNum; A Pre-Christian Reworking of the Septuagint', *HTR* 70 (1977), pp. 39-50; E. Ulrich, 'The Greek Manuscripts of the Pentateuch from Qumran, Including Newly Identified Manuscripts of Deuteronomy (4QLXXDeut)', in *De Septuaginta. Studies in Honor of J.W. Wevers on his Sixty-Fifth Birthday* (ed. A. Pietersma and C. Cox; Missiauga, Ont.: BenBen, 1984); C.H. Roberts, 'On Some Presumed Papyrus Fragments of the NT from Qumran', *JTS* ns 23 (1972), pp. 321-25; A.C. Urban, 'Observaciones sobre ciertos papiro de la cueva 7 de Qumran', *RB* 8 (1973), pp. 16-19; A.R.C. Leaney, 'Greek Manuscripts from the Judean Desert', in *Studies in New Testament Language and Text* (ed. J.K. Elliott; Leiden: Brill, 1976), pp. 283-300. The authors of these essays refute J. O'Callaghan's reading of these fragments as NT texts (*Los papieros griegos de la cueva 7 de Qumran* [BAC, 353; Madrid, 1974]); see also Tov, 'Hebrew Biblical Manuscripts', pp. 18-19; and, D. Barthélemy, *Les devanciers d'Aquila* (VTSup, 10; Leiden: Brill, 1963).

4.   Van der Woude and van der Ploeg, *Le Targum*.

5.   See Talmon, 'Institutionalized Prayer'.

the heading *hiẓonim*,[1] such as *Jubilees*,[2] Ben Sira,[3] *Enoch*,[4] and the *Testaments of the Twelve Patriarchs*.[5]

The *Yaḥad* members considered many, if not all, of these works to have been authored under divine inspiration, and invested them with the sanctity which attaches to the biblical books. *Jubilees* is expressly cited in the *Zadokite Documents* (CD 16.3-4) as the book in which 'the divisions of times according to jubilees and sabbath years' are authoritatively explicated. That opus is thus presented as the source which proves the exclusive legitimacy of the Covenanters' particular calendar reckoning. This issue was an important factor of contention with the main community and eventually led to their dissent from it.[6]

In addition, the Covenanters ostensibly attached inspired sanctity to some works of a legal nature which are in no way Bible-connected and were authored by their own members. They considered these books pillars of the Renewed Covenant that God had established with them, and held them in highest esteem. It suffices to refer, *inter alia*, to the *Manual of Discipline* (1QS) and the related *Serek Ha'edah* (1QSᵃ), the *Temple Scroll* (11QTemple), the *Zadokite Documents* (CD), and the yet unidentified *sfr hhgw/y* which is mentioned there

1.   Manuscript fragments of a variety of such 'extraneous' books issued from the 'smaller' Qumran Caves (2–10). See Baillet, *Les 'Petites Grottes' de Qumrân* (DJD, 3; Oxford: Clarendon Press, 1962).

2.   2Q19 and 2Q20. Baillet, Milik, and de Vaux, *Les 'Petites Grottes'*, pp. 77-79; further M. Kister, 'Newly-Identified Fragments of the Book of Jubilees: Jub. 23.23-23, 30.31', *RevQ* 48 (1987), pp. 529-36; J. VanderKam, *Textual and Historical Studies in the Book of Jubilees* (HSM, 14; Missoula, MT: Scholars Press, 1977); A.S. van der Woude, 'Fragmente des Buches Jubiläen/aus Höhle XI (1QJub)', in *Tradition und Glaube. Das frühe Christentum in seiner Umwelt* (ed. G. Jeremias, H.W. Kuhn, H. Stegemann; Göttingen: Vandenhoeck & Ruprecht, 1971), pp. 140-46.

3.   Y. Yadin, *The Ben Sira Scroll from Masada* (Jerusalem: Israel Exploration Society and Shrine of the Book, 1965).

4.   J.T. Milik, *The Books of Enoch, Aramaic Fragments of Qumran Cave 4* (Oxford: Clarendon Press, 1964).

5.   J.T. Milik, 'Le Testament de Lévi en araméen. Fragment de la grotte 4 de Qumran', *RB* 62 (1958), pp. 498-506; for the *Testament of Judah* (4Q484TJud), see Baillet, *Qumrân Grotte 4* (DJD, 7; Oxford: Clarendon Press); J.T. Milik, 'Ecrits préesseniens de Qumran', in *Qumrân, sa piété, sa théologie et son milieu*, pp. 91-106.

6.   See Talmon, 'The Calendar of the Covenanters'.

together with the titles of several other works (CD 10.6).

The continuance of inspired literary activity in the biblical mode supports the proposition that the Qumran Covenanters did not see the biblical period as a closed chapter in the history of Israel. Far from it; in their *Eigenverständnis* they viewed their community as a new link in the reconstituted generation-chain of biblical Israel (CD 1.1-10).

The Living Bible

Many *Yaḥad* compositions are manifestly couched in an archaizing style and wording which reveal their authors as epigones who intentionally infused biblical linguistic coinage into their vernacular mishnaic Hebrew. However, other Qumran works, which by theme and content are more closely related to canonical writings, display linguistic, terminological, and stylistic characteristics reminiscent of distinctive features which are intrinsic to the language, style, and spirit of the biblical literature. Against the background of these compositions, we can better appreciate the ongoing literary creativity at Qumran in diverse genres, and their distinctive essence which marks the books of the Hebrew Canon.

The following examples will illustrate the persistence of biblical literary styles at Qumran:

1. Several noncanonical songs which are interspersed among 'canonical' psalms in the Psalms Scroll of Cave 11 (11QPs[a]) give evidence to the preservation at Qumran of extrabiblical psalmodic creations which for one reason or another were not included in the canonical book of Psalms. We find in that scroll a variant version of Sir. 51.13-30 (11QPs[a] 21.11-17; 22.1) and three Hebrew songs (cols. 18–19). The latter are extant in a Syriac translation which the eleventh-century Nestorian patriarch Elias of Anbar had included in his homiletical opus *Kitab 'al 'Anwa'r* (together with two others which are not attested at Qumran). The Covenanters invested these songs and similar, hitherto unknown, psalm-like compositions preserved in 11QPs[a] and other cave manuscripts,[1] with the same aura of sanctity which they attached to the canonical psalms.

We cannot say for certain whether those supernumerary psalms

---

1.   See E.M. Schuller, *Non-Canonical Psalms from Qumran: A Pseudepigraphic Collection* (HSS, 28; Atlanta, GA: Scholars Press, 1986) and bibliography cited there.

originated *in toto* or in part at Qumran, or whether they were brought there by recruits who joined the *Yaḥad*. It is safe, however, to conclude that the art of biblical psalmody was still practised in the Covenanters' community and in all likelihood also in other contemporary sectors of Second Temple Judaism.

2. The self-identification of the *Yaḥad* with biblical Israel shows in the liberty which Qumran men of letters took in rearranging tradited biblical psalmodic materials and changing their textual formulations. A case in point is the sequence of the 'canonical' psalms in 11QPs[a],[1] which diverges from the order in the MT, and the internal restructuring of several 'canonical' psalms with the obvious aim of casting them in the form of the *responsorium*. This mode of recitation is pre-eminently suited to their use in prayer worship. Moreover, going beyond the liberal restructuring of biblical psalms, they extracted constitutive parts from diverse songs and rearranged and combined them into new compositions which are moulded after the typical patterns of biblical psalmody or else resemble them closely.

These features presumably evidence the use of the Psalms Scroll as a breviary[2] in the prayer service which the Covenanters instituted as replacement for the sacrificial service in the Jerusalem Temple from which they had withdrawn.[3] 11QPs[a] shares the postulated breviary character with the prayer manuals that in mainstream Judaism became current in post-biblical times. It is therefore of importance to point out a prominent difference between the two sets of liturgical traditions. The authors, redactors, and arrangers of the later normative Jewish synagogal compendia never had recourse to such a liberal

---

1. The editor of 1QPs[a] defined the MS as a copy of the biblical book of Psalms. See J.A. Sanders, *The Psalms Scroll of Qumran Cave 11 (11QPs[a])* (DJD, 4; Oxford: Clarendon Press, 1956), and 'Cave 11 Surprises and the Question of Canon', in *New Directions in Biblical Archaeology* (ed. D.N. Freedman and J. Greenfield; Garden City, NY: Doubleday, 1971), pp. 113-30, and 'The Qumran Psalms Scroll (11QPs[a]) Reviewed', in *On Language, Culture, and Religion. In Honor of E.A. Nida* (ed. M. Black and B. Smalley; The Hague: Mouton, 1974), pp. 19-99.

2. The presentation of 11QPs[a] as a biblical MS has been questioned by scholars who would rather view it as an early liturgical composition. See M. Goshen-Gottstein, 'The Psalms Scroll (11QPs[a]). A Problem of Canon and Text', *Textus* 5 (1960–66), pp. 22-33; S. Talmon, 'Extra-Canonical Hebrew Psalms from Qumran: Psalm 151', *WQW*, pp. 244-72.

3. See Talmon, 'Institutionalized Prayer'.

revamping of canonical psalms. When incorporating passages from Psalms and other biblical books in their compilations, the sages and later rabbinic authorities took pains to preserve the borrowed materials in their transmitted forms and textual formulations. The firm adherence to the hallowed tradition clearly indicates that in this matter rabbinic authors and authorities assumed a consciously *post-biblical* stance.

The Qumran authors' attitude is the exact opposite. They freely adapted canonical texts to the particular requirements of their community and their time. Their procedures reflect that pronounced *inner-biblical* attitude towards the texts which has already been pointed out and which is akin to the posture maintained by the biblical psalmists.

Psalm 108 is an instructive example of this liberal, structurational technique which biblical poets were wont to use. Several originally independent elements (e.g. Ps. 57.8-12 and 60.7-14) were combined in this song to form a new comprehensive unit.

Another illustration is provided by the textual and structural divergencies between two versions of one and the same psalm which are extant in different books of the Hebrew Bible or even in the Book of Psalms itself. For example, there are two versions extant of David's *Mizmor*, one found in 2 Samuel 22, the other in Psalm 18. Similarly the opening passage common to Psalms 31 and 71 is preserved there in variant formulations.

Quotations and paraphrases drawn from one or several biblical books will result in the constitution of a new song, as is the case with Psalm 86 or with Jonah's psalm (Jon. 2.3-10). One can further compare the liberal use of excerpts from Psalm 107 (vv. 40-42) in Job 5.16; 12.21, 24; 22.19.[1]

Even more persuasive is the comparison of the Covenanters' approach with the compositional methods to which the Chronicler had recourse when he inserted in his work a hymn (1 Chron. 16.8-36) which is constituted of several pieces drawn from a variety of canonical psalms (105.1-15; 96.1-13; and 106.1-2, 47-48).

The author or compiler of 11QPs[a] (or possibly one of his predecessors) seems to have pursued this course when he set about the

---

1. The borrowing may have been in the reverse, but this would not affect our argument.

rewording and restructuring of some canonical psalms which he adopted into his compilation. Other Qumran literati proceeded along similar lines.

3. A Qumran biblical manuscript will at times exhibit a variant text that diverges from the MT in the same characteristic details and overall manner in which differ the MT readings of a pericope which is preserved in parallel versions in two canonical books, and occasionally in one and the same book. The phenomenon can be illustrated by making reference to a few of these well-known textual doublets or triplets.

The concise note about the capture of Samaria by Sennacherib's forces is recorded in 2 Kgs 17.5-6; 18.9-12 in two significantly different readings, one possibly preserving an Ephraimite, the other a Judaean tradition.[1]

Again, the much more extended report on the siege which Sennacherib's army laid on Jerusalem is extant in 2 Kgs 18.13–19.36 in a reading which diverges textually and structurally from the parallel in Isa. 36.1–37.38. A third, evidently compressed, version turns up in 2 Chron. 32.1-22.

Similarly the conquest of Judah and the destruction of Jerusalem by Nebuchadnezzar's troops are reported in 2 Kgs 25.1-21 in a wording and composition which differ substantially from the parallel found in Jer. 52.1-27. Another version of this account in the book of Jeremiah (39.1-10) exhibits a text and literary structure that do not tally with either of the aforementioned sources.[2]

It stands to reason that a great number or possibly most of these variant formulations resulted from a variety of secondary phenomena which affected one pristine *Vorlage* in the process of transmission, whether involving scribal lapses or premeditated linguistic and theological/ideational changes.[3] But there is room for another explan-

---

1. See S. Talmon, 'Polemics and Apology in Biblical Historiography: 2 Kings 17.24-41', in *The Creation of Sacred Literature: Composition and Redaction of the Biblical Text* (ed. R.B. Friedman; Los Angeles: UCLA, 1981), pp. 57-68.

2. We should also mention the preservation of two divergent wordings of a pericope as pivotal as the Ten Commandments (Exodus 20 and Deuteronomy 5). Their ascription to two different 'sources' is of no concern in the present context.

3. The assumption underlies, e.g., the attempt to reconstruct an original common *Vorlage* for the two extant versions of David's psalm: F.M. Cross and D.N. Freedman, '2 Sam. 22 = Ps. 18', *JBL* 72 (1953), pp. 15-34.

ation of the emergence of such variations in the biblical text tradition, both in the original Hebrew and in the ancient versions. I have suggested that some such variants persisted from a precanonical stage in which traditions could still be transmitted legitimately in somewhat differing formulations which did not affect the intrinsic content of the text. Such diverging readings should be judged 'original'.[1]

This understanding of the data differs from a prevalent appreciation of the facts, as E.A. Speiser has succinctly argued: 'The canonical tradition...much older than the pentateuchal writers, older indeed than the time of Moses', conferred a binding sanctity upon the narratives, and no biblical writer 'would have felt free to recast them in terms of his own time and environment'.[2] The very opposite appears to be the case. Compilers, redactors, and even copyists of the biblical age acted in varying degrees as the authors' minor partners in the creative literary process, occasionally injecting their personalities into the materials which they transmitted.[3] Whenever they deemed that textual adjustments were called for, they would not abstain from adapting formulations which they found in their *Vorlagen* to their own preferences and predilections. At times they would go beyond what appears to have been tacitly accepted as a 'legitimate latitude of variation' in respect to wording, style, and structure.[4]

The Persistence of Biblical Literary Genres at Qumran

The variance in attitude toward the biblical world that, as proposed, distinguished the *Yaḥad* from rabbinic Judaism and at the same time

---

1.　See S. Talmon, 'Double Readings in the Massoretic Text', *Textus* 1 (1960), pp. 144-84; 'Synonymous Readings in the Textual Tradition of the Old Testament', *ScrHier* 8 (1961), pp. 335-85; and 'The Old Testament Text', in *Cambridge History of the Bible. I. From the Beginnings to Jerome* (ed. P.R. Ackroyd and C.F. Evans; Cambridge: Cambridge University Press, 1970), pp. 159-99 = *QHBT*, pp. 321-400.

2.　See E.A. Speiser, 'The Biblical Idea of History', *IEJ* 7 (1956), pp. 201-16, esp. 206-209 = *Oriental and Biblical Studies* (Philadelphia: University of Pennsylvania, 1967), pp. 187-200.

3.　See S. Talmon, 'The Textual Study of the Bible: A New Outlook', *QHBT*, pp. 321-400.

4.　We cannot accurately define the extent to which such variation was considered legitimate. For some of the relevant phenomena which seem to be involved, see Talmon, 'Textual Study'.

evidences the Covenanters' 'biblical stance', is not exhausted by a review of the divergent procedures in the handling of the hallowed biblical texts and traditions and the continuance of biblical linguistic and stylistic conventions which obtained at Qumran. It also shows in the persistence of biblical literary genres which evidently relapsed in the rabbinic literary tradition.

Qumran Law Literature

The formulations of Qumran enactments bear a close resemblance to the characteristic style and structure which mark the Pentateuchal legal compilations. The similarity shows both in the extrapolation and amplification of biblical laws and in the wordings of new ordinances which pertain in particular to the *Yaḥad* membership. The following examples may serve as illustrations of this phenomenon.[1] The supplementary Sabbath prescriptions listed in the *Zadokite Documents* are introduced severally by the biblical conclusive *'l* formula, *'l (y's, ythlk, yš'b)*, which parallels the biblical apodictic *'al/lo'* model. Both preclude the voicing of any objections or dissenting opinions (CD 10.2-12.16; cf. Exod. 3.5; 12.9; 16.29; 19.15; Lev. 10.6, 9; 25.14; etc.). At times that same formula precedes intrinsically Qumranite purity injunctions (e.g. CD 10.10-14; 10.21, 12.2, 12-15) and other precepts which are derived from and enlarge upon biblical legislation.

Qumran legislation is sometimes couched in wordings which resemble the biblical casuistic mode,[2] e.g. *kl ('yš) 'šr* (CD 12.2) or *wkl 'šr* (CD 12.4), etc. (cf. Lev. 20.9-21; etc.).

Practically all formulae which Qumran authors apply in the expansion and amplification of biblical laws are also applied in the distinctive *Yaḥad* legislation; one may cite phrases such as *kl 'dm* or *kl' 'yš* followed by a verb (CD 9.1, 2), which turn up in a roster of precepts regulating the life of the community. The violation of these statutes engendered harsh punishment (CD 9.1-10.10).

The roster of purity laws in the halakhic compilation *miqṣat*

---

1. The issue can only be touched upon here. The required detailed analysis must be undertaken in a separate framework.

2. These terms were introduced into the discussion by A. Alt, *Die Ursprünge des israelitischen Rechts* (Leipzig: Hirzel, 1934) and have recently come under criticism from various quarters. See the review of the discussion *apud* Childs, *Introduction*, part 2; and R. Rendtorff, *Das Alte Testament. Eine Einführung* (Neukirchen–Vluyn: Neukirchener Verlag, 1983).

ma'asei/dibrei hatorah (4QMMT) is arranged in units of itemized related phenomena, each introduced by the protasis *'l*. The same superscription is found in the *Zadokite Documents: 'l hthr bmym* (CD 10.10); *'l hšbt* (CD 10.14). A similar purpose in the organization of legal materials is served by the standard phrase *zh hsrk* (CD 10.4; 12.19, 22; 13.7; 1QS *passim*), and equally by the typical biblical collocation *w'lh hḥ(w)qym* (CD 12.21). This latter structurational model may be compared with the formula *zo't hatorah* or *zo't torat*, which in biblical law texts precedes and/or summarizes the enumeration of distinct categories of statutes (e.g. Lev. 6.7; 7.1, 11, 37), especially in reference to ritual purity (Lev. 11.46; 12.7; 13.59; 14.1, 32, 54; Num. 5.29-30).

In contrast, rabbinic legal literature is predominantly cast in the form of *shaqla weṭarya*: the presentation and evaluation of discordant views leads to the promulgation of normative statements based on majority decisions or on past pronouncements of acknowledged authorities. Unlike Qumran tradition, the style and procedures which denote these rabbinic debates[1] are fundamentally distinct from the ones which predominate in the legal corpora of the Hebrew Bible.

Qumran Historiography

Early rabbinic Judaism evidently did not cultivate the historiographical genre. Rabbinic literature does not comprise any composition which is similar to the inclusive biblical historiographies, such as the Pentateuch and the Former Prophets, or Chronicles and Ezra–Nehemiah, which offer wide-ranging surveys of past events and also encompass contemporary occurrences and situations. The comprehensive presentation of history in perspective will re-emerge only in mediaeval times, when a compilation such as *Seder 'Olam Zuta* (sixth–eighth centuries) presents an overview of events from the creation of the world to the days of the Babylonian exilarchs in the sixth century CE.[2]

---

1. See Neusner, 'The Meaning', pp. 1-33, and see his 'Mishnah and Messiah', in *Judaisms and their Messiahs at the Turn of the Christian Era* (ed. J. Neusner, W.S. Green, E. Frerichs; Cambridge: Cambridge University Press, 1987), p. 267: 'The framers of the [Mishnah] code. . . barely refer to Scripture, rarely produce proof texts for their propositions, never imitate the models of speech of ancient Hebrew, as do the writers of the Dead Sea Scrolls at Qumran'.
2. See M. Grossberg (ed.), *Seder Olam Zuta* (London: Narditzky, 1910);

This late work draws heavily on the *Seder 'Olam (Rabba)*,[1] which the third-century Palestinian *amora* R. Jochanan ascribes to the second-century *tanna* Jose b. Halafta (*b. Šab.* 88a; *b. Yev.* 82a-b; *Nid.* 46b). In the present context, it is of significance to note that this earlier opus is dedicated in its entirety to a presentation of the biblical era. Only one part of its final chapter contains a compressed summary of events from Alexander's conquest of Persia to the Bar Kochba revolt. It appears that this excerpt, a mere literary torso, stems from the pen of an editor who was evidently 'uninterested in post-biblical history'.[2] The chronological discontinuity between the end of the biblical period and the ensuing period invites the conclusion that the author of *Seder 'Olam (Rabba)* deliberately refrained from directly linking the 'post-biblical' rabbinic age (including his own times) with the biblical era.

The sages' distinction between the biblical period and their own world invites the conclusion that the nonexistence of the specifically biblical genres of historiography, prophecy, and psalmody in rabbinic literature is not accidental but rather points up a premeditated discontinuance.

An altogether different picture emerges from the Qumran finds. *Yaḥad* authors purposefully added new features to the rich canvas of past events which their biblical predecessors had bequeathed them, and spun out anew the historical thread which had snapped some four centuries prior to their own times. They present the experiences of their community as another link in the narrative chain which opened with the creation tradition, related the story of biblical Israel's progress in history, and was severed when the Babylonians put an end to Judah's sovereignty in 586 BCE (CD 1.1-2.1 *et al.*).

A partial account of events in the Covenanters' history is contained in the *Zadokite Documents* whose overall literary structure is reminiscent of the Pentateuch and especially of the book of Deuteronomy: a core of legislative material is embedded in a historical–narrative

M.J. Weinstock (ed.), *Seder Olam Zuta ha-Shalem* (Jerusalem: Metivta Torat Hesed, 1957); J.M. Rosenthal, 'Seder Olam', *EncJud* (Jerusalem: Keter, 1972), XIV, pp. 1092-93.

1. B. Ratner (ed.), *Seder Olam Rabba* (Vilna: Romm, 1897), repr. with an introduction by S.K. Mirsky (Jerusalem: Rabbi Kook Foundation, 1966); A. Marx (ed.), *Seder Olam* (Berlin: Itzkowski, 1903).

2. Rosenthal, *EncJud*, XIV, pp. 1091-92.

framework which consists of a series of addresses, probably delivered by the 'Righteous Teacher', the Moses-like spiritual leader of the *Yaḥad*. Further pieces of historical data are found in the *pesharim*, e.g. 1QpHab, 4QpNah, and 4QpPs, and in other Qumran documents of different literary genres.

There is also ground for assuming that *Yaḥad* writers authored comprehensive historiographies as well. Some such opuscules are mentioned by title in the Qumran literature. However, no copies of them are extant among the published manuscripts, just as no copy of the above-mentioned *sfr hhgw/y* has yet been found. These works may have been somewhat similar to the lost compositions to which biblical writers, especially the authors of Chronicles (1 Chron. 29.29; 2 Chron. 9.29; 12.15; 20.34; 32.32; etc.) and Kings (1 Kgs 11.41; 14.19; 15.31; etc.) refer,[1] occasionally recording quotations from such works (Num. 21.14; Josh. 10.12-13; 2 Sam. 17–18; and possibly 1 Kgs 8.13, LXX).

In this context we should give special attention to the *mspr*, viz. the *sefer*, mentioned in the *Zadokite Documents*, which was most probably a written account couched in the style of a chronicle (cf. 2 Chron. 24.27). That work evidently contained a record of events in the Covenanters' history, from their 'Exodus' after the destruction of the Temple and their experiences in 'Exile', to the 'Return' to the land, together with a reference to an as yet uncharted future age[2] termed *'ḥryt hymym*:

> The returners (and/or repenters)[3] of Israel (*šby ysr' l*)... who had left the land of Judah[4]... they are the elect of Israel, the men of renown who (will) arise *b' ḥryt hymym*. Here is the roster of their names according to their families (*ltwldwtm*), and the appointed time[5] of their *constitution* (as

1. Leiman, *Canonization*, counts 24 lost books, which number would correspond to the number of books included in the Hebrew Canon. See also Talmon, 'Heiliges Schrifttum', p. 55, and *Literary Guide*, pp. 368.

2. For the understanding of the Hebrew term, see S. Talmon, *Eschatology and History in Biblical Judaism* (Occasional Papers, 2; Tantur: Jerusalem Ecumenical Institute, 1986).

3. *šwb* is employed here by way of a *double entendre*, similar to some of its uses in biblical Hebrew.

4. Undoubtedly an allusion to the enforced deportation of Judaeans in the wake of the debacle of 586 BCE.

5. This is the predominant connotation of *qṣ* in the Qumran writings as, e.g., in

a community) (*qs m'mdm*); the account, *mspr* of their afflictions (during) the years of exile (*šny htgwrrm*); here is (*hnh*), the (overall) exposition of their affairs (CD 4.2-6).

I presume that this compilation was in fact a Qumran parallel of the biblical reports which pertain to the returned exiles and are preserved in the books of Haggai, Zechariah, Malachi and Ezra–Nehemiah. Those reports also include various detailed lists of returnees arranged according to their paternal houses (Ezra 2 = Neh. 7; Ezra 8.1-14; 10.16-43; Neh. 3.1-32; 10.1-28; etc.), and itemized accounts of the events which befell them (*passim*), together with an unmistakable reference to the future era of *'aharit hayamim* in the prophecy which closes the book of Malachi: 'the day when I (God) will (again) make (them) my (special) possession and will have mercy upon them as a man has mercy on his son who serves him' (Mal. 3.17).

It is of interest that the formula *hnh*, which in the *Zadokite Documents* introduces the reference to that historical account (no longer extant), echoes incipits which in the Hebrew Bible precede several comparable allusions to books that are not preserved in the canon: (2 Sam. 1.18; 2 Chron. 16.11); *hinam* (1 Kgs 14.19; 1 Chron. 29.29; 2 Chron. 20.34; 27.7; 32.32); and *halo' hinam* (2 Chron. 25.26).[1] Especially noteworthy is the resemblance of the Qumran phrase *hnh prwš šmwtyhm ltwldwm* to the collocation *wekol yisrael hityaḥsu ketubim,* which prefaces the post-exilic inventory of returning families in 1 Chron. 9.1.

It seems plausible that the *mspr* which bridged the gap between the ending of biblical Israel's history and the early stages of the Covenanters' community was actually a component of a comprehensive historiographical account in which the 'appointed epochs', were set out in their sequential order, *wkl qṣyhm ldwrwtm* (1QS 4.13). The writer of

---

gmr qṣ (1QpHab 7.1-2). The term has the same signification in some late (post-exilic) biblical books. This meaning becomes especially apparent when *qeṣ* is used coterminously or in conjunction with *'et* (Ezek. 21.30, 34; 35.5; Dan. 8.17; 11.35, 40; 14.4, 9) or *mo'ed* (Dan 8.19; 11.27). We can also compare the rabbinic collocation *qeṣ mashiaḥ* (*b. Meg.* 3a); further: *Gen. Rab. 88 ad Gen 49.1* (ed. J. Theodor-C. Albeck; Jerusalem: Wahrmann, 1965), p. 1251. In the sense of 'end', *qṣ* is only rarely used in the Qumran literature. See e.g. 4QpNah 3–4 ii 4–6. See S. Talmon, 'Qeṣ', *ThWAT* 7 (1990), col. 84-92.

1.   *halo' hinam* may have arisen from a conflation of *hineh* with the parallel formula *halo' hy'* (Josh. 10.12; 1 Kgs 15.31; 2 Chron 9.29; 12.15).

that composition had recorded the divinely imparted information concerning the 'years of (their) existence and the full account of their epochs, for all that was and is, unto what will befall them in their (future) epochs for all times' (CD 2.9-10).

That opus and similar compositions inspired other Qumran authors to employ in their own creations (which are not necessarily of the historiographical genre) the specific vocabulary and imagery used there.[1] A striking example may be found in the series of speeches which the *Zadokite Documents* ascribe to the Righteous Teacher.[2]

Exile-and-Return Phraseology and Imagery

The conceptual proclivity to identify with and present themselves as biblical Israel finds a salient expression in the socioreligious vocabulary of the *Yaḥad*. When recording their community's history, the writers of Qumran appropriate the idiomatic phraseology which the authors of the post-exilic biblical books employ in the presentation of the period of the Return. This tendency can be illustrated by some pivotal examples:

1. The triad *šub/šibah–midbar–golah*, in which the essence of the biblical exile experience is concretized, also figures prominently in the Covenanters' literature. This is true, e.g., of a *pesher* in CD 7.14-17 (not expressly stated but clearly implied), where the author extrapolates from Amos' visionary threat of Israel's deportation to the north of that city a prospective allusion to the divine 'Covenant in Damascus' of the *Yaḥad* (Amos 5.27).

Similarly the reference to the Righteous Teacher's flight into the desert (of Qumran), is also couched in exile terminology. The Wicked Priest pursued him and his adherents *'byt glwtw* (1QpHab 11.4-6), so as to prevent them from observing the Day of Atonement at a date

---

1.   Thus we read, e.g., in the first *Hodayah*: *hkwl ḥqwq bḥrṭ zkrwn lkwl qṣy nṣḥ wtqwfwt mspr šny 'wlm bkwl mw'dyhm*. The phrase *ḥqwq bḥrṭ ṭzkrwn* is not attested in biblical Hebrew, as J. Licht, *The Hymn Scroll* (Jerusalem: Bialik, 1965 [Hebrew]) correctly points out. It may be a paraphrase of Mal. 3.16, with an adjustment of the biblical text to the typical *Yaḥad* vocabulary.

2.   His historiographical sermons appear to be modelled upon the paraenetic speeches ascribed to Moses in Deuteronomy. Cf. the prayers of Daniel (Dan. 9), Ezra (Ezra 9), and Nehemiah (Neh. 9), which also bear the stamp of the historiographical genre.

which accords with their special calendar.[1]

The same concept permeates the depiction of the future aeon. In the *War Scroll* the Covenanters are termed *bny lwy wbny yhwdh wbny bnymyn* (1QM 1.2-3; cf. Ezra 1.5; 4.1; Neh. 11.4; further, Ezra 2.1, 70 = Neh. 7.6, 72; etc.). They are the *gwlt bny 'wr*, viz. *gwlt hmdbr* who 'will return... from the *mdbr h'mym* camp in the *mdbr* (outskirts) of Jerusalem'.[2] From there they will launch their victorious attack on the city and its inhabitants, who are the Wicked Priest's followers and the implacable adversaries of the *Yaḥad*.

2. The intended existential implantation in the conceptual 'Returners' matrix may shed some light on the Covenanters' pointed employment of the biblical term *Yaḥad* as the most conspicuous designation of their community. In biblical Hebrew *Yaḥad* serves prevalently as an adverb. Only rarely does the word occur as a noun. The most important one for our purpose is found in the opening passage of Ezra 4, which reports on an encounter between the repatriated Judeans and their 'adversaries' who offer to join with the returnees in the rebuilding of the Temple. Zerubbabel, Jeshua the high priest, and the leaders of the people, *rashei ha'abot*, reject these overtures. They maintain that only they have been instructed by King Cyrus to undertake this project and that they alone are permitted to carry it out: *'anaḥnu yaḥad nibneh* (Ezra 4.3).

I have proposed that in this instance *yaḥad* serves as a noun which circumscribes the community of the repatriated exiles, to the obvious exclusion of the petitioners who are referred to as *šarei yehudah ubinyamin* (Ezra 4.1).[3] It may be presumed that the letter *hē* was elided in the MT, possibly due to a *lapsus calami* involving a quasi-haplography, and that the text originally read *'anaḥnu hayaḥad nibneh*, viz. '(only) we, the *yaḥad* (of the returnees) will rebuild (the Temple)'. This conjecture restores a reading in which *yaḥad* is used as a noun. It is also the only instance in which it serves as a socio-religious term that defines solely the community of the erstwhile exiles. The Qumranites' appropriation of this singular designation

---

1. See Talmon, 'Yom Hakippurim in the Habakkuk Scroll', *Bib* 32 (1951), pp. 549-63 = *WQW*, pp. 186-99.

2. For this meaning of the term, see Talmon, 'midbar' *ThWAT* 4 (1983).

3. See Talmon, 'The *Yaḥad*, a Biblical Noun', *VT* 3 (1953), pp. 133-40 = *WQW*, pp. 53-60.

again reveals their intention to present themselves as the only true successors of predestruction Israel.

3. Nevertheless, against the background of the evident linguistic similarities, a telling difference between the Qumran and the biblical vocabulary pertaining to 'exile and return' should not go unnoticed. In post-exilic historiography the notion of a return to the Land is preponderantly expressed in words belonging in the semantic field *'lh*, which connotes physical movement from a remote place (in the Diaspora) towards the Promised Land. Viewed in their totality, vocables derived from *'lh* constitute an ideational motif. They serve as signifiers of the returnees and their community (Ezra 1.3, 5, 11; 2.1, 59 = Neh. 7.6, 61; Ezra 4.2; 7.7, 9, 28; Neh. 7.5; 12.1; etc.), which distinguish them from the inhabitants of the Land. In contradistinction, *'lh* vocables are used in Qumran literature in the general sense of 'rise, go up' or in the technical connotation of 'sacrifice', and are seldom found in texts which have a socioreligious import.[1]

At the same time vocables derived from the root *šwb* which can also denote a 'physical return', are comparatively rare in post-exilic historiography.[2] As against this, one registers a plethora of words in the *Yaḥad* documents belonging in this semantic field. It is significant, however, that Qumran authors employ *šwb* terminology predominantly with the connotation of 'moral repentance', with the concomitant muffling of the notion of physical movement. The preference for the ideational over the physical aspect of *šwb*, both of which are within the twofold semantic range of the root in biblical Hebrew, appears to be intentional. These data suggest that for the *Yaḥad* authors, *šwb* terminology and related language signify moral-credal repentance rather than spatial return. The entire complex of exile and repatriation imagery in Qumran literature pertains to a religious 'turn of the mind' and should not be construed as evidence for a 'bodily return', which the Covenanters presumably experienced in a sociopolitical reality.

---

1. S. Iwry ('Was There a Migration to Damascus? The Problem of *shavi Yisrael*', in *W.F. Albright Volume* [EI, 9; Jerusalem: Israel Exploration Society, 1969], pp. 80-88) remarked on this circumstance en passant (p. 87), but failed to discern its heuristic importance.

2. Only three instances of *šwb* are extant in Ezra–Nehemiah (Ezra 2.1 = Neh. 7.6; Ezra 6.21; Neh. 8.11).

4. The correlation of significant Qumran vocabulary and imagery with equally important post-exilic biblical phraseology did not escape the attention of scholars. However, one is usually content with simply registering the fact. At best this similarity of language and wording is taken to reveal the evident temporal proximity of the composition of the latest biblical books and the earliest Qumran writings.[1] Mention should be made, however, of some attempts to probe the significance of this similarity beyond the merely linguistic aspects. The probe led some scholars to interpret this circumstance as revealing a real-historical connection, or else a parallelism between the *Yahad* and the community of returnees of which the biblical books speak.

Assigning a much earlier date to the Qumran scrolls than is generally assumed, J. Brand suggested that the Covenanters were in actual fact a group of erstwhile Ephraimites who clashed with the repatriated Judaeans and Benjaminites in the days of Nehemiah.[2] But a variety of palaeographical, historical, and scientific criteria make this early date untenable, *a fortiori* the dating of the *Vorlage* which underlies the *Zadokite Documents* in the fifth century BCE. Thus Brand's theory did not come under serious discussion.

S. Iwry's real-historical interpretation of the exile motif and the 'return' vocabulary found in the Covenanters' literature is better attuned to the prevalent dating of the Qumran manuscripts and the emergence of the *Yahad* in the second century BCE. He opines that the Covenanters were a group of Jews who, for reasons that are no longer ascertainable, had left the Land at some juncture after Nehemiah's days. Coming from Damascus where they had established their

1. See, *inter alia,* C. Rabin, *The Historical Background of Qumran Hebrew* (ed. C. Rabin and Y. Yadin; ScrHier, 4; Jerusalem: Magnes Press, 1958), pp. 144-61; R. Polzin, *Late Biblical Hebrew: Toward an Historical Typology of Biblical Hebrew Prose* (HSM, 12; Missoula, MT: Scholars Press, 1976); A. Hurvitz, *A Linguistic Study of the Relationship between the Priestly Source and the Book of Ezekiel* (Cahiers de la Revue Biblique; Paris: Gabalda, 1982); E. Qimron, *The Hebrew of the Dead Sea Scrolls* (HSS, 29; Atlanta, GA: Scholars Press, 1986).

2. J. Brand, 'The Scroll of the Covenant of Damascus and the Date of its Composition', *Tarbiz* 28 (1959), pp. 13-39 [Hebrew]. More recently H. Stegemann has also argued in favor of dating the original composition of some Qumran works, foremost the *Temple Scroll*, in the third or even fourth century BCE. See H. Stegemann, 'The Origins of the Temple Scroll (11QT)', *Congress Volume, Jerusalem 1986* (ed. J.A. Emerton; VTSup, 40; Leiden: Brill, 1988), pp. 233-52.

Covenant (CD 8.35), they actually returned to Israel in the first half of the second century BCE.[1]

This theory derives some support from the Wadi Daliyeh documents from which it can be deduced that the population of the province of Samaria, and possibly of Yehud, experienced persecution and malevolence at the hand of the Persian authorities in the early fourth century BCE.[2] But there are no ancient reports of a voluntary or forced exodus of Jews from the Land of Israel at the height of the Persian rule which could eventually have triggered the actual return to the homeland of a group such as the *Yaḥad*. The silence of the sources and the arguments presented above militate against the theories of Iwry, Brand, *et al.*, which take the Covenanters' exile-and-return language and imagery at face value, investing them with a real-historical signification.

The Qumran Schema of Israelite History

In the Qumran tradition the entire history of Israel is fitted into a schema of four major eras which, however, was adapted to the requirements of the secondary literary setting in which it is now found: the world epochs (cf. 1QS 6.16; 9.9) are no longer recorded in their chronological order. Their sequence is determined, rather, by the flow of the orator's arguments. However, a synoptic view of the texts leaves little doubt that the references in question were in fact extracted from a properly structured piece of historiography[3] in which the *qṣym* in the Covenanters' history were detailed as follows:

1. *gṣ hr'šwnym*, the epoch of the former (i.e. the pre-destruction) generations (CD 1.16; 4.6; 8.17, 31) when the first founders of the

1.   Iwry, 'Was There a Migration?'

2.   See F.M. Cross, 'The Discovery of the Samaria Papyri', *BA* 26 (1963), pp. 110-21; and 'Aspects of Samaritan and Jewish History in Late Persian and Hellenistic Times', *HTR* 59 (1966), pp. 201-11; and 'Papyri of the Fourth Century BC from Daliyeh: A Preliminary Report on their Discovery and Significance', in *New Directions in Biblical Archaeology* (ed. D.N. Freedman and J. Greenfield; Garden City, NY: Doubleday, 1971), pp. 34-39.

3.   The presumed structure and the content of that comprehensive schema can be given here only in bare outline. A detailed treatment of the matter will be presented elsewhere. For the present, see J. Licht, 'The Doctrine of "Times" according to the Qumran Sect and Other "Computers of Seasons"', in *E.L. Sukenik Volume* (EI, 8; Jerusalem: Israel Exploration Society, 1967), pp. 63-70.

(divine) Covenant (CD 3.10; 4.2; cf. 1.4) established the fundamental tenets by which the *Yaḥad* members were to be judged (CD 20.31).

Like the appellation *hanebi'im harišonim*, which in Zech. 1.4; 7.7, 12 designates the prophets of the age of the monarchies, *qṣ (hdwrwt) hr'šwnym* in the *Zadokite Documents* refers to the First Temple period,[1] possibly to the inclusion of the preceding times (CD 3.4) which are recorded in the Hebrew Bible. That age ended with the 'destruction of the Land'. At that time God punished the 'transgressors of the (established) norms, *msygy hgbwl*, who had led Israel astray' (CD 5.20-21) and gave them up 'to the sword' (CD 1.3-4) because they had forsaken the divine covenant (CD 3.10-11).

2. *qṣ hdwrwt h'ḥrwnym*, the 'epoch of the latter (rather than 'last')[2] generations' (CD 1.12; 1QpHab 9.45). This expression defines the post-destruction generations who had returned from the exile with Zerubbabel, Ezra and Nehemiah. It pertains also to their successors, the antagonists of the *Yaḥad* in actual history.

The 'latter generations' were in no way better than the 'former'. At first they steadfastly adhered to the divine commandments. But they soon went astray, misled by 'the scoffers' (*'nšy hlṣwn*, CD 5.34) and the 'latter [i.e. the 'contemporary'] priests of Jerusalem' (*kwhny yrwšlym h'ḥrwnym*, 1QpHab 9.45). That group was headed by the 'Wicked Priest'. He too had acted truthfully when he was appointed, but once safely installed in office he became haughty (cf. Deut. 17.20) and forsook God (1QpHab 8.8-10). The post-exilic period, viz. the days of 'the return', which God had assigned as the *qṣ hbryt*, 'the epoch of the (reconstituted) covenant' (CD 1.4-8) became in fact a *qṣ ḥrwn*, another 'epoch of wrath'(1QH 3.28).

The wrong-doings of the 'latter generations' caused 'all discerners of righteousness', *ywd'y ṣdq* (CD 1.1), viz. the followers of the Righteous Teacher, to separate themselves from their contemporaries.

3. *hqṣ h'ḥrwn*, 'the latter' (i.e. the present) epoch (1QS 4.16-17; 1QpHab 7.7, 12) now opens for them.

This phase in the Covenanters' history coincides with the final stage of the *qṣ hdwrwt h'ḥrwnym*. At that time the *Yaḥad* established *habrit haḥadašah* (Jer. 31.31), the 'new [better 'reconstituted'] Covenant',

---

1. For the connotation of *rišonim* and *'aharonim*, see Talmon, 'Eschatology'.

2. The translation 'last' misconstrues the meaning of the Hebrew term. See Talmon, 'Eschatology'.

from which all others are excluded. The Covenanters are the chosen ones who alone will be saved of all the sinful. Unlike the contemporary Jews who adhere to the 'false temple' which their predecessors had erected, the *Yaḥad* will build the true *byt htwrh* (CD 8.33, 36) which is destined to become the fundament of the ultimate redemption of Israel.[1]

The term *hqṣ h' ḥrwn* designates the days of the actual existence of the *Yaḥad,* when all the events detailed in the Qumran writings occurred: the Covenanters' initial dissension, the conflict with the Wicked Priest and his followers, the emergence of the Righteous Teacher, their retreat into the desert, and so on. During this span of time they had expected to experience the ultimate redemption, when they would assume the succession to biblical Israel and inherit its glory of old. This hope did not come true, and its realization was *nolens volens* deferred to an uncharted future.

4. This future was the *qṣ 'ḥryt hymym* (CD 6.11; 1QpHab 1.5-6; 9.6; etc.) in which the Twin Messiahs of David and Aaron will make their appearance on the historical stage (1QS^a 1.1).[2]

This four-tiered schema brings to mind the vision of four successive empires presented in the latter part of the book of Daniel (ch. 11), in which four periods in the post-exilic age are detailed. In comparison with the more comprehensive overview offered by the Qumran work, the scope of the Daniel text is chronologically limited. But their evident interdependence is pointed up by the shared basic concept of a tetrad of historical eras and by the culmination of both schemata in an account of the ultimate triumph over the enemies of Israel (Dan. 12.1-3),[3] and of the Covenanters (1QM), which will precede the establishment of the messianic age (1QS^a).

The similarity is highlighted by the presence of a distinctive vocabulary in both the book of Daniel and in that *mspr* (as in Qumran literature generally); *qeṣ* (Dan. 11.13, 27, 35, 40; possibly to be restored also at the end of vv. 24 and 35); *maskilim* (Dan. 11.33, 35; 12.3); *ḥalaq(laq)ot* (Dan. 11.21, 32), especially *yaḥanif baḥalaqot*

---

1. The true *byt htwrh* stands in opposition to the 'illegimate' temple, *byt*, which those who returned with Zerubbabel, Ezra and Nehemiah had built and which the Covenanters did not recognize for various reasons.

2. See Talmon, 'Waiting for Messiah'.

3. See Talmon, 'Daniel', *The Literary Guide*, pp. 343-56.

(Dan. 11.32), for which cf. *dwršy ḥlqwt* (1QH 2.15, 32; 4.10-11; CD 1.18; etc.); *'ozbei brit qodesh* (Dan. 11.30); *marshi'ei brit* (Dan. 11.32); and cf. *bqwm rš'ym 'l brytk* (1QH 2.12); etc.[1]

Chapters 1–11 of Daniel are attested at Qumran by fragments of eight manuscripts, of which 4QDan[a] 'is closer to the time of the original composition of its text than any other extant manuscript of a book in the Hebrew Bible'.[2] It stands to reason that in emulating the quadripartite Daniel schema of post-exilic world history which affects Israel directly, the *Yaḥad* members purported to integrate themselves into a late biblical historiographical pattern, thus once again emphasizing their spiritual, even existential, identification with the biblical people.

The First Returnees from the Exile

The Covenanters' self-integration into biblical Israel culminates in their assumption of the status of 'the first returnees to the Land' after the deportation which came in the wake of the destruction of Jerusalem. In retying the historical thread which was then severed, the Qumran authors completely disregard the 'Returners from the Exile' of whom the post exilic biblical sources speak (Haggai, Zechariah, Malachi, Ezra and Nehemiah). These biblical books, which pertain most directly to that period, are the most poorly represented in the Qumran finds of biblical manuscripts.[3]

The return of Judaeans to the Land, and the leading figures of that period, are passed over in silence in the Qumran writings. Those

---

1. Also the depiction of the *kytym* in 1QpHab is presumably dependent upon the portrayal of the warring empires in Daniel 11, but was developed beyond the biblical text.

2. See Ulrich, 'Daniel Manuscripts from Qumran'.

3. We have as yet no definitive roster of the biblical fragments from Qumran. Therefore the statement made here may need to be revised in the light of future information. No MS finds of Haggai, Zechariah, Malachi, Ezra, Nehemiah or Chronicles were listed by J.A. Sanders, 'Palestinian Manuscripts 1947–1972'. J. Strugnell has kindly informed me that fragments of some of these books were found in Cave 4 (4Q XII[a,b,c,e]). The book of Nehemiah, however, is not tangibly represented. The single (?) fragment of Ezra can attest to the presence of Nehemiah at Qumran only if we assume that Ezra–Nehemiah were already constituted there as one book. This question is discussed in commentaries and introductions. See also S. Talmon, *Ezra and Nehemiah (Books and Men)* (IDBSup; Nashville, TN: Abingdon Press, 1970), pp. 317-18.

earlier generations had applied to themselves the honorific title *zera'*
yisra'el (Neh. 9.2) and had also claimed for themselves the exclusive
right to the auspicious designation *zera' haqodesh* (Ezra 9.2) by which
the prophet Isaiah had designated the remnant that will be divinely
saved from the debacle which he foresaw (Isa. 6.13).

The author of the *Zadokite Documents* pointedly appropriates that
very title for the *Yaḥad* members alone (CD 12.21-22). He ostensibly
denies it to all other contemporary Jews and casts the Covenanters
unhesitatingly in the role of the 'holy seed' and of the 'first returners'
to the Land after the exile of 586 BCE:

> For when they were unfaithful and forsook him, he (God) hid his face
> from Israel and his sanctuary and delivered them up to the sword. But
> remembering the covenant of the forefathers, he left a remnant for Israel
> and did not deliver them up to (utter) destruction (cf. Jer. 5.18; 30.11;
> 46.28; Neh. 9.31). In the age of wrath. . . he remembered them (cf. CD
> 6.2-5) and caused the root he had planted to sprout (again) from Israel and
> Aaron to take possession of his land and enjoy the fruits of its soil (cf.
> Isa. 6.11-13; Hag. 2.18-19; Zech. 3.10; 8.12).

Moreover, there is no explicit reference in the *Yahad* literature to
Jeremiah's vision of a restitution of Israel's fortunes after seventy
years (Jer. 25.11-13; 29.10; Dan. 9.2), which had been a source of
(impatient) hope for the Judaean exiles.[1] The repatriates who returned
with Zerubbabel and Jeshua the high priest, with Ezra and Nehemiah,
saw this prophecy realized in the edict of King Cyrus (Zech. 1.12;
7.5; Ezra 1.1; 2 Chron. 36.21-22).

The *Yaḥad* substituted for Jeremiah's vision and the cluster of
pivotal texts connected with it, Ezekiel's prediction of a period of
punishment for Israel destined to last 390 years for the Northern
Kingdom and forty years for Judah. The prophet is divinely
commanded to carry the years of Israel's and Judah's castigation
symbolically, first by lying for 390 days on his left side and then for
forty days on his right side (Ezek. 4.4-6).[2]

---

1.   The deportees of 597 BCE apparently refrained from adjusting to the diaspora
conditions, even for the span of the predicted 'seventy years'. Their 'impatient hope'
caused Jeremiah to send a missive, in which he exhorts them to prepare for a longer
stay in exile than they had expected (Jer. 29.1-9). See S. Talmon, 'Exil und Rückkehr in der Ideenwelt des Alten Testaments', in *Exil, Diaspora, Rückkehr*
(ed. R. Mosis; Düsseldorf: Patmos, 1977), pp. 31-55.

2.   That passage seemingly fused two biblical traditions drawn from the Exodus

The author of the *Zadokite Documents* read a message of hope in Ezekiel's punitive oracle by construing the implied ending of the foreseen time of woe as the concomitant starting point of the redemptive history[1] of the *Yaḥad*: 390 years after God had given Israel (actually Judah) into the hand of Nebuchadnezzar, he remembered his people and implanted them again in his (their) land (CD 1.5-8).

The forty years of Judah's punishment are captured in a statement about a period of twenty years, during which the founders of the Covenant 'groped like blind men' (CD 1.9-10) awaiting the consummation of Ezekiel's prophetic vision. The reading 'twenty' instead of the MT's 'forty' years (Ezek. 4.6) may be an ancient variant which the Qumran tradition preserved, or else an intentional textual emendation.[2] In any event, when examined against the background of the *Eigenverständnis* of the *Yaḥad*, this reading becomes another witness to the Covenanters' intended self-integration into the framework of biblical history.

The sum of several schematic-symbolical data given in the Qumran literature results in the total of 490 years. This span of time is seen as intervening between the past destruction of Jerusalem and the future restitution of the Covenanters' 'New World' in the aeon designated *'ḥryt hymym*, after the vanquishing of all their enemies in the cosmic battle which is portrayed in the *War Scroll* (1QM):

> 390 years of Israel's punishment
> 20 years of 'groping' (CD 1.9-10)
> 40 years of strife with their adversaries in history (CD 8.26-38)
> 40 years of the final cosmic war (1QM).

The sum total of 490 years is patently identical with the transition

story, which in the primary account, however, pertain to two independent episodes. The representation of one year by one day evidently reflects a pattern which ties the forty years of wandering in the desert to the forty days in which the faithless scouts spied out Canaan: 'Your bones shall lie in this wilderness; your sons shall be wanderers (reading *to'im* for MT *ro'im*) in the wilderness for forty years, paying the penalty of your wanton disloyalty. . . forty days you spent exploring the country, and forty years you shall spend—a year for each day—paying the penalty of your iniquities' (Num. 14.33-34). On the other hand, the sum total of 430 years undoubtedly echoes the statement in Exod. 12.40-41 which gives that same figure for the duration of the Egyptian bondage.

1. See Talmon, 'Waiting for the Messiah'.
2. Talmon, 'Waiting for the Messiah'.

period of 'seventy (year) weeks' of which Daniel is advised in his vision as being 'marked out for (Israel) your people and (Jerusalem) your holy city, (when they will pass) rebellion shall be stopped, sin brought to an end, iniquity expiated, everlasting right[eous might] (*ṣedeq*),[1] ushered in, vision and prophecy sealed, and the most holy anointed' (Dan. 9.24).

The three Hebrew terms *ṣedeq, nabi', mashaḥ-limshoaḥ* are used here as catchphrases which announce the reinstatement of the public office holders who in the First Temple period had together constituted the pillars of the Israelite society: king, prophet, and priest. Like the predominant biblical vision, the Qumran *Vorstellung* of the future ideal aeon foresees this same triad again becoming the fundament of Israel's renewed polity.

The future prophet (1QS 9.11) is conceived in the image of Elijah, who in the concluding passage of the biblical corpus of prophetic literature is portrayed as the harbinger of 'the great and terrible day' which will precede the envisaged era of sublime reconciliation (Mal. 3.22-24). That prophet will be the forerunner of 'the anointed of David and Aaron'. The vision of Twin Messiahs who are expected to arise in that future age, a prominent feature of Qumran theology, is most probably patterned after a post-exilic biblical (prophetic) tradition. The book of Zechariah (Zech. 3–4; 6.9-15) appears to propose this bicephalic system as a blueprint for the desirable structure of the Returnees' polity.[2]

Once again it can be shown that the Covenanters derived a pivotal facet of their spiritual universe directly from the world of ideas of the post-exilic community, utilizing it as a sign and symbol testifying to the existential continuum of their own history with the history of biblical Israel.

A Substitution Theology

The results of the above examination of some central aspects of the *Yaḥad* literature lend credence to the theses that were advanced at the outset:

---

1. For this understanding of *ṣedeq*, see Talmon, 'Biblical Visions of the Future Ideal Age', in *KCC* (Jerusalem: Magnes Press, 1986), pp. 147-61.
2. See Talmon, 'Waiting for the Messiah'.

1. The specific *Yaḥad* documents were produced by a particular Jewish community of the Second Temple period. This community is not explicitly mentioned in the pertinent classical sources and thus was unknown prior to the discovery of the hoard of manuscripts in the Qumran caves. A renewed scrutiny of the ancient Jewish, Hellenistic, and early Christian literature may reveal veiled or implicit references which pertain to that community but which were hitherto not recognized as such.[1]

2. In their totality, the Qumran finds mirror the Covenanters' *Eigenverständnis* and show the *Yaḥad* to have been a *sui generis* socioreligious phenomenon. The particular spiritual profile of that community and its unprecedented social structure demand that the Qumran documents should first and foremost be appreciated on their own merits before the community that produced them is compared or identified with any other contemporaneous socioreligious Jewish entity known from the classical sources.

3. An unprejudiced analysis of the Qumran literature brings to light the Covenanters' particular existential stance: the *Yaḥad* members viewed their community as the direct and only legitimate heir of biblical Israel of the First Temple period. They purged from their literature and their construction of Israel's history all memories of the generation of the Return documented in the post-exilic biblical literature. Concomitantly they inserted their community into the resulting historical hiatus, appropriating for themselves the glorified status of 'the first returners from the exile'. In their eyes they were the divinely saved remnant of the deportees whom Nebuchadnezzar's army had abducted to Babylon after the conquest of Jerusalem.

The Qumran Convenanters' *Eigenverständnis* constitutes the first instance in Jewish history of *Substitution Theology*.

---

1. Echoes of the calendar dispute with the Covenanters, which were not recognized as such, presumably still reverberate in rabbinic literature. See Talmon, 'The Calendar', *WQW*, pp. 174-83.

INDEXES

INDEX OF REFERENCES

OLD TESTAMENT

INDEX OF AUTHORS